Time to Reconcile

Southern Voices from the Past: Women's Letters, Diaries, and Writings

This series makes available to scholars, students, and general readers collections of letters, diaries, and other writings by women in the southern United States from the colonial era into the twentieth century. Documenting the experiences of women from across the region's economic, cultural, and ethnic spectrums, the writings enrich our understanding of such aspects of daily life as courtship and marriage, domestic life and motherhood, social events and travels, and religion and education.

Time to Reconcile

THE ODYSSEY OF A SOUTHERN BAPTIST

Grace Bryan Holmes

The University of Georgia Press | Athens and London

Acknowledgments for the use of copyrighted materials appear on
pages xi–xii, which constitute an extension of the copyright page.

Published by the University of Georgia Press
Athens, Georgia 30602
© 2000 by Grace Bryan Holmes

Designed by Kathi Dailey Morgan
Set in Fairfield Light by G&S Typesetters
Printed and bound by Maple-Vail
The paper in this book meets the guidelines for
permanence and durability of the Committee on
Production Guidelines for Book Longevity of the
Council on Library Resources.

Printed in the United States of America

04 03 02 01 00   C 5 4 3 2 1

Library of Congress Cataloging-in-Publication Data
Holmes, Grace Bryan.
   Time to reconcile : the odyssey of a southern baptist /
   Grace Bryan Holmes.
      p. cm.
   Includes index.
   ISBN 0-8203-2217-2 (alk. paper)
      1. Holmes, Grace Bryan.   2. Baptists—Georgia—Biography.
3. Spouses of clergy—Georgia—Biography.   I. Title.
BX6495.H555 A3 2000
286′.1′092—dc21
[B]   00-036386

British Library Cataloging-in-Publication Data available

This book is for my mother,

Lila Smith Bryan

(1895–1978)

CONTENTS

    24. The Revolutions *171*
    25. Losses and Gains *178*
    26. The Misfit *181*
    27. New House, Old Misery *191*
    28. Buried Treasure *199*
    29. Nincompoop and the Grown-Up 208
    30. Love on Lindsay Street *213*
    31. Beautiful Horses Running Wild *221*
    32. Tattnall Square *224*
    33. A Woman's Liberation *229*
    34. A Badge of Honor 235

Book Four: Reconciliation

    35. Providential Pulpits *245*
    36. To Make Amends 255
    37. To Go Home Again 260
    38. We Shall Overcome 267
    39. My Heart Can't Express 277
    40. Discontent at Holmeland *287*
    41. Harp and Song *295*

    Epilogue *300*
    Index *301*

ACKNOWLEDGMENTS

I am indebted to my late husband, Thomas Joseph Holmes, for his encouragement, assistance, and forbearance through the years I worked on this book. I also wish to express gratitude to our daughter, Kathy Holmes Simmons; my granddaughter, Rachel Grace Nell Simmons; my brother, Gainer Bryan; his wife, Mary Anna Bryan; my editor, Kistler London; and Malcolm Call, Senior Editor, University of Georgia Press.

I wish to express thanks to Blair Trewhitt, Deborah Gough, Norma Finley, Tish McCutchen, Virginia Davis, Janice Daugharty, Stuart Woods, Tom Herndon, Jane Roughton, and Dot and John Knox for their help and support.

I am grateful to Bill and Leslie Madden for their expertise in indexing.

The author and publisher gratefully acknowledge the following permissions to quote from copyrighted materials:

Chapter 32: Martin Luther King Jr., "I Have a Dream," August 1963, courtesy of Intellectual Properties Management, Inc.

Chapter 34: "An Ineffably Sad Story" by Ralph McGill, September 2, 1966, with permission from The Atlanta Journal and The Atlanta Constitution.

Chapter 35: "The Two Atlantas," May 12, 1968, with permission from The Atlanta Journal and The Atlanta Constitution. "Pastor Fired in Macon,

BOOK ONE

Segregation

Prologue

Last night I dreamed I went back home. And once again I was six, the chubby daughter of a young and fair mother afraid for her Little Girl to leave the safety of her skirts, afraid to let me go out into the wasteland that was our village. On that sunny September morning in 1925, the last day of summer and the first day of school, every sandy yard in the hamlet except ours was deserted of its children. Every white school-age child except Lila Bryan's was tripping off to the old red schoolhouse next door.

Built when Washington County flourished under master and slave and cotton was king, the schoolhouse had been the site of Mount Vernon Academy. Both the school and our white-columned Greek Revival cottage, once the home of the institute's first president, had survived the Civil War, Sherman's army, and Reconstruction. The red building was topped by a belfry that enclosed a great bronze bell.

Once more it tolled its call to learning.

And I wept as I watched every sunburned boy and girl skipping toward this shimmering excitement. I alone was forbidden to answer that call.

1   *The Washerwoman*

Way back in 1859, the African slave Dole had neglected to join two fence boards, allowing me a slit of window to the west, to the world outside the severe confines of Mother's. With one brown eye pressed close to the peephole, I watched Rachel, my father's young sister and my own play-mate, in the midst of the other children trooping up the timbered steps of the faded-red schoolhouse.

And I suffered, alone, behind that high wall of unpainted, weathered boards that surrounded our backyard. Barefooted, I wore a pink dress Mother had created with her skilled hands and treadle sewing machine. Minus a collar, the frock had sleeves to the elbows to protect my olive skin from the sun. Long gold hair drooped in loose curls around my sad shoulders, and the bothersome sun hat lay upside down at my feet.

Boys in the schoolyard wore faded denim overalls and cotton shirts. But girls were decked out in new cotton dresses with short puffed sleeves and Peter Pan collars. Their flowered frocks ended a few inches above the knee and sported matching bloomers that showed an inch below the hemline, 1920s style. They were fashioned from patterns and colored cotton bought at the counter of Cudn Bill's store a block down the unpaved street. On their feet the girls wore white ankle socks and black-laced slippers.

A yellow bus deposited children of rednecks and country crackers, whose unkempt hair and faded clothes gave them a dull, ragged appearance. The ragtags carried wrinkled brown sacks or tin lunch boxes stuffed with ham biscuits and cold baked sweet potatoes grown on their fathers' farms. But all the children ran and yelled in a merry hodgepodge of tousled heads, swinging sashes, and flying feet.

As I saw Rachel's blue skirt disappear into the mysterious schoolhouse door, my heart broke into little pieces as fine, as numerous as the sands beneath my toes. Between me and the children's shrill voices and all the joy of that golden Indian summer morning stretched only a few hundred feet of sunbaked dirt. But planted firmly in it, separating me from those coveted comrades, were a barbed wire fence, a narrow patch of dead corn, a towering wooden wall—and Mother. She who had been a teacher before her marriage had decided to tutor her daughter at home.

Digging a suntanned toe into soft earth, I kicked my straw hat off to the direction of the shriveled peach tree in our side yard. I knew a misery that was exquisite. Why couldn't I be like Rachel?

My aunt, blue-eyed Rachel Bryan, was just my age, her slender body, dainty feet, and merry mouth always ready with laughter or words of wisdom. She, of the honey-colored hair covering her pretty head with a cap of waves and ringlets bobbed to her dimpled ears, was free as the March wind and beautiful as the June sky. The music of my life had gone up steps and into a classroom where I could not follow. Rachel would share our song with children I was jealous of.

Yesterday afternoon, my thirty-one-year-old father put on his Sunday suit and red bow tie. His right coat sleeve hanging empty by the side of his navy blue striped jacket, he carried his suitcase to the black Ford parked near the kitchen door. "Be back Friday night," he said. "Help Mother with Little Brother." He kissed each of us good-bye and smiled at me before driving through the wide gateway at the left of the backyard and over the wooden bridge spanning a ditch. Guiding his Model-T with his large left hand, he turned left on Harrison Road, then left again in front of our house up dusty Sandersville Road, west to Mercer at Macon to get an education.

Where Macon and Mercer were, I didn't know. What an education was, I didn't care. I only knew that Daddy, with his soft voice, tender smile, and velvet brown eyes, was gone. Gone too was the automobile that took us on Saturday afternoons to Sandersville, where we could buy new shoes, fresh-parched peanuts, and hot dogs with mustard and onions. Gone was the short, slender slip of a man Mother called Gainer.

Gone also was the enchantment I'd always found in our backyard, a quadrangle dominated by a huge pecan tree towering in the middle. Its ample arms stretched wide and round, giving shade in summer, dropping tiny nuts and leaves in fall all over the grassless dirt that Lucy Riddle, our mulatto nurse and maid-of-all-work, swept on Friday afternoons. The sun-silvered well, outhouses, and fences Abe and Dole had built in slavery days formed a symphony of southern antiquity.

Near the southeast corner of the house, to the left of the kitchen doorstep and in a corner formed by the fence, pungent wood chips lay scattered and heaped amidst short logs split to arm-size lengths just right for Mother's black kitchen range. Near the woodpile a wash pot, covered with soot from the fires of both weekly clothes boiling and monthly soap making, lay upside down. On this Monday morning Aunt Lou, our aging black washerwoman, had already drawn water to fill the wash pot set on its four prongs. Around the pot a fire crackled, boiling soil out of white bedclothes and shirts.

And just inside the gate, in the southeast corner of the yard, stood Uncle Abe's one-room cabin. Like the columned cottage, it had been built seventy years before by the Jewish immigrant Wescoloski, who came to this country to escape the pogroms in his native Poland. The cabin had never known the stroking of a paintbrush. But decades of summer suns, spring winds, and winter rains had silvered its sides to the patina of a mockingbird feather. It now made a cozy playhouse for Rachel and me and our dolls. At the rear of the backyard, Lou Howard's "laundermat"—two zinc tubs on a crude stand—stood against the dove gray fence where it backed the smokehouse.

Silence fell at the schoolhouse. The bell stopped its clangor and children ceased their chattering. Now the roar of Uncle Tom Fulghum's cotton gin down the unpaved street to the west could be heard all around our little village. I heard the sluggish snort of a mule and the pokey rumble of a faded green farm wagon carrying a load of cotton past the cemetery for whites to the gin. September sun already lay hot upon my back.

Mother scurried around in the kitchen amid the click of china and rattle of silver-plated forks and spoons. She was cleaning up after breakfast, hastening to set the house straight and get to the business of my lessons. Thirty-year-old Lila yearned to give her daughter the fine education she herself had been denied. She wore a faded dress, handmade from red plaid cotton, and wine red bedroom slippers ordered year before last from Sears Roebuck. Her little toes peeped from holes worn through the felt. Mother had nice new dresses and black patent leather pumps in the wardrobe. But these were saved for Sunday and rare afternoon excursions to visit the neighbors: Grandma Mary, Aunt Clara, or Cudn Ophelia.

Face powder and rouge were saved also. Mother never put on makeup in the mornings. Lipstick was not worn at all except by carnival women at the county fair. Eye makeup was unheard of. Sections of Mother's hair were coiled and held by flat metal curlers for afternoon "fixin' up" after housework was finished.

My teacher did not present a pretty picture to her lonely pupil. But there was nothing I could do about it but feel hurt in my heart and sadness in the pit of my stomach for myself and my overworked mother. Already this Monday morning Mother had cooked breakfast, made beds, swept floors, fed chickens, and fetched in buckets of water from the well and more wood for the stove.

In the kitchen Little Brother sneezed and whined. Three years old, Mother's only other child was a victim of hay fever. He was a cute little fellow with eyes as brown as acorns in autumn and hair the color of candied sweet potatoes. Over his diaper he wore a blue checkered apron Mother had sewn on the Singer machine. Buttoned up the back and self-belted in the front, the garment came to his knees.

In the yard Aunt Lou trudged back and forth between tubs, wooden well, and sooty wash pot. I peered through the fence and dug my toe in the dirt again. And I muttered, *Oh, to be like Rachel, to have blue eyes and bobbed hair, go to school with her and Pauline, Jessie, and Jack!*

Behind me Aunt Lou drew water. I could hear the creak, creak, creak of the chain and the slosh, slosh of the water. I turned to stare at the sixty-year-old widow who every Monday walked half a mile from her sagging shanty on the western edge of our hamlet to do our family wash. She wore a faded blue cotton dress, a white apron, and ragged black shoes run down at the heels. Her black hair sprinkled with white was neatly parted into squares, then screwed into braids all over her head.

With hands big and brawny she lifted the overflowing well bucket, strained her back forward under the thirty-pound weight, and poured the cool liquid into another pail, wetting her clean dress. Squaring her shoulders, she hauled the pail over to the hand-hewn stand where the tubs waited. Heaving the bucket once more, she dumped the water in, sighed, and then trotted back to the well for more.

"Gra-ace," Mother called urgently, "it's time for your lessons now. Come on in the house. Hurry up! Where is your hat?"

In the combination living-bed-schoolroom in the front corner of our house, Little Brother settled with his toys beside the white-painted iron crib. Mother waited in her favorite oak rocking chair, her crossed leg swinging impatiently. There were deep furrows between her brows, and her mouth formed a thin, hard line, for her little girl was stubborn. "You're brown as a nigger! Just won't keep on your sun hat."

The lesson began.

"Repeat after me," commanded my teacher. "Five plus five equals ten; six plus four equals ten; four plus six equals ten."

Seated at the little yellow desk, I parroted the sums. Then I wrote them as instructed. I already knew how to write numbers and had learned that two plus two make four. But my thoughts were not in that room. They were in the rust red schoolhouse with the belfry on top, where Rachel was learning arithmetic. "Mother," I whined in my timid voice, "why can't I go to school with Rachel?"

"It's a sorry school! With sorry teachers!" she said. "I can teach you better at home. And you might get hurt, break a leg or something, running and ripping. They go wild up there at recess." Her voice turned more sharp and resolute. "Now put your mind on your work. Mother is always right, you know. Your mother is your best friend. She loves you more than anyone else in the world and knows what's best for you."

I did not argue, remaining outwardly docile. But inside rebellion seethed with all the fury of a storm brewing at sea. And so we finished arithmetic and started reading and spelling, the big tan clock on the green mantel over the fireplace metronoming the minutes and punctuating the hours. Finally it struck ten times in unison with the ringing of the bell in the belfry.

"Now you can have recess," said Mother, "while I put dinner on." She hurried into the kitchen to make a fire in the black range and set pots to boiling for the noonday meal. "Put on your sun hat!" she reminded me.

Flinging my pencil down, I grabbed the hated hat and ran through the kitchen, on through the porch that was a continuation of the central hall of our house, and down the wooden back steps to peer through my tiny opening in the wall.

From the playground rose squeals of joy as pretty little people frolicked. "Red Rover, Red Rover, let Rachel come over." "Red Rover, Red Rover, let Jessie come over." How sweet it would be to hear them yell "Red Rover, Red Rover, let Grace come over." I saw Rachel, Jessie, and Pauline run and fall into the dust, cry and get up, run again, the sashes of their ging-ham dresses bobbing, their short, straight hair swirling freely around their heads. *Mother is always right. But I wish it was right for me to run and rip and get hurt the way other daughters do.*

Certainly it would do no harm to be as close as possible to the gaiety. So I stole to the small gate in the west wall toward the school. When I unlatched the gate, I could see the top of our privy, which Mother called The Closet. The three-holed outhouse squatted behind a fig bush, in a corner of our vegetable garden.

But I had no urge to go. Instead, being careful to latch the gate to keep our scratching chickens in the yard, I crept across the corn patch, slipped between a walnut and a pecan tree, and hid behind the pome-granate bush leaning against the barbed-wire fence. Removing my hat, I tossed it defiantly to the ground and yanked a red pomegranate off the thorny bush. I tore into the pink seed with a hungry mouth before I real-ized I was only a heartbeat away from Rachel and her buddies in the schoolyard beyond. They mustn't know how different I was, how much I wanted to be with them.

But they'd already heard the leaves rustle. I cringed as they burst upon me at the playground's outer boundary, faces flushed and wet with sweat, hair awry, voices breathless.

"What you doin' back here, Grace?" asked the jolly Jessie. "Why don't you go to school with us?"

"Her mama won't let her," said Rachel just as the end-of-recess bell pierced the air. Turning, they ran back to the schoolyard, each clawing the other to be first in line.

Alone again behind the barbed wire, I crunched the acid fruit and watched forlornly until the last merry sash and denim-clad leg were swal-lowed by the ancient schoolhouse. A hush fell over the village. All you could hear were the whir, whir, whir of the cotton gin and Aunt Lou sing-ing about her troubles as she scrubbed in our backyard.

"Her mama won't let her." So Rachel knew! Her words made me feel suddenly naked, stripped of dress and bloomers. There must be something wrong with Mother. No, she's "always right. Mother is your best friend. She always knows what's best for you."

Wounded and angry, I turned toward the backyard and Aunt Lou's song.

Aunt Lou often sang as she scrubbed. Her voice was loud and sorrowful and unrefined, her words more like a wail than a song.

I must tell Jesus all of my trials;
I cannot bear these burdens alone;
In my distress, He kindly will help me,
He ever loves and cares for His own.

Shifting my steps into the lumbering tempo of the widow's wailing, I picked my reluctant way back over dry brown earth and dead cornstalks toward the gate, the house, and the inevitable little yellow desk and infantile babblings of Baby Ray in my primer.

Aunt Lou and I must be kin—she's sad and I'm sad. But she's not really my aunt. She's "colored." Mother says they don't like to be called "nigger" or "nigra." Call them "colored." When you speak to older ones, call them "aunt" or "uncle." Of course, Mother says "nigger" when she's mad, but she always says "Aunt Lou" to Aunt Lou's face. That's what Rachel calls her, and so do Grandma Mary Bryan, Daddy, and Uncle Frank. We also call Aunt Lou's white-haired sister "Aunt Nannie" and her husband "Uncle Dole." It's because they come to the back door and the backyard, I suppose, to help Mother when she's tired and hot and has too much to do. And Mother always feels better when one of them comes. Her worried face becomes smooth and pretty again. She smiles and jokes, and we all laugh.

Today Aunt Lou is sad because she's got so many clothes to wash and buckets of water to draw. And I'm sad because I can't go to school with Rachel, and Daddy's gone to Macon and won't come home tonight to take us for a ride.

I moved closer to the washtub, stood, and listened to Aunt Lou's lament. Her voice rose and fell deep into her bending body, rose again with the resonance and intensity of heartbreak. The dark head jerked back and forth, her entire person keeping rhythm with the washing. Bronze hands galloped up and down the metal ridges of the scrub board, in and out of white, bubbly soapsuds—black hands, white clothes, black hands, white suds, black, white, black, white, soapy water sloshing onto bare feet spread comfortably upon shadowed sand. Beside her lay another mound of soiled garments—my ruffled dresses, Little Brother's shirts and pants that Mother made, Mother's rose-strewn towels and red aprons trimmed with white rickrack—waiting for the slap of Octagon soap and the skill of the washerwoman's hands.

Every Monday it was the same, had been all my life, all Aunt Lou's life, I supposed. Now she threw her woolly head back and raised her voice for the chorus:

I must tell Jesus, I must tell Jesus,
I cannot bear these burdens alone;
I must tell Jesus, I must tell Jesus,
Jesus can help me, Jesus alone.

Listening to the words fall from her thick, rolled-out lips, seeing the contortions of her flat nose and square face and the tears trickling from her white eyes down the wrinkled bronze velvet of her cheek, I sensed the anguish in her heart and found relief in my own. I loved Aunt Lou. She who wasn't my aunt was somehow kin to me just the same.

"Gra-ace, come here, take this to Aunt Lou," called Mother from the kitchen door. In her hand was another soiled towel for Lou's scrub board. Furrows deepened between Mother's eyes. "Then you come on here. Don't be slow. It's nearly eleven o'clock, and we've got to have a writing lesson."

"Mother," I said as I took the towel, "I want to go to school with Rachel, Jessie, and Pauline. Please Mother! Everybody's going to school but me. Please let me go with them."

"Now don't you start that again," Mother said firmly. "I've already told you no! You're going to school at home. I'm going to teach you every day. You'll learn more than they do. Besides, you can't do what everybody else does. Now hurry up and quit worrying me."

Then Mother lashed me with the words that never failed to shut me up, render me docile and afraid. "You'll be sorry you worried me so when you see my cold, dead body."

Mother had a notion that she would die young. Death had already been a frequent visitor to her family. Her father, Zachariah Smith, succumbed to typhoid fever when Mother was an infant. Her beloved sister Lucy died of meningitis at twenty-six. And just recently Daddy's sister, Annie Ola, at only thirty-six, had left five motherless children. As I trudged toward the tubs, I imagined Mother lying, still and dead, in a soft white-and-gray casket at the front of a church that smelled like pink carnations. I trembled. What would I do without Mother? I'd go to school with Rachel. But I couldn't imagine coming home without Mother in the kitchen cooking and caring for Little Brother and me.

When I delivered the towel to Aunt Lou, she stopped singing and grumbled, "I ain't never goin' get through this here washin' if'n y'all don't quit bringin' towels, such as that, out here."

From the street came the clang and clatter of the Coca-Cola truck. Diagonally across the intersection I could see the driver climb to the top of his red vehicle and unload new crates of bottled drinks he delivered from the plant at Sandersville, the county seat, ten miles to the northwest. He disappeared into the red brick store Grandpa John Bryan had built, and the screen door slammed again and again as he carried in full crates, brought out empties, loaded them onto the truck.

Guilt squeezed my heart as I ran back toward the kitchen door of our cottage: *I don't want Mother to die! I'd better not beg anymore to go to school with Rachel. If I worry Mother, she might die. And I can't bear to think of that!*

I must not let Mother know I love Aunt Lou, either. She's a Negro, and Mother says: "You mustn't be too friendly with them, or they'll get uppity."

All my young life, in stores, on sidewalks and porches, and around fireplaces I'd heard people say, "You have to keep a nigger in his place," and "Give 'em too much freedom and they'll rule over us."

Still, to see Aunt Lou weep and not weep with her . . . to watch her wash my dresses, cook my bread, labor and sweat for me, and not let her know I cared . . . when others forsook me and I derived comfort from her black strength, but I could not return that comfort—how could those things be? Hadn't I learned at Sunday school that I should love my neighbor as myself?

It was all too bewildering.

2 Lucy Riddle of Riddleville

The sun had climbed to the top of the sky when the school bell clanged again, sending dinnertime signals all over the village. Children poured through the front door, down the timbered steps, and out into the hot sunshine to enjoy an hour's pause for their noonday meal. Rachel and the town children skipped merrily along streets and sidewalks to eat a hot dinner at their mothers' kitchen tables. Ragtags from the country found shady places around massive oaks on the schoolyard. Sitting in laughing groups, they lunched upon the contents of their wrinkled brown bags or fragrant lunch boxes.

In our schoolroom the clock struck twelve. Little Brother, whom Mother had helped into his white-painted crib while my lessons went on, awoke. He raised his red head, stood up, and, clinging to the crib's railing, blinked at Mother and me. Pleased with the morning's work in her household, she laid her reading book down, crossed her stockinged leg, swung her bedroom-slippered foot, and looked lovingly at her little daughter. It was at moments like this that Mother was most charming. The washerwoman sang in the backyard, the sun rode high in the sky, black-eyed peas bubbled in the pot, and the morning's lessons were done. She smiled, her brown eyes sparkling, and called me by my pet name. I loved the smile and the sparkle in her eye. But I hated the name.

"Little Buttermilk," said she, "you can stop now. Go tell Aunt Lou to come make me some corn bread for dinner." To my little brother she said, "Whatchu doing, Bucky Snort?" She rose from her rocking chair, lifted her little boy out of his bed, set his bare feet on the bare floor, and hastened to the kitchen.

I ran to deliver the message. Lou Howard laid down her thin bar of Octagon soap and her scrub board. Wiping her sudsy hands on her white apron, she spat out a dark stream of snuff upon the ground near the fence and scuffed into the house on bare feet.

"Well," said Mother in cheerful voice to Aunt Lou, "I see you've got your shoes off."

"Yessum," said Aunt Lou in her hoarse, gravelly voice. "I can't work with my feets hurtin'. I have to git my feets outa my shoes."

The screen door slammed behind the black woman. I paused on the back porch to watch the ragtags devour their lunches. How I wished to join their circle beneath the oak trees! I imagined how they'd all stop and smile, offer me a ham biscuit and sweet potato. I recollected one memorable day, after we'd spent the night at Grandma Sally's, when Mother had let me go to school with Aunt Evelyn, who was a teacher at Indian Hill. At lunchtime the children took me to their favorite trysting place underneath the pines for a picnic. They treated me like a princess, because I was their teacher's niece and a visitor from town. For one golden moment on a perfect spring day, I'd been one of the crowd.

"Little Buttermilk!" called Mother, shaking me out of my trance. "Come on and eat your dinner!"

The dining-room table was laid with a blue checkered cloth. As soon as I sat down, Mother bowed her head and asked the blessing. Then she filled our plates with fragrant cabbage, fried chicken, black-eyed peas, and golden crisp corn bread.

"How do my bread eat?" asked Aunt Lou from the kitchen table, where she ate from a tin pan.

"Oh, your bread's good," said Mother, between bites. "Buttermilk makes it better. Mama gave me that gallon jug of fresh buttermilk yesterday." Then, looking at me with mischievous glints in her dark eyes, she added: "Little Buttermilk didn't spill it this time."

There was that name again. Although Mother's laughter was like the lapping of lake water, my heart grew heavy, as it always did when she or Daddy called me that.

It happened when I was four years old and Little Brother, wrapped in a blue blanket and whimpering, was a baby in Mother's arms. At almost dusk on a winter Sunday afternoon, Daddy drove the four of us in his Model-T into the backyard. Grandma Sally owned a tenant farm. This day she had given us turnips and cabbage from her garden, sausage and ham from her smokehouse, butter and buttermilk from her churn.

Although Mother was tired and troubled about many things, her face anxious, her voice cross, I loved her so. I wanted to help her and recapture that lost realm of sweetness and security I'd once had in her arms.

I wore a brown coat trimmed with fur. I was so proud of it, and Mother was too. Seldom did she buy new clothes; the wool coat would have to last until it was up to my thighbone. All of us got out of the car, Mother carrying the baby. Wanting to carry something, too, I picked up the biggest thing I saw, the gallon jar of buttermilk. But halfway up the back steps I fell and dropped the white stuff.

The big jar broke, buttermilk spreading upon the steps like snow in January. I tumbled into the liquid, spattering it all over the new coat and fur. Mother was horrified.

I was humiliated. All I had wanted to do was help my parents and win their praise. But I had failed, and Mother couldn't see inside my soul. All she saw was the wreckage of glass and milk and coat. Her dark eyes narrowed. "Now just look at you! You've ruined your new coat. I'll never be able to clean it." Her sharp tongue cut at me. "You should have left it alone. You should have known it was too big for you. I was going to bring it in."

Uttering a short, nervous laugh, Daddy helped me up with his strong left hand. The buttermilk and the coat didn't matter much to him. Only I mattered. But he always said that Mother was right. This time he tried to make light of it, calling me an endearing term. He said, "Come, get up, Little Buttermilk."

The hated nickname stuck like the buttermilk stains. They were too much for even Mother's scrubbing strength and persistence. Once smooth and soft, the fur stayed matted in tight little knots like unpopped kernels of popcorn. Every time I wore the wrap and smelled the soured milk, and every time they called me "Little Buttermilk," I was defeated all over again.

So the familiar misery followed me again today until Aunt Lou had finished her dinner and gone back to the splashing tub, until Rachel and the ragtags had returned to their desks, books, and blackboards. Then Lucy Riddle entered the backyard through the back gate. My heart grew light when I heard her say, "Hello, Aunt Lou, hi' you?"

"I's just tol'able. Tryin' to git through with this here washin' so I can git home and rest my feets."

"I got to go to the fiel' myself. Gotta pull foddah."

"Who you goin' pull foddah fo'?"

"Mistah Tom, over to the back fiel'," declared Lucy.

"Gonna be hot pullin' foddah today."

"Sho' is. But I gotta have a dollah to buy my snuff and rashions with, ain't I? Gotta eat. Gotta have snuff. Gotta have somethin' to putt in my mouf. I ain't got nothin' to putt in my mouf. He say I pull foddah two days, he give me a dollar Sad'dy."

"Lawd, Lawd," said Aunt Lou, bending over the washtub, "the troubles I see."

Our nurse climbed the back stoop, opened the screen door without knocking, crossed the kitchen linoleum, and leaned against the dining room door. No matter how dreary the day, Lucy brought sunshine with her. She seemed to belong or wish to belong to all the white folks in the village. At one time or another, she'd nursed and helped to raise all its pale-faced children. Since the turn of the century she'd bathed and dressed, cooked and cleaned, swept and scrubbed for the Bryans and their children and grandchildren.

A curious crossbreed of Africa, Europe, and America, Lucy Riddle was born in our county in 1882, seventeen years after Emancipation. Her father had been born into slavery, the son of a white plantation owner and his slave cook. Lucy was of medium height and slender build, and she was bow-legged. Her strange dark eyes, patrician nose, and small mouth were inherited from her white grandfather. The thin mulatto skin of Lucy's gentle, loving face seemed to slip over its finely chiseled bones. Her high cheekbones delighted me by dancing up and down when she smiled and talked. Beautifully arched black eyebrows continually rose high onto her forehead, then descended into a V above her nose.

The poor widow was an enigma to everyone in the village. White people found it difficult to keep Lucy "in her place," and black people said she acted like she thought she was white. She was an object of scorn and ridicule, until her loving heart and willing hands were needed to wash clothes or nurse the young or sweep the yards. Then she seemed to sense our need and appear at our door when that need was greatest. Often she'd forget and come to the front door instead of the back, kiss a white child on the cheek, or even talk friendly to a husband. Sometimes at a family gathering on the front porch in summer, she could be seen sitting on the crude, slatted bench behind the rocking chairs just as if she were one of us. Grandma, aunts, and uncles would ignore her until she opened her mouth to join the conversation. Then they'd say, "Ah, Lucy! Go wash the dishes," or "Go sweep the back porch," or "Bring in a turn of stove wood." Lucy would disappear into the rear of the house, but not before throwing a twinkling eye and a mischievous glance at Rachel, Bucky Snort, and me.

No one ever paid her much for her labors. No one in the village, black or white, had money. When Lucy finished a job, her white employer would say, "Well, Lucy, how much do I owe you?" And Lucy would say, "Jes' give me ha'f a dollah an' a dime fo' a can o' snuff." When this was done, sometimes the housewife, feeling appreciative and not a little guilty, would throw in a faded, ragged dress or shirt for Lucy or one of her offspring. Lucy'd go home at sundown to cook a supper of fatback and corn bread, which she'd eat from a tin pan.

Today Lucy wore a white apron over a clean but ill-fitting cotton dress Mamie Brett had tired of. An empty Buttercup Snuff can bulged from her apron pocket. Her straw sun hat was pulled down over braided black hair. On her feet she wore brown-and-dingy-white saddle oxfords Aunt Emma had cast off.

"Well, where'd you come from?" asked Mother.

"I come from Miz Bryant's," said Lucy, raising her black eyebrows high onto her forehead to denote pride that she'd been asked to work for my grandmother, who was Aunt Mary to half the folks in Riddleville and Cudn Mary to the other half.

"Ah, her name's not Bryant. It's Bryan, B-r-y-a-n—Mrs. Bryan," said Mother, explaining to Lucy for the hundredth time how to pronounce our name.

"I cooked dinner there for Mistah Herbert, Mistah Frank, Mistah Cecil, Mistah George, and Mistah Amos," continued Lucy.

These were Daddy's brothers, ranging in age from twelve to twenty-five. They ran the red-brick country store that joined Grandma Bryan's rambling Victorian with the wraparound porch. Grandpa Bryan had died in 1922, when he was sixty-four, leaving Grandma with ten children aged three to thirty. My playmate Rachel was her youngest.

"Well, I've been trying to see you," said Mother between bites. "I want you to come Saturday and help me take the children to the fair."

"Sure, I'll come, Miss Lila." Her high cheeks leaped up and down as she smiled. Turning to me, she said, "What you doing home, baby? Why ain't you at school? Rachel at school. Pauline at school. All the other chil'ren at school."

I wanted to run to my nurse, bury my face in her red and white checkered lap, and cry. I wanted to feel her brown hands stroke my head and hear her soothing words.

But I dared not, because this would displease Mother. She often complained, "Lucy kisses you when I leave her with you. Lucy don't know her place. She thinks she's white." I knew my nurse would understand my sorrow and say, "You oughta let her go to school with the other chil'ren, Miss Lila," and that would make Mother angry.

While I was trying to decide what to reply, Mother spoke sharply: "Ah, Lucy, you talk too much. You'll make her dissatisfied." Moving out of her chair, Mother cleared her throat. She went to the stove, pushing strands of hair from her damp forehead. "Weather's so hot," she said. "Wish it would rain. Here, Lucy, you want something to eat?" said Mother, lifting the aluminum lid from the pot of peas. "Got plenty."

"Nome, I done et. Et at Miz Bryant's."

"You mean 'ate,' Lucy, not 'et,'—a-t-e, ate."

Lucy giggled. Her cheeks slid up and down. "You know I cain't say hit, Miss Lila. I ain't never went to school none. Papa made us work in the fiel' when us was li'l."

"You could learn if you wanted to," said Mother in her schoolteacher voice. She was moving rapidly now from dining room to kitchen table to range. Her bedroom slippers made soft hissing sounds as they brushed across the green linoleum. She cleared and stacked plates, then put away leftovers in the warming closets high up at the back of the stove that stood in the middle of the kitchen. Lucy followed her around obeying instructions. Little Brother sneezed and threw his spoon onto the floor. I sat down in Grandpa Zachariah's little wagon chair in the corner of the kitchen by the west window with its view of washtubs and well, wishing Lucy would stay the rest of the day.

"Grace's too little to go to school," Mother continued as though she must convince Lucy that she was doing the right thing. "She might get hurt, running and ripping with the children. They go wild up there at recess."

"Sho' do," said Lucy, now in perfect agreement with the white woman. "They ain't the onliest ones what goin' wild. They anothuh killin' las' night."

"Another killin'. Where? Who?"

"Up to Breezly Hill. Hit were Mose. Anothuh niggah kilt him with a knife. Say he been botherin' his wife. They was drunk, I think."

"Lord-a-mercy, I pray! What'd they do with the nigger?"

"They ain't cotched him yet. Got the bloodhoun's atter him, though."

"Lord-a-mercy, I pray! Liquor's gonna be the ruin of this country. Ole bootleggers make me sick. I don't know why people want to fool with the stuff. Samp came to town drunk Saturday afternoon staggerin' all over. They found him in a haystack Sunday morning. I don't know what's gonna become of the world if people don't stop drinkin' and fooling around. Makes me think of that lynchin'. Lord, those were terrible times. Men from all over the country drivin' through town with guns poked out of car windows. Guns goin' off all night, just like war. All night, just like war. And burnin' up that boy."

"Sho' did. They burnt up Li'l Cha'lie. Jes' tied 'im to a tree and burnt 'im up. They made his daddy bring the wood, made his mother light the fire. And she were pregnant. Both them crying like they hearts would break."

"It was horrible. I can't stand to think about it."

"Shoot, I'm goin' to Dee-troit, myself." Lucy always said that when there was trouble in the village. "I'm goin' to see my baby, goin' to see Claudia."

"When have you heard from Claudia?"

"Hit been a munt' since I heared, seem to me like."

"You mean a *month*. Here, Lucy, you can have some of these peas and corn bread for supper. Cleophas, Gozella, and Evalena'll love my victuals. Went to Mama's yesterday, and she gave me some buttermilk. It makes the best corn bread!"

"Mother, what's a lynchin'?"

"You're too little to hear about that."

"Who was Little Charlie? Why'd they burn him up?"

"Oh, they claimed he killed the mail carrier, Mrs. Kitchens. She was driving alone on that lonely road, and she was murdered one day about dinnertime."

"Sho' was. And they blamed Li'l Cha'lie. But he ain't the one what done hit."

"And the Negroes left here in droves. Went in the middle of the night."

"Sho' did. They cotched the Shu-fly at Davisboro."

"Went to Detroit, Philadelphia, Atlanta," agreed Mother.

"They ain't never come back, neither. They scairt."

Lucy went into the dark pantry and found an old tin pan to put the leftovers in, thankful to have food for her family, something besides fatback. "I wishen I could hear from my baby," she said. "Wishen I could hear from Claudia."

It was so cozy to have Lucy there. I wished she'd stay and talk to me. "Lucy, stay with us this afternoon. Please don't go away."

"Lawdy, chile, I gotta go to de fiel', gotta pull foddah," said Lucy, scowling, her eyebrows drawn down in a V over her nose. "I sho' wish I had some snuff to putt in my mouf. Ain't got nothin' to putt in my mouf."

"Ah, Lucy, you ought not to use that nasty stuff."

"What's foddah?" I asked pushing my damp hair back from my forehead, feeling sorry for Lucy, who had to go to the dusty field on this sizzling day.

"Dat's what they feeds hosses, mules wid, such as dat."

"It's corn blades," said Mother. "Dead cornstalks. Farmers use fodder to feed cows, horses, and mules."

"Well, I wish you didn't have to pull foddah, Lucy. I wish you could stay with us."

"Grace, take Little Brother out of this hot kitchen," said Mother. Sweat dripped from her chin as she lifted her little boy out of his high chair and set his bare feet upon the green linoleum. "Take him into The Room and play with him until I get through in this hot kitchen.

"Lucy, come help me with these dishes and I'll give you a dime to buy yourself a can of snuff. And I need a bucket of water and a turn of stove wood for the box. Didn't Mrs. Bryan pay you today?"

"No, Ma'am, she goin' pay me Sad'dy."

"Now, Lucy, don't forget to come Saturday. I need you to come at eight o'clock, help me get ready to get off to Sandersville."

"Mistah Gainah goin' be home?"

"Yes, he's coming Saturday morning. Now don't forget," Mother repeated. Lucy sometimes overestimated her strength and promised more than one family that she'd come on a certain day.

The mulatto made her standard reply: "I come, Miss Lila, if'n I live and don' die and the good Lawd spare me."

3   Always Be like Jesus

When Mother said "The Room," I knew she meant the one with pea green walls where we did most of our living. Other rooms were closed off to keep them neat for company and to save fuel. But instead I took Little Brother across the hall to the parlor, opened the door, and eased in, reveling in its cool respite from stifling heat.

The parlor was my favorite space. I loved its papered walls and the wool rug Mother called an art square. It was patterned in bunches of pink roses scattered across a background the color of wheat. I loved to play on the carpet, to lie down and gaze at the picture of horses over the mantel—see their manes and hooves flying—and to dream. But the best thing about the parlor was the long, narrow window that faced the now quiet schoolhouse. Maybe I would see Rachel when the bell rang again.

All up and down its five streets, the village settled into its regular afternoon siesta. From the William Gainer Bryan ancestral home on the hill at the east end of town to the Fulghum family home at the northwest corner near the cemetery for whites, merchants, farmers, and housewives paused for relief from sweltering, semitropical sun. Farmers despaired that it would ever rain again.

At the Wescoloski-Bryan cottage, our clock on the mantel struck twice. Its pendulum swung right and left and right and left in tick-tock rhythm. Aunt Lou drew more water at the well for rinsing. I heard creaking chain, sloshing water, the singing of her song. Lucy slung dishwater out the back door, scattering cackling hens. She picked up her dime and pan of leftover cabbage and peas, clamped her hat tighter upon her woolly head, and headed home by way of the back door, then around through the front yard and along the sidewalk that went by the town well and past the schoolhouse. Cutting across the churchyard, she walked alongside the little colonial church with white columns where whites worshiped every Sunday, and proceeded south a quarter mile on the road to Mount Moriah. Her hut on the other side of the road was hidden from our view by the church.

Mother took Little Brother and lay down for her nap, and in the parlor

I lay still on the rug and stared at the picture on the wall. A screen door slammed at Bryan's General Store across the street, then the village was tranquil again.

Finally the bell rang, the clock struck three, and Little Brother cried. Weary children poured from the school building. They yelled, called, whooped, and woke up the somnolent village. And I was a lonely little girl again on a hot wool rug, my dress and hair wet with sweat. Springing to the west window, I peered at the surging mass, searching for Rachel, hoping she would disengage herself from Jessie and Pauline and come play with me.

Soon I saw her skipping down the sandy street toward our house. My heart missed a beat as I ran to the front window. She was passing the town well, where a rider had stopped to draw a bucket of water for his horse. Her bobbed hair shone gold in the sunlight. Now she was in shadow as she stooped beneath the huge oak tree to examine an acorn. Oh, I hope she's coming to see me, I thought, and then she was unlatching the front gate of the white picket fence. Hurrying out the front door, I met her on the columned porch.

Standing at the foot of the steps, Rachel squinted up at me, her right eye closed against the brilliance of the sun, the other as blue as lake water. Her hair was disheveled, bangs parted at the cowlick side. The right pocket of her flowered frock was torn almost off. In a dusty black oxford her right foot turned demurely on its side. "Grace," she said, her voice fairylike, "come and play with me. Ask Sister Lila to let you."

At that moment Mother pushed the screen door open and walked onto the porch with Little Brother following. "Mother," I said, "I want to go home with Rachel."

Mother sat down in her green rocking chair. The baby crawled to her red polka-dotted lap. "I 'spect you'd better stay here," she said softly.

"Ah, Mother, I want to go home with Rachel. I've been here all day."

"No," said mother, her voice firm, "you can't go. There's been a killing in town, and they haven't caught the nigger yet. I'm afraid for you to be out on the streets. You might get hurt. These are bad times." Worry knitted her brows, drew her mouth into a thin line, and set her narrow nose into a point as sharp as a streak of lightning on a summer night. "Makes me think of that lynching."

"Ah, I won't get hurt," I cried, "I'm not scared!" A wave of hopelessness, quickly followed by resentment, engulfed me, stinging my eyelids with hot tears.

"Please, Sister Lila," begged Rachel. "Just let her go for a little while."

Angry now, Mother spoke louder.

"I said she can't go, Rachel. Don't you know what 'no' means? And you ought not to be out on the streets either. You ought to be at home with your mama where you belong. It's dangerous for a little girl like you to run about so freely. Something might happen to you." Then Mother checked herself, fearing she'd said too much to the twelfth child of her mother-in-law. She grew more patient but no less firm. "I 'spect you'd better go home and leave Grace alone. I'll take her to see you tomorrow."

Rachel wheeled and raced out the front gate. I turned, yanked open the screen door, ran down the hall and out the back door, bawling.

Aunt Lou was hanging clothes on the wire line stretched diagonally from the corner of the back porch, across the yard to the corner of the garden gate. Clamping a clothespin onto a damp apron, she heard my cries and asked, "What's-a-matter, chile?"

"Mother won't let me go home with Rachel," I said between sobs.

"Mother knows best, honey. Be glad you got a mother. She your best friend, sure is. Wish I had a mother."

I stumbled across the yard, through the wide opening that led to and through the empty barn. It held Daddy's Ford when he was home. Behind the barn, I climbed the wire fence and let myself down on the other side. Sitting down on the crunchy brown leaves beneath Uncle Tom's pecan trees, I leaned back against the wire and wept, sputtering, "I hate her! I hate her! I hate my mother!" until I was satisfied.

But just as soon as I found relief, shame and fear tugged at my conscience. I recollected Mother's voice saying, "Your mother is your best friend. Mother always knows best."

"Grace," called Mother from the kitchen door. "Gra-ace, where are you? Come here!"

Fearful that she knew what I'd been thinking, I jumped up, climbed the fence, and ambled stubbornly to the back door where she stood frowning, holding out my sun hat. "Here, put this on now, and keep it on. You'll get burned up in this sun." Beads of perspiration stood on her forehead. "Wish it would rain and turn cooler."

But the hot orb was high and fierce and deliberate in its trek toward the west.

The clock struck four. I put on the hat and walked over close to Aunt Lou. She was pouring out the water now, her day's work done and drying beneath the summer sun. The cool, soapy liquid wet our bare toes and splattered droplets of sand onto legs and skirts. Then Aunt Lou turned the tubs upside down on the stand, grabbed the thin bar of Octagon soap, the scrub board, and her shoes, and trudged toward the house to receive her wages. I plodded behind her, my emotions spent.

Mother went into The Room and unlocked her cinnamon-colored wardrobe. Taking the black patent-leather purse from a shelf where she kept slips and teddies and stockings, she sat down in her rocking chair.

Aunt Lou sat across from her and took a brown glass jar of snuff from her apron pocket. Pouring a little pile of the dark tobacco into the beige palm of her left hand, she put the tobacco behind her lower lip, making it poke out. Her hands were shriveled and wrinkled from hours in the water.

"You ought not to use that nasty stuff," said Mother.

Aunt Lou laughed hoarsely and rubbed her hand across her bulging mouth. "It my comfort," she said in a muffled voice. "Lawd, Lawd, the trouble I see."

"What's the matter? What's bothering you?"

Aunt Lou scratched her curly head, shifted her tobacco wad to the other corner of her lip, and said, "It's Nannie Lee. She done had anothuh chile. And Li'l Baby, he done run away." Nannie Lee was Lou's nineteen-year-old daughter, and Little Baby was Nannie Lee's husband.

"Lord-a-mercy!" said Mother, knitting her brows into a frown. She crossed her legs and opened her purse. "How many does that make? Little Brother, get off the chair!"

"It make four, two of them's twins. And Nannie Lee, she poorly and she cry all the time; and the baby, he cry with the colic, and them chil'rens, they hungry all the time." Aunt Lou spoke in a husky drone, her words indistinct because of her full mouth.

Mother counted the money in her purse—two dimes, a fifty-cent piece, a few pennies, and two rolled up one-dollar bills. I knew she was hoping to buy material for new clothes in Sandersville. And she hoped Gainer would bring home a check Saturday, although it would be for only fifty dollars and there would be the house note to pay October first, the car note, the insurance, the grocery bill. Impossibly, she also wanted a piano so the children could take music lessons. Oh, she so wanted her children to play the piano! Indeed, she wanted to play herself.

Little Brother began jumping up and down on the bed. "Get down from that bed!" Mother commanded. "You'll dirty up my counterpane."

"Mistah Tom Fulghum, he say I can pick cotton for him next month, but it don't pay nothin'."

"You're still washing for Miz Page, aren't you?"

"Yes, ma'am, I goes there tomorrow."

"Here's fifty cents," said Mother, "and I've got some old clothes for you." She closed her pocketbook, put it away, and went into the adjoining room. Throwing back the lid of the trunk in which she'd carried her clothes to Charlottesville the summer she attended the University of Virginia for teacher's studies, she searched through faded and ragged garments and Daddy's artificial limb bulletins.

"I want to give you some buttermilk, too," said my generous mother, "and a sack of cornmeal."

"Yes, ma'am," said Aunt Lou as she rushed to the back door to relieve her lower lip of its juicy accumulation. Carrying her trove of goods, she trudged toward the west, as Lucy had, but stayed on the Sandersville Road to reach her hut well beyond the white cemetery.

When cool darkness came at last, my young mother again sat in her rocking chair in The Room. A kerosene lamp on the oak bureau behind her chair furnished the haven with a dim light. All doors and windows were locked and shades drawn, and the only sound in the village was the sound of Mother murmuring to her children and the swish of her brush through her long brown hair. She'd changed into a loose-fitting gown that ended at her ankles, and her lustrous hair flowed about her shoulders. She brushed it a hundred times, counting the strokes.

From my place on a low stool she'd fashioned from an empty tobacco box and a square of colorful cretonne, I admired the woman who was my mother, father, teacher, cook, nurse, and protector. She was the single most beautiful creature in my world. My heart softened like melted butter. I wished I hadn't hated her, because I loved her so much. Gone were all my reasons for resentment. Here instead were love and my intense need for her smile, her lilting voice, her comforting presence.

Her grooming finished, she removed the strands from the brush, rolled them into a little wad, and deposited it in the empty fireplace. She laid the brush down and picked up her big black Bible. With Little Brother clad in Wedgwood blue pajamas in her pink cotton lap and me on a stool at her feet, she read to us from Genesis.

Mother had been brought up in the Primitive Baptist church at Mount Gilead, where her mother was a member. She had recently been converted during the August revival to Daddy's faith, Missionary Baptist, and baptized. She was very diligent about reading the Bible to her children.

And the Lord said unto Cain, Where is Abel thy brother? And he said,
I know not: Am I my brother's keeper?

Then she told us the whole story, how Cain had slain his brother and tried to hide the deed from God. She impressed on us to watch out for our little brothers.

I watched the red head of my brother nestled close to her breast and was needled by prickly fingers of envy where I wanted to feel only love. Then the business of hate raised its ugly head again in my brain, and I pushed it down into my darkest corner, thankful that, although God knew, at least I could hide it from Mother—whose wrath I feared more than God's. Mother was always in my presence. I didn't know where God resided.

She heard Little Brother say his prayer and put him in his bed. Then I knelt at her knee for mine, repeating the words she'd taught:

Now I lay me down to sleep,
I pray the Lord my soul to keep;
If I should die before I wake,
I pray the Lord my soul to take.

I understood all the other words, but one was a puzzle. "Mother," I asked, "what is the soul?"

"The soul?" she said, her big brown eyes searching mine, her thin mouth fumbling for words. "Why, the soul," she seemed bewildered, her soft hands covering mine, "the soul's you. Your soul's yourself."

Then she pressed me close to her bosom, which smelled of Coty perfume, and ran her fingers through my long locks. And I felt secure again.

"Always be like Jesus," she said. "His was the most perfect life ever lived. He went about doing good. He fed the hungry, healed the sick, and stilled the stormy sea. He made the lame to walk and the blind to see; and He gave His life for you and me. Always be like Jesus, mind your mother."

"Yes, ma'am."

4 *Never Tell These Things I Tell You*

When I awoke Tuesday morning, Mother was in the kitchen putting a fire in the stove to cook breakfast and heat water. I could hear the iron door open and close as she placed wadded-up newspapers and sticks of light'ard into the firebox. She struck a match, and I could smell the match after she blew out the flame.

Rural kitchens of the 1920s, like plantation kitchens of the 1860s, were dominated by that energy saver, the wood range. Ours was tall and wide and made of black iron, with the trade name Southern Comfort on the oven door. And it was accurately named, for the kitchen stove was a main source of comfort in that deprived region. Food, warmth, and the center of companionship were all supplied by this dear monstrosity.

It had a firebox on the left side, a reservoir for water on the right, and round cooking "eyes" all in between. The back rose taller than Mother's head and furnished warming closets. There she kept biscuits soft and warm for afternoon snacking.

Day after day, delectable odors poured forth from the oven: biscuits browning, pound cakes baking, yeast breads rising, cornpones crisping, peach pies bubbling. On the eyes I could see the pots and pans; I could smell the chicken, ham, or fish frying, the golden corn stewing to a thick and milky succulence, the blackberry juice thickening into jelly.

Now Mother opened the oven door and put a pan of split, buttered biscuits left from Monday onto the rack to brown for breakfast. Then she hurried back on slippered feet into The Room. "Grace, *ma chère,* it's time to get up now," she said sweetly as she lifted Little Brother out of his crib, laid out a clean yellow apron for him. "Help Bucky Snort get dressed and we'll have toasted biscuit and blackberry jam for breakfast."

Pausing before the mantelpiece, she opened the glass door of the clock, clutched a key, wound the spring, and waited. The timepiece had stopped in the night, and Mother couldn't be sure of the hour until the bell rang at the old academy.

Presently the bell clanged in the belfry. Children laughed and yelled as they trotted to books and blackboards. Mother moved the long right hand around and around, stopping it at the figure twelve when the short hand reached for the figure eight. The clock struck eight times. Mother closed the door, talking both to us and to herself. "Get up now! It's getting late. We've got to have breakfast and your lessons. I've got to iron today. Got a big ironing to do, all those clothes Aunt Lou washed yesterday. It's cloudin' up like it's gonna rain. Got to bring in stove wood and buckets of water. It's been dry and hot so long, when it does start, I 'spect it'll set in and rain a spell.

"Got to fill up the wood box. Wood won't burn when it's wet. I need Uncle Dole to come and cut up some wood. Got to try to get word to him today."

When the breakfast dishes were done, Mother went out the kitchen screen door, fetched in a load of wood, and built up the fire. She took two black flatirons from the top of the warming closet and set them on the stove to heat for the ironing.

Lifting an empty gallon pail from the shelf beside the back door, she raced to the well and drew water. Leaning to the left to balance the thirty-pound weight in her right hand, she brought the full bucket into the house and poured it into the stove's reservoir. Then she went back for another pail and another. The reservoir was kept full at all times for bathing, cooking, dishwashing. Two pails were kept on a kitchen shelf for drinking, along with a pan for washing hands and another for washing dishes.

Mother settled her cooing toddler into a corner of the kitchen with his teddy bear and building blocks for company. Then she went to work inside her hand-hewn but cozy country kitchen. The walls were fashioned from wide pine planks. Exposed beams formed the ceiling. The floor featured wide, bare boards the color of pewter from many scrubbings with home-made lye soap and a cornshuck mop.

Mother spread a white sheet on top of blue-checked oilcloth on the old tulipwood table that her father, Zachariah Smith, had made for his bride, Sally, in 1881. Then she dipped her hand into a basin of water and sprinkled the mound of clothes and bed linens Aunt Lou had scrubbed the day before. I watched while she dampened Daddy's starched shirts, one by one. She rolled each into a tight ball and placed the balls side by side in the center of the sheet. On top of these she placed my rolled-up cotton dresses and hers, red-checked, blue-dotted, pink-flowered, along with Little Brother's green pants and his shirts.

Her sprinkling finished, she wrapped the corners of the sheet around the clothes to form a huge ball as big as the stump of an oak tree. She moved the day's work to the dining-room table momentarily, while she spread a handmade quilt on top of the kitchen table oilcloth. Over this padding she placed another old scorched quilt to transform the eating table into an ironing board.

"Now let me get you started on your lessons," she said. "Bring your primer here, and your tablet and pencil, while I get your desk and chair from The Room." Hopping around like a squirrel in the grass, Mother placed her pupil's yellow desk adjacent to her day's work.

The kettle hissed, the fire popped. The ironing and the education commenced.

With a hot pad Mother picked up an iron off the stove. Turning it sideways, she wet the forefinger of her left hand on her tongue and touched it to the bottom of the iron. If it went "smack" it was hot enough. She set the iron down on a trivet.

Unrolling the sheet, she took out a damp dress of mine, spread it out on the padded boards. The hot iron moved up and down the lavender skirt, in and out of the gathered waist. I could see steam rising and smell the hot starched cotton as Mother's skilled hands transformed damp wrinkles into a beautiful garment for her unhappy daughter.

"Mother," I whined, "I want to go to school with Rachel. I want my hair bobbed like Rachel's."

"Now don't go to worrying me about that again. You ought to be thankful you don't have to walk two miles to school, like I did when I was a little girl. You ought to be glad you don't have to carry your dinner in a syrup bucket."

"Two miles?"

"All the way to Smith Grove, squishing on the ice on cold winter mornings. There were no school buses then, no cars, only horses and buggies. And Mr. Jordan wouldn't hitch up the horse just to drive us to school. He was always sick and cranky. I was scared of him. You ought to be glad you don't have a mean stepfather like I did."

I felt sorry for Mother, recalling how Grandpa often growled at me when I ran through Grandma's hall and let screen doors slam behind me with a bang.

"He'd been to that terrible war, been a guard at that old prison camp, Andersonville."

"What war?"

"Oh, that old War Between the States. He wasn't but fifteen when they took him off, just a boy."

Mother finished the lavender dress, hastened to The Room, hung it up in the wardrobe.

She put the cold iron back on the hot stove, saying, "Now you must not ever tell anybody these things I'm telling you. Little girls must be seen and not heard."

She started me on my reading lesson. While I read aloud, she turned to the stove and moved an eye, set it down on another eye, and put more wood into the firebox, saying, "I've got to chunk up the fire." Sweat dripped from her rolled-up hair, dropped off the end of her nose, fell into the fire and sizzled. "I hope it does rain and turn cooler. This hot cloudy weather is so oppressive, and ironing makes me so hot! I'm afraid the well's gonna run dry if it doesn't rain soon. But I hope it doesn't start 'til after dinner, 'cause we've got to get in stove wood."

Now the eye was back in place and turning red hot. The lid to the blue pot began dancing up and down. The kitchen was filled with the aroma of black-eyed peas simmering with ham hocks. Mother "smacked" another hot iron and went to work on my pink-and-blue-flowered dress. As the iron smoothed wrinkles from fragrant cotton, the sad story of Mother's life unfolded from her lips.

I cried inside for Mother. But all I could do was sit still and quiet, listen, and let my heart break for her. *I'll try not to worry Mother, just stay close to her and be sad with her. That's the way I can help her, make her smile. How happy I'll be when Mother gets through ironing, puts on her pretty dress, brushes out her hair and puts it up with hairpins, and we go to see Grandma and Rachel!*

A knock sounded at the front door.

"Now who in the world can that be at this time of the morning?" said Mother. "Lord-a-mercy, I pray, I've got so much to do." She plunked the iron on the stove and hastened up the hall to open the wood door with the decorated frosted glass on the top half. "Haven't got time to be bothered."

It was Lucy, standing on the porch, a sheepish look on her ginger face, her sun hat clamped on her head.

"What do you want? What are you doing at the front door?" Mother spoke sharply, exasperation on her face.

"Miz Bryant done sent me after some thread. She done run outa red thread. And she tryin' . . ."

"Go around to the back door, Lucy. What do you mean coming to the front door? Miz Clara's liable to see you, and Aunt Emma." Mother slammed the door and raced back to the sewing machine in The Room. Opening the drawer, she took out a spool of red thread and bucketed to the kitchen in time to meet Lucy at the back door.

"Miz Bryant's done run outa red thread. She say please send her a spool if'n you is got some to match this here piece a te-te-real . . ."

"You mean material, Lucy," said Mother, taking the scrap and matching it with the proper color of thread. "Have they caught the killer yet?"

"Yes, ma'am. Cotched him yesterday with the bloodhoun's."

"Thank the Lord! Poor boy, what'd they do with him?"

"They put him in the jailhouse in Sans-ville."

"You mean Sandersville. Well, I'm sure glad he's safe. Glad they didn't lynch him. Lord, that lynching was an awful thing. Negroes left here in droves. The whole region was terrified."

"Shoot, I'm goin' to Dee-troit myself."

"It was an afternoon in May right after dinner. Little Brother was a baby, two months old. Roses bloomed on the fence, robins sang in the trees. It was such a pretty day, I decided to sit on the porch and rock the baby. Then all of a sudden, I heard guns going off. And hundreds of cars came tearing down the road, with hundreds of guns poked out of windows. Have you heard from Claudia yet?"

"Nome, I ain't heared nothin' from my baby, I hope I hears today. I gotta go now, take Miz Bryant this here thread so's she kin finish Rachel's dress. Gotta cook some corn bread."

"Be sure and come Saturday, Lucy, and help me take the children to the fair. Gainer's coming home Saturday and drive us to Sandersville."

"I tol' you I'd come, Miss Lila. 'Clare 'fore Gawd, I be here, hope to die."

"Well don't forget."

"I'll be here Saturday mornin', sunup, if'n I live an' don't die and the good Lawd spare me."

"Lucy, all those sayings mean the same thing," Mother said, laughing.

Lucy laughed too, her cheeks going up and down.

"If you see Uncle Dole, tell him I need him to come cut up some stove wood."

"Yes, ma'am." The screen door banged behind Lucy.

Mother put her restless redhead in his crib in The Room for his morning nap. She built up the fire in the stove, lifted the lid, and stirred the peas with a long-handled spoon. "Peas sure do smell good," she said. She started me on my writing lesson, resumed the ironing and the education.

At noon the school bell rang for dinner. Children galloped down the steps, the sidewalk, the dirt road. I could hear screen doors of stores and homes banging behind them.

"Lord-a-mercy, I pray. It's twelve o'clock and I've still got Gainer's shirts to iron. Got to finish dinner. Here, take your dresses, hang them in the wardrobe. Come back, get the sheets and pillow cases, and put them away in the drawer."

At the open wardrobe I hung my dresses and counted seven in all with the Sunday frock. It was pink, like the Dorothy Perkins roses that bloomed on our white picket fence in May, and trimmed with ribbons and lace. Looking at all the dresses Mother had made for her little girl, I was ashamed of myself, guilty about having seven when my poor mother had had only one when she was little.

In the back bedroom–office, where Daddy kept a desk and typewriter, stood a bureau with wide drawers and a tall mirror. It was here that Mother kept the bed linens. I opened the drawer, and Mother, holding the pressed, ragged white sheets with both hands, laid them down on top of new sheets—some hand-embroidered, some hemstitched, others trimmed with her handmade tatting. All were white and lovely and unused.

"Mother, let's use these pretty sheets sometime."

"Oh no, we have to save these for company, for special occasions." Then pointing to a tatting-trimmed sheet, she said, "I want you to tell them to cover me with this one when they lay me out."

"Lay you out?"

"When I die, they will lay me out on the bed like we did Lucy, my sister. Then I want you to give them this sheet to cover me with. They will draw it over my face and head."

"Oh, Mother! Don't die. Please don't die and leave me," I cried with terror as we walked back to the hot kitchen.

"I hope I don't die till you're grown, *ma chère*. But you never know when death will strike. The surest thing about life is death and taxes. We're born to die, the preacher said, born to die. We have to live right every day, so we'll go to heaven when we die. Obey your mother and daddy. Don't worry me. Don't run away. Always be like Jesus. Mind your mother like Jesus did."

"Oh I won't worry you anymore, Mother. I won't ever worry you again to go to school with Rachel. Mother, what does *ma chère* mean?"

"It's French for 'my dear.'"

"I love for you to call me *ma chère*," I said softly, feeling warm inside.

Sweat dripped from stray curls at the nape of Mother's neck as she dipped the brown peas from the pot into a bowl and set the bowl on the dining-room table. Sweat trickled down onto her red dress as it had all morning; now it was soaked.

The round oak table had a pedestal and modified Queen Anne chairs. Mother put the corn bread and boiled country ham ends on the table, then opened a jar of golden peaches she had picked, peeled, and pickled when the July sun sizzled. Setting the Mason jar on the oilcloth, she lifted Little Brother, placed him in the oak highchair, washed his hands with a wet rag. The clock on the mantel struck once as the end-of-dinner school bell rang.

"Wash your hands, Grace, let's eat dinner," said the weary woman.

I went to the back porch and poured a dipper of cold water into the white enamel pan. Picking up green Palmolive soap from a china dish, I washed my hands while watching Rachel, Jessie, Pauline, Jack, and Jacob line up in front of the schoolhouse, march up the steps, disappear into the antique building. Silence fell upon the village as we gathered around the dinner table.

"Hold down your heads, *mes chèrs*, while I ask the blessing. Close your eyes."

"Dear Father in heaven," Mother voiced, "we thank you for this food and all our many blessings. Bless Gainer yonder at Macon." Mother hesitated. "Bring him home safely." Mother's voice broke into a sob. I looked up and tears were trickling down her cheeks, falling into her plate.

I froze with fear. My throat tightened, my stomach hurt. *What is the matter with Mother? Is Mother going to die like Aunt Lucy?*

She took a handkerchief from her apron pocket, wiped her eyes and nose, wiped sweat from her face and neck. Stuffing the handkerchief back into her pocket, she served our plates with the peas. Dark brown pot likker covered the white plates all the way to the cluster of pink roses near the edge. Our nostrils were filled with fresh vegetable fragrance.

"Eat your dinner now. Hold over your plates. Don't spill food on your clothes. Keep them clean so I won't have so much ironing to do next week."

"Yes, ma'am," I said, cramming my mouth with crisp corn bread and bits of ham.

Mother's voice broke again. Tears fell into her peas. She wiped her eyes with her handkerchief again, by now sopping wet. "My daddy died when I was a baby. My husband went off and left me with these little children to raise by myself. And all this work to do alone. I get so lonesome and scared and tired with everything to do by myself.

"He just would go. I just couldn't keep him from going. He just went crazy over church work and the BYPU. Just went crazy. Tearing all over the country, starting BYPUs in other churches—Bartow, Wadley, Harrison, New Bethel, Deepstep, Sunhill, Mount Moriah. Uncle Pete was right. He said, 'Gainer lost his head over the BYPU.' Just lost his head and went off and left me.

"Mama was right. She didn't want me to marry him. Said a one-armed man wouldn't be any good around the house. I should have listened to Mama. Now God is punishing me because I disobeyed my mother. Punishing me with all this hard work and loneliness. I didn't want to be left alone. I wanted companionship, a husband home every night to help me draw the water and raise the children. I wanted somebody to talk to."

My heart broke for Mother, and for Daddy, too, who had gone away and left Mother alone and sad. Food turned to sawdust on my tongue. *What is the BYBU?* But I couldn't ask her. Terrified about Daddy losing his head, I'd lost my voice.

Suddenly a thunderclap roared at the bowels of the earth outside, interrupting my poor mother's lament.

"Lord-a-mercy!" said Mother, looking out the tall window. "Lord-a-mercy, I pray. There's a black cloud comin' up. It's gonna rain."

She jumped up from her chair, snatched Brother from his, set his bare feet upon bare floorboards. The she picked up two empty water pails and dashed out the screen door, calling behind her, "Come help me, Grace. Get in some stove wood while I draw the water. Brother, you stay in the house."

Thunder rumbled around the horizon. Lightning split the sky. Dark clouds lowered. The old pecan tree tossed its branches around to right and left and crape myrtles littered the grassless ground with blossoms the color of watermelon meat.

I put three sticks of wood into the crook of my left arm. *What is the BYBU?* Little Brother opened the screen door. I threw the fuel into the wood box behind the range, grieving because Daddy had lost his head, left Mother, and made her cry.

Mother set the gallon pails upon the kitchen shelf, reached for her straw sun hat, and placed it over her curlers to keep her hair dry.

She hurried down the steps calling: "Gotta get the chickens in. Come help me. Bring in some more stove wood. It's gonna set in and rain a spell. It's been dry so long. Wood won't burn when it's wet. Wish I could see Uncle Dole."

Mother hightailed it to the old gray barn, calling: "Chick, chick, chick, come here, chickens. Come on here. Get in your coops. Chick, chick, chick."

Finally, we rounded up the Rhode Island Reds and the Dominica hens, shut them safely inside their foul-smelling coops, and latched their screen doors. Big drops of rain splattered the ground. We ran up the kitchen steps just ahead of the gully-washer.

Lightning cracked like firecrackers on the Fourth of July. Thunder roared, boomed. Rain fell in sheets.

"Come help me pull the windows down," Mother called urgently. "Be quick, before everything gets wet."

We jumped from kitchen to dining room to bedrooms, unlatching Wescoloski's eighteen windows, pulling out props, letting them drop with a thud. Then Mother ran to the front porch, turned the three green rocking chairs over, propped them against the wall. She started dragging the settee across the floor. "Here, help me bring the settee inside to keep it dry."

We placed the cane-bottomed seat against the wall in the middle of the hall.

"Now, let's sit here," she said, pointing and running to close front and back doors. "Sit in the middle of the house so lightning won't strike us. If lightning strikes us, it might kill us."

Electricity flashed, thunder rolled, raindrops galloped on the shingled roof. We huddled together on the settee. Through the rectangular glass panes surrounding our front door, we watched wind and rain lashing our cedars' branches.

"We'd better pray," said Mother. "Better be still and pray. Ask God to keep us safe through this storm. Wonder what Gainer's doing?"

But I didn't know how to pray anything but "Now I lay me down to sleep." I wondered what the BYBU was, and I worried about Daddy losing his head. I heard my voice ask, "Mother, what's the BYBU?"

"The BYPU?" She broke into sudden laughter. "Ah, that means Baptist Young People's Union! It meets at the church every Sunday night. They train young people for Christian service, to read the Bible daily, learn how to pray, speak for Jesus."

I began to whimper.

"What's the matter with you?"

"I'm afraid Daddy will die without his head. You said he lost his head."

"Ah, that's just a saying," she said, laughing more, her brown eyes glowing like fireflies. "He hasn't really lost his head. He's all right." Then anxiety narrowed her eyes. "You must never tell anybody these things I tell you. Little girls must be seen and not heard."

"Yes, ma'am."

5   Southern Comfort

Mother's prophecy came true. It set in to rain a spell. Rain danced on the roof, splattered on upside-down washtubs and puddled at kitchen doors. Mother laid a long plank adjacent to the back steps to prevent soaked feet when we had to go outside to the well or The Closet or to feed the chickens.

On Wednesday morning, the school bell clanged, our clock struck, Little Brother chattered. But The Room was dark, the shades still drawn. Mother lay motionless in the double oak bed and as silent as a corpse. No breakfast smells wafted from the kitchen range. No fire burned in the wood stove.

Mother had migraines, one every two weeks as regular and depressing as the ashes that collected daily underneath the firebox of the Southern Comfort. I knew she wouldn't eat all day, wouldn't talk except to give instructions. The ancient house was so still I could hear the silence buzzing like a drove of tiny insects.

"Grace," Mother finally called weakly from her pillow, "get up and get dressed. Help Little Brother put on his shirt. I've got a sick headache today. You'll have to help me. I'm so nauseated I can't cook breakfast, can't eat. You'll have to eat corn flakes. Fix Little Brother some."

"Yes, ma'am."

After corn flakes I waited at the foot of Mother's bed on a stool beside the narrow window. She lay silent and still, fully clothed and covered with a white cotton counterpane, on her back. A white handkerchief covered her closed eyes to shade them from the light. I knew by her breathing she was not asleep. Bedroom slippers waited as mutely and patiently as a small puppy might for its mistress to resume her walking.

Our solitude was broken now and again by Little Brother's chattering and the ticking of the clock on the green mantel. I watched the pendulum swing back and forth, back and forth. Now it struck ten times and fell silent again except for its tick-tock, tick-tock, tick-tock.

It always made me melancholy when Mother was sick and silent. Afraid to open my mouth or move around lest I make her worse, and knowing Mother liked little girls to be nice and quiet, I kept as still as a cat sleeping in the sun, my hands folded in yellow-flowered lap. I hoped my presence would somehow help my poor mother get well.

From my lonely window I could see most of Riddleville. The village held about one hundred people, one-third of them "colored." Through the drizzle to the east, I could see three stores, one filling station, Grandma's house, the icehouse and the one-room jail with bars at the windows. Once the jail had been used to lock up "uppity niggers" and rowdy drunks until they sobered. Now it was overgrown by weeds and vines and never used. There was no police force to remove alcoholics from the sandy sidewalks. When one had drunk too much bootleg whiskey and couldn't find his way home, he simply fell into the nearest ditch, haystack, or barn.

If a black got "uppity," refusing to bow and bend before a white, he was dealt with quickly by the nearest white or group of whites. Where lowly blacks were concerned, "superior" whites throughout the South didn't always wait for due process of law.

Our village had no paved streets or sidewalks, no green lawns or evergreen shrubs. Few trees colored the landscape with autumn beauty. Homes had no electricity, no plumbing, no indoor toilets. There were only four telephones. One of the black contraptions hung on the wall of each of the three stores; the fourth hung in Grandma's hallway.

We saw few automobiles. Most people traveled on foot or by horse and buggy. Beside the street, just outside the narrow corn patch next to our house, was the public well, a relic of the eighteenth century, where travelers still stopped to water their horses.

At the close of the Revolution in 1784, when the nation was young, proud, and victorious, our county was established to give land and homes to patriots who'd sacrificed everything they owned in winning freedom for the colonists from the British. Freedom meant that white people would be free to pursue life, liberty, and happiness. Washington County was originally composed of all the land lying between the Ogeechee and Oconee Rivers, land nurtured by an ancient Asian race for perhaps ten thousand years. By wagon train the patriots came from Virginia and North Carolina. They were the sons and daughters of Ireland, England, Scotland, and

France who'd crossed the sea on sailing ships. These Revolutionary veterans built log cabins, planted corn and cotton and roses.

Anderson Riddle arrived in 1815, got rich off cotton and slaves. It was he who donated three hundred acres for the purpose of educating young people, with the stipulations that the village springing up around the Mount Vernon Academy be named for him and that no liquor be sold within its borders.

Energetic yeoman farmers erected large houses near their log cabins and turned the cabins into slave quarters. One was William Gainer Bryan I. His grandfather William Gainer had been a soldier in the Revolution and received a grant of 250 acres near the Ogeechee River in 1790. Bryan built a handsome house on the hill and moved his wife, Martha, and baby son, John, there from the Gainer plantation. John Fulghum settled on the other side of the school. In 1859 the town that had sprung up around the institute was named Riddleville and incorporated by an act of the Georgia legislature.

The clock ticked away the minutes until finally both hands folded at the top, and I counted twelve strikes. The school bell rang for dinner.

Mother's voice, weak and sad, spoke from her pillow: "Maybe if you will go to The Store and get me a Co'-Cola, I will feel better. Then I can fix you and Brother some dinner."

Startled from my reverie, I jumped from the stool.

"Get a nickel out of my purse, and put on your sun hat. Be sure it's cold," added Mother. "I want it to be icy. Can't stand a Co'-Cola if it's not as cold as can be."

I bounded down the front steps and raced through the gate. All happiness and gaiety lay outside my home, away from Mother. But today as always, sweet freedom mixed with pangs of guilt. Clutching the nickel in my sweaty palm, I ran, contemplating The Store with its chocolate candy kisses, peppermint sticks, and Uncle Herbert. Bare brown feet carried me across the sloppy road just as school children filled up the streets on their way home to dinner.

Once inside the store, I dawdled, fascinated and frightened by the gaggle of country rednecks hanging around. Bums and loafers, Mother called them. Clad in faded denim overalls and high-top, mud-caked shoes, they smelled of bootleg whiskey. In their group near the door, they shifted from one foot to the other snapping red suspenders, chewing tobacco, guffawing as callous men do when swapping dirty jokes — or "nigger" stories.

But Uncle Herbert was different. He was tall and handsome and twenty-five. All the girls loved him. He parted his dark curly hair in the middle. His brown eyes were kind, his voice soft and caring. "What do you want?" he asked gently as he pulled away from the cracker group and walked toward his niece with the pounding heart.

"A Co'-Cola for Mother, a very cold one," I murmured.

"Is Mother sick today?"

"Yes, she's got a sick headache."

"I'm sorry," he said, thrusting his clean white hand into the crimson tank stuffed with cracked ice, water, and soft drinks. Fishing around in the icy waters, he brought up a 6-ounce bottle filled with what I knew was dark, sweet liquid. Bits of ice clung to the frosty glass. "This will be just right for Sister Lila."

His hand, reddened from the frigid waters, stuffed the Coca-Cola into a small brown paper sack. He handed it to me, and I gave Uncle Herbert the nickel, then stayed to watch him move back to the cluster of rednecks. Forgetting about Mother, I studied the men. In sharp contrast to the country laborers, my uncle wore polished brown slippers; they wore scuffed boots. His laughter was low and refined; theirs, raucous and loud. He smoked thin white cigarettes; they spat out brown tobacco juice, which stained the concrete apron in front of the store and attracted swarms of flies. I thought of Uncle Herbert's Chrysler with a rumble seat and their buggies and wagons. He was always patient and adoring; the other men ignored me.

I love Uncle Herbert. When I grow up, I'm going to marry him. I watched the group disperse for dinner. They went out screen doors one by one until there was no one left except my heartthrob and me. Mesmerized, I clutched the thawing drink in my chubby hand and longed for a word of admiration from Uncle Herbert, just a word. "You're a pretty little girl," he's sometimes say. And sometimes he'd even say, "Let's go to ride in my car."

But it was not to be. "You'd better go home now," he said gently. "Mother'll be waiting for you."

His sweet voice, soothing like a stroking hand on my back, was enough.

I went out the door just as Mother called from across the deserted street. Everyone in the village had gathered around their dinner tables or school lunch boxes except Mother and her boy and girl.

"Gra-ace! Come on here!" Mother's voice split the air. She stood on the porch in her red-dotted dress, ragged bedroom slippers, and disheveled hair.

Fear constricted my heart. I ran as fast as I could.

But it was too late. The drink was no longer icy. Mother had no ice in the cottage, no refrigerator, no electricity. And she was sick and hungry. Her wrinkled brows showed anger. "Why did you fool around so? I told you to hurry back."

I had no answer.

She removed the wet, smelly sack from the Coke, anger etching her face, voice heavy with disappointment. "You never can do anything right. Always fooling around, slow as Christmas. Looks like to me you would help me when I'm sick after all I do for you, all the sewing, cooking, ironing. You ought to be ashamed of yourself! You're going to be sorry when you see my cold, dead body."

I hung my head. I'd failed Mother again while waiting for a word of admiration from my beautiful uncle.

But the next day, Mother was out of bed long before the school bell rang. The Coca-Cola had worked its miracle, cured her headache. She'd munched on saltines in the afternoon, sipped chicken soup for supper. An anthill of activity, she had gathered figs from the bush by the garden gate and eggs from the hen nests before eight o'clock Thursday morning.

"I got to make fig preserves today," she said, lighting a fire in the stove. "I'm so hungry after yesterday's fast, think I'll cook some of Mama's ham for breakfast, make scrambled eggs and grits. Then, while the figs are cooking, we'll have your lessons."

The rain had started again in the night and puddled at the back door. Now a gentle mist descended on the roof, on barn and well, on Abe's cabin.

Soon the delicious smell of country ham frying permeated the air. A timid knock sounded at the back door. Mother opened it, and there in the rain and mud stood the former slaves Aunt Nannie and Uncle Dole. The two Africans were as black as our iron stove. Uncle Dole's back was bent with age, for he was past eighty. His head was covered with a battered black hat and he leaned upon a crooked, hand-hewn cane. Aunt Nannie huddled beside him, clad in black-and-white-checked rags.

Uncle Dole bowed and removed his hat. Raindrops splattered upon his graying head. "Is you got a li'l somethin' to eat, Missy? Us poor old niggers hungry."

"Uncle Dole, where in the world have you been?" Mother said, her voice gentle. "I've been trying to see you for days. I wanted you to cut some wood for me. But you can't work in this rain."

"I think it gonna quit after while; I cut you some then."

Smiling, Mother was already opening the screen door. She said "Y'all come on in here out of the rain. I'll give you some breakfast in a minute. Then maybe it'll slacken up a bit and you can chop me some wood."

"Yessum."

My heart was jumping with joy. Mother was well and smiling, ham was frying, Uncle Dole had come to help Mother.

He picked up the empty water pail. "Miss Lucy say you done send after me. Would-a come yesterday, but it were rainin' bullfrogs, and I were down in my back."

"What's the matter with your back?"

He opened the door. "It the 'ralge, somethin' other like that."

"Neuralgia," Mother said. "Mama has that sometimes."

As he headed toward the well, I could hear his lament: "Lawdy mercy, how many buckets of water I done drawed this here well. Ever since Massa bought me, brung me here. Ever since me and Nannie jumped the broom, I's been drawin' water this here well."

"We was drawin' water that there well when the Yankees come through that warm day in the fall '64," said Aunt Nannie. "They callin' theyselves settin' us free. Us poor niggers ain't free yet. What us got now, worse'n slavery. Leastways us had 'nuff to eat then."

Finally the food was cooked and set upon the oilcloth, and we all sat down—Mother, Brother, and I at the kitchen table, the blacks in chairs pulled up close to the stove "to dry out," they said. They balanced their plates of ham, gravy, and grits on their knees and smacked their lips mightily with every morsel. It tasted good to me too.

"It been a long time since us done et this good," said Uncle Dole. He poured his hot coffee into his saucer, then set the cup on the stove. "I's goin' sasser and blow my coffee," he said. Then while balancing his plate of food upon his knees, he grasped the saucer with both hands, blew the coffee with his lips pursed, then slurped in obvious enjoyment.

"Corn all burnt up in the field long ago," said Aunt Nannie. "Garden gone all 'ceptin' a little okra pods. Ain't nothin' in the house to eat 'ceptin' some little old beans I canned. I was sick in June, July, couldn't can much of nothin'."

"I'm sorry," said Mother. "What was the matter?"

"Rheumatiz in my knees and hands and back. I just hurt so bad, can't hardly walk none. Can't hardly see neither. I's feared I's goin' blind. It's all I kin do, cook us a little fatback, corn bread. Just ain't no 'count. Me and Dole neither one ain't no 'count. Us pore ole niggers 'bout plumb wore out."

I stared at their black faces fringed with white hair, their black fingers twisted and gnarled like old trees in the pecan orchard behind the barn. I worried about the dear old folks, aged, bent, clad in smelly rags. *They aren't really my aunt and uncle, but somehow they're close to me just the same, and I am happy Mother is letting them eat with us. It's so cozy to have them here in the kitchen and seated around the warm stove while Rachel and the other children are up at the schoolhouse.*

Friday, after lessons, Mother cleaned house. "Come and help me," she said, giving me an oily dustrag. "You wipe the dust off the dresser and tables while I sweep. It's a pretty day. Let the blessed sunshine in!" She pushed up the windows, propping up each sash. "After dinner we'll dress up and go visiting. And tomorrow Gainer's coming, and we're going to the fair."

"Can we go to see Rachel today?"

"Yes, we're going to see Rachel this afternoon."

"Oh, boy!" Gleefully I wiped dust from the oak dresser, knocking Mother's hairbrush to the floor in my enthusiasm.

By three o'clock the seven rooms and wide hallway were as clean and shining as a Greek temple, and Mother's smile was like the sunshine as she fixed us up to go visiting. My heart light as a cloud puff, I stood by the oak dresser with the big mirror and watched Mother put on her red dotted-Swiss dress, comb and brush her long dark hair. She dressed me in a pale pink frock that had hand-embroidered flowers on the bodice and bloomers that matched the dress. Little Brother wore an apron fashioned from green-striped cotton. Finally she put on our white socks and black slippers, fastening them with straps that buttoned at the ankles.

At last, Mother strapped her pocketbook over her arm and clutched one hand of her "Bucky Snort," and we walked down the sandy sidewalk. Crossing the unpaved road, we passed the icehouse and its filling-station gasoline tanks, then stepped onto the paved porch of The Store.

A festive Friday atmosphere had spread through the village. White men and women milled up and down the porch. Our marketplace was filled with chattering country folk clad in calico. They'd come to town to purchase weekly supplies, kerosene and wicks for lamps, seafood for pots and frying pans, cigarettes, coffee, flour, and sugar. White males in blue denim overalls leaned against the counters and bantered with khaki-clad clerks. These were Daddy's four teenage brothers—Cecil, Frank, George, and Amos, white shirts open at their throats—all good-looking, all adored by me.

In the back corners blacks waited in silent dejection until all the whites were served. They never mingled with whites in public. It behooved them to stay in their places.

Mother, clutching our hands, nodded to each white and said, "Good afternoon." But in the South in the twenties, black men were invisible to a white woman. I was instructed to ignore them. "Never look a colored man in the eye. He might harm you. If you meet one on the street, turn your head the other way."

But when I saw Lucy's sons, twenty-one-year-old Willie and eighteen-year-old Cleophas, I wanted to greet them with a "Hey!" I couldn't help looking at them out of the tail of my eye. They were huddled together with Ambrosia at the back entrance of the red brick store. Dressed in dirty overalls that smelled like grease, grime, and sweat, they had cowed looks on their desolate dark faces and rolled cigarettes by sprinkling tobacco from a Sir Walter Raleigh can into tiny cupped rectangles of thin white paper.

We walked on down to Grandma's house, also on the north side of the street. Grandma sat in her rocking chair by the fireplace. But there was no fire on this warm day. The white bedspread she was crocheting filled her lap.

Rachel danced in and flopped down on her mother's padded lap. Grandma gently moved her youngest, took up the spread, and set it in a brown basket on the floor. While Mother chatted with Grandma, I stared enviously at Rachel's curly top.

Uncle Herbert strode up the steps and into "Mama's Room." He clutched a newspaper-wrapped package that smelled like the seashore. "I brought some fish, Mama, and oysters for supper. I saw Lucy in The Store, and she said she'd come cook 'em for you and wash the dishes."

"All right," said Grandma. "We'll have fried fish and oyster stew. Lila, y'all stay and eat with us."

While the stove heated, Lucy appeared as though summoned, took the mullet out to the backyard, and drew a bucket of water. With a sharp knife she cleaned and scaled the smelly fish, cut off the bloody heads and threw them to the cats. In the kitchen Grandma set an iron griddle on the hot stove and started the corn bread. Mother chopped onions and poured milk into the pot for the oyster stew. Soon the big house was rampant with mouthwatering smells.

In carnival mood, we children laughed and ran up and down the wide hall from back to front door and all around the porches. Such freedom and fun could only be had at Rachel's house.

The village lay in darkness when we left Grandma's to walk back home. There was no light at all except starlight, moonlight, and dim lamplights glimmering from the windows across from Grandma's at Cudn Ophelia's and at Aunt Clara's. We hurried through the gate of our white picket fence and up the steps.

"I would have taken my flashlight if I'd known we'd be gone so long. I didn't mean to stay so late," said Mother, taking her key from her purse. "I meant to be home 'fore dark. Now I'm scared to go in the dark house by myself." Little Brother whimpered at her knees. My heart pounded with fear while Mother unlocked the door.

"Y'all stay here by the door," she said as we stepped inside the threshold, "while I find a match and light a lamp." My brother and I clung together. "Don't cry, Little Brother, don't cry," I said, patting his little shoulder.

We heard the pine boards squeak as Mother stepped carefully across the hall and into The Room to find the kerosene lamp on the bureau. "Click" went the glass chimney as she lifted it off the lamp. She struck a match and turned up the wick. A tiny flame flickered.

Brother and I burst into laughter, scampering toward Mother and the light.

She moved it to a table, barely setting it down before she exclaimed, "Whoa! The light's going down into the kerosene. It'll explode! Lord-a-mercy, I pray—what'll I do?"

We froze as Mother flew to the window, threw up the sash, and knocked the screen out onto the ground. Quick as a flash she dashed back, picked up the flaming lamp, and flung it out the window. It landed in the garden by the tall crape myrtle. Briefly flaring bright orange, the lamp went out like a snuffed candle flame.

"Lord-a-mercy," Mother cried, "it could have exploded and burned up the house! That was a close call!"

Now all was darkness again. Mother fumbled her way to the next room and found another lamp, another match. This time the light glowed perfectly inside its globe. Then my brother and I held hands as Mother carried the lamp from room to room checking the house. The old boards creaked and groaned. An owl hooted from the tall, spooky cedar tree. Mother peered behind doors, in corners, in the closet, under the four beds, in the kitchen pantry. When she finally deemed the house safe, she replaced the window screen and we all climbed into the two double beds in The Room.

I didn't know how long we'd been sleeping when there was a rap on the window screen. A gentle voice called out of the blackness, "Little Shug, Little Shug, unlock the door. It's me, Gainer. I'm home."

Daddy! Heart leaping, I lay perfectly still under the sheet, listening. Mother muttered, "Why did he have to wake me in the middle of the night? Thought he was comin' home tomorrow. Never can tell what he's gonna do." Mother got out of bed, pushed her feet into her felt slippers, and fumbled for a match. She lit the lamp, carried it to the front door, and unlocked it.

Daddy stood in the doorway, holding his black satchel in his left hand, his right coat sleeve limp and empty. A big smile creased his face.

Mother never noticed. "Why did you come in the middle of the night waking me up?" she grumbled. "Thought you were coming tomorrow."

"I wanted to see you, Little Shug," said Daddy. "I got through early and decided to drive on home tonight, Little Shug."

"It's dangerous driving at night. You're liable to have a wreck."

"I drove carefully and slow."

"You could have been robbed or killed."

"I'm all right. How are you, Little Shug?" Daddy opened his satchel. It smelled like toothpaste and shaving cream. "Did you miss me?"

"I'm sleepy and tired, worked hard all week. A lamp nearly exploded tonight. It would have burned up the house and us too if I hadn't thrown it out the window. Now I don't have but two lamps. And I wasted kerosene."

"I'll buy you another lamp at The Store tomorrow and get you some kerosene."

"It's rained all the week. Stove wood got wet, wouldn't hardly burn. I like to never found Uncle Dole to cut me some more."

"I'll find Uncle Dole tomorrow."

"Ah, he finally came. But it was raining so, he couldn't do nothin' but eat. Grace fell over at Mrs. Bryan's tonight and cut her chin jumping on beds. Your mama just lets Rachel run wild, do anything she wants to do. And Grace loses her head when she gets with Rachel. I had a sick headache Wednesday. And Grace broke all my cups trying to fix breakfast."

I didn't lose my head! Didn't break all the cups, only three. I didn't say anything out loud. I was sleepy, and besides, I'd lost my tongue again.

"What time do you want to leave tomorrow for the fair?"

"About eleven o'clock, I guess, after I get through cooking breakfast, washing dishes, drawing water. Lucy's coming to help me with the children."

"I've got some book reports to type before we go," said Daddy as he blew out the light. "Got a kiss for me, Little Shug?"

I drifted back into slumber, thinking of my father's wide smile, seeing his limp right sleeve.

6 His Right Arm

Tragedy came to my father when he was nineteen.

The second of twelve children, William Gainer Bryan II quit school in ninth grade to help his father run the farm and the J. Y. Bryan and Sons country store, where everything from farm plows to chewing gum was sold. On spring afternoons he liked to plow his father's fields, walking in the furrows behind an old brown mule. With the smell of freshly turned earth in his nostrils and a cloudless blue sky above his head, he was content. What more could a man ask of life? What need had he for a high school diploma? He would settle here in the village, where few men went beyond the ninth grade and fewer still ever dreamed of going to college, and become a merchant-farmer and a cotton ginner like his father and his grandfather.

Sundays, because his father and little brothers did, he went to the little white church on the hill. His young sisters sang in the choir, and he was expected to be there too. From his corner on the back pew, he listened absentmindedly to the sermons and the singing of such hymns as "Amazing Grace" and "Jesus, Lover of My Soul."

But all this changed abruptly one warm September morning in 1913.

About 8:30, William Gainer picked up the reins of Old Rhoady, the gray mule, to drive a wagonload of cotton three miles to his father's gin. Shortly after nine, the young man stood on the second floor of the Bryan's reproduction of Eli Whitney's invention. He watched, fascinated by the new machinery he had only last week helped to assemble. Sixty giant steel saws shifted back and forth in swift precision, separating cottonseed from cotton, combing and cleaning, cleaning and combing, and turning into a five-hundred-pound bale the bolls he had helped to grow and gather beneath the summer sun.

He stood transfixed, alone, the thunderous whir and roar of machinery in his ears, the floor vibrating beneath his feet. He thought of the dollars the fruit of his hands would bring, and of his sweetheart, Sally. *I will buy her a ring when we sell the cotton. And maybe at Christmas we will marry.*

His brown eyes steadfastly on the saws, he saw them clogging with errant cotton. He would just lift the breastwork as he had seen other men do and with his right hand quickly, carefully clean away the offending bits.

But the swift teeth caught his hand, their massive sawing, chewing fingers grinding flesh and bone, severing his arteries and veins up the arm almost to the elbow. Blood spurted in every direction, and the youth's agonized cries rose above the thunder.

Men clad in faded overalls came running and quickly stopped the mammoth. Only gasps and moans echoed in the now silent gin. In disbelief the men watched as John and Mary Bryan's boy withdrew from the cruel steel his mangled right hand and chewed-up arm, his life's blood flowing to the floor.

But while William Gainer was in school, he'd learned well the lessons from his physiology book. Now those lessons were to save his life. With his left hand, he reached around his back to his right hip pocket, pulled out a clean, white handkerchief, and calmly instructed the frantic men to tie it tightly around the arm above the elbow. As soon as the tourniquet was knotted with nervous fingers, blood slowed to a trickle.

Button Connell, driving his horse and buggy past the gin to the village, saw the new machine wasn't running and stopped. Still on the seat of his buggy, hands holding the reins, Button saw Gainer, face ashen, arm bloody and dangling, being led down the steps. Aghast, Button knew immediately what he must do.

As soon as the pale young man was helped onto the seat of the carriage, Button stood, cracking his long leather whip to make the horse go faster and faster, carrying the wounded man and his ruined right arm back to The Store, the flight of the horse stirring the sluggish September wind, which whipped in turn at Gainer's wounds.

A cloud of dust rose from the dirt road, flew behind the speeding horse and carriage, and swirled around them all when the horse was halted in front of The Store. A crowd gathered, his mother, Mary, wringing her hands and crying to her husband, "I told you not to send Gainer to the gin. He's too little."

Quickly the only doctor in town and the only car were summoned. Twenty agonizing minutes later Dr. Davis arrived in his horse-drawn buggy and Uncle Tom Fulghum in his automobile. The doctor gave the boy a "puncture" to relieve the pain. Then Uncle Tom's little red Maxwell carried the three of them at its top speed of forty miles an hour to the nearest hospital, ten miles away in Sandersville.

At eleven o'clock in the morning the young man was asleep on the operating table and attended by five doctors. His arm was amputated just below the elbow. It was a morning that was to reach out and touch every other morning of his manhood. Never again would he plow a furrow in an open field or lift the reins of a horse or mule with two hands. He would not become a merchant-farmer-ginner. Nor would he marry Sally.

At four o'clock in the afternoon he awoke in a strange room at Rawlings Sanitarium. From his white hospital bed he saw, sitting in a chair on his right, a nurse in a stiff white uniform. Immediately he went back to sleep.

When he awoke again at six and slowly became conscious of pain in the area of his right elbow, dreadful reality began to take shape in his mind. The smell of antiseptic burned in his nostrils. Turning his head, he saw what was left of his right arm, neatly swathed in white bandages, propped on pillows.

Beside his bed the chair was now empty. Just beyond it a window opened to the west, bathing the room in the bright glow of the setting sun. In the quietness came fully what had happened. Was it yesterday? He had slept so long. *No, it was this morning. I lost my hand and my arm, my right arm, in the cotton gin.*

Then he became aware of another Presence in the room, in the chair where the nurse had been. The Person also bore the marks of violence, in both hands. Peace reigned. A new conviction arose within the young man: *I need never cry or complain about what is gone, or worry about what I will do, how I will manage.*

When William Gainer left the hospital six days later and went back to the home of his parents, he was not the same young man. Nor was Riddleville the same town to him. There was nothing in the farming village a one-armed man could do. So his father sent him to Atlanta to enter business school. After completion of the course he got a job in the bank at Davisboro.

But the business world was not the world for this newborn Christian. Now every Sunday found him at church because he wanted to be there. And that compelling Presence stayed by his side every day until William Gainer Bryan II was changed to the core.

Now a new man must have a new name. And so he changed his name to Gainer E. Bryan.

He was elected president of the Baptist Young People's Union in his church. The BYPU became his obsession. Through this organization Daddy learned to speak in public, tell the Good News of the Gospel, and help others do the same. Once a week young Gainer led his group on cotton-picking parties, earning money to give to the children's home at Hapeville and other mission programs. Soon he learned to drive a car with his left hand and filled his father's Ford with sisters, brothers, cousins, friends, driving them to other churches in the county to start BYPUs until there was one in every church in the Mount Vernon Association.

He had long since given up the idea of marrying Sally. Instead, on December 28, 1915, the man from Riddleville married the maid from Indian Hill. He was twenty-one, and his dark-haired bride, Lila Smith, was twenty. She had a creamy, flawless complexion and lovely brown eyes. She had taught school in the village for more than a year, having come from the one-room schoolhouse near Oconee via Charlottesville and a summer school session at the University of Virginia.

The bride and groom bought all their furniture before their winter wedding day. Pooling their resources, his thirty and her thirty dollars a month, they saved throughout the spring, summer, and fall of 1915. They ordered bed, bureau, tables, chairs from Bagby Furniture Manufacturers, Baltimore, Maryland, and from Baltimore Bargain House. With loving care they placed the pieces in a four-room colonial cottage on Harrison Road loaned to them by Grandma Mary. It had two outside brick chimneys and a kitchen and dining room on the back connected by an open porch that formed a breezeway. Their first home was shaded by water oaks in summer and warmed by hickory logs burning in the fireplaces in winter.

Into this charming setting I was born on April 9, 1919.

That fall Daddy, who was twenty-five, returned to high school after twelve years' absence to complete the work for his diploma. His maternal grandfather, William H. Fulghum, died, and we moved into Grandfather's

Greek Revival cottage on Main Street. Daddy quit the banking job to devote his life in ministry to God.

In 1924, when he was thirty, Daddy entered Mercer University, driving back and forth the seventy miles. By 1925 Gainer Bryan, the student, would also be teaching at Mercer and working with the Rehoboth Association, making one hundred dollars a month. He was gone more than ever, and I was a prisoner of my mother's desire to shelter me at home.

But now my daddy was home, as he had promised.

7 The Fair

Mother was frying eggs for breakfast Saturday morning, her hair still in curlers and wrapped with the pink cotton cap, when Lucy made her appearance in our backyard. Mother looked up from the iron skillet and popping grease, frowned, and exploded, "Lord-a-mercy, there comes Lucy dressed fit to kill."

Lucy pranced up the back steps. She wore a red crepe dress with long sleeves and fringed skirt, high-heeled black pumps with gold buckles on the toes, and a scarlet hat with feathers and plumes. Around her neck hung a rope of crimson beads. Long gold earbobs dangled from her ears. She had powdered and rouged her ginger skin and topped off her costume with a cast-off, moth-eaten fur neckpiece.

Opening the back door, she paused there in all her handed-down finery, raising her eyebrows high onto her forehead as though yearning for compliments. But none were forthcoming from Mother.

"Where do you think you're goin' all dressed up like that?"

"Us goin' to the Fair, ain't us? You ax me to come, Miss Lila, help you with Grace, Li'l Brother. You ax me Monday when Aunt Lou was here washin' y'all's clothes."

"I know what I said. But how are you gonna work dressed up fit to kill? Hat and high heels and fringed skirt, bracelets and earbobs! And you sure don't need fur. It's gonna be a hot day. You'll burn up in that thing!"

Lucy lowered her eyebrows and frowned, sliding the muskrat from her shoulders. "I take it off 'til us gets ready to go." She put it and the pink-plumed scarlet hat on a back-porch shelf next to the can of kerosene. Then she stomped back into the kitchen, pushing up her long sleeves, clumping along as awkwardly as a thirteen-year-old girl in her first pair of high heels.

"Those shoes are too little for you. Your feet'll be hurting all day. Who gave you them things?"

"Miss Mamie, she done give 'em to me."

"Well, if you can walk to the well in them things, I want you to draw some water, fill the reservoir and all the buckets, wash the dishes after breakfast, sweep the kitchen, feed the chickens, bathe the children, get them dressed—if you can get around in them spike heels."

"Yes, ma'am," said Lucy. She headed for the well with empty pail and swinging skirt. "I see Mistah Gainuh come home last night. See his car in the barn. Good mornin', Grace," she said to me as I edged into the kitchen.

Soon Mother and Lucy had transformed the cubicle between The Room and the dining room into a bathroom. Lucy placed a white enamel pan of warm sudsy water on the brick hearth, the green soap in a dish nearby. She sat in a cane-bottomed Shaker chair Grandpa Zachariah had fashioned in the 1880s, dipped the washrag into warm water, lathered it with soap, dipped it into the water again. Then she scrubbed my face, neck, ears, and arms, talking sweet talk all the while. "You my baby. I been bazin' you, nussin' you since you was a li'l ole bitty baby. You didn't know nothin' when I started nussin' you."

I enjoyed the ritual. The bath water was as warm and soothing as my nurse's voice. The soap smelled good. Lucy herself smelled like soap, powder, and hair cream; her gold earbobs dangled; her cheeks sprang up and down.

She toweled my arms, tummy, and back and kissed me on the neck. Then she helped me pull on clean underwear. Sitting on a stool, I put both feet into the pan of warm suds. And Lucy, bending over until her beads clicked against the enamel pan, bathed my feet, the soapy cloth going in and out and between all ten toes. Then she spread a towel on her fringed skirt and rubbed my feet and toes one at a time until they were bone-dry.

She hugged and kissed me again. "Now put on this here dress, baby," she said, unbuttoning the blue gingham down the back, spreading the sash.

I heard Daddy pounding his typewriter in the back-room office, typing book reports with his left hand. "Mistah Gainer printin'," said Lucy.

Lucy's high heels slowed her down to a slug's pace, so Mother washed the dishes, swept the floor, fed the chickens, brought in stove wood and more water. Then, standing in front of the washstand, she sponged off and put on her cool navy-and-white cotton for the trip to the fair. "Bucky Snort, get off the bed. Come here now, let Lucy bathe you."

Our nurse went to work on my grubby little brother. He squealed and hollered. Lucy's bracelets and earbobs dangled as she unbuttoned the little redhead's apron and he pulled with all his might to get away. She pulled harder, her red fringe swaying like the grass skirt of the Hawaiian dancing doll on Aunt Pency's mantelpiece. "Don't be nawsy, Junior. Be still so I kin baze you."

"Nawsy," Mother laughed while brushing my hair. "You mean *naughty*, Lucy."

"Ah, Miss Lila, you know I cain't say hit."

Carefully Mother wound my yellow curls around her forefinger. She combed and wound, combed and wound until she was satisfied I looked like a Mary Pickford doll. She sputtered, "All I can hear is 'When are you gonna bob Grace's hair?' Bob Grace's hair? You better leave your typewriter, Gainer, and get dressed. It's nearly twelve o'clock."

Daddy pulled on a clean shirt, tucking the tail into navy pants, and buttoned up the front with his left hand. Winding the right shirt sleeve around his right elbow, he secured it with a rubber band. With his one hand he placed a red-striped tie underneath his collar and tied it expertly. Then he began to search for his tie clasp, stirring around Mother's hairpins and hand mirror on the bureau.

"What're you looking for?" asked Mother, her tone anxious.

"I can't find my tie clasp. I thought I put it here last night."

Mother left my curls and joined her husband in the search.

"I ain't had hit," said Lucy; "'clare 'fore Gawd, I ain't seed Mistah Gainuh's tie clash, hope to die."

Lucy always got nervous when a thing was lost around the house. Past accusations in other households had not been forgotten. "I ain't had Mistah Gainuh's tie clash, Miss Lila, 'clare 'fore Gawd, hope to die," Lucy repeated while soaping my little brother's legs and feet.

Watching our nurse, I couldn't tell which was moving the faster, the washrag, the red fringed skirt, or Lucy's mouth.

"Ah, Lucy, you talk too much," said Mother. "Nobody's accused you of taking the tie clasp."

"Well, I ain't seed hit. I ain't seed Mistah Gainuh's tie clash, 'clare 'fore Gawd, hope to die. Be still, Junior, so I kin baze you, put on you li'l green suit your mama's done made you. Hit got buttons all around the tail of the shirt. See, buttonholes in the top of you short britches, so we kin button 'em up to the shirt. You wants to ride on the merry-go-round, don't you? Ride the Ferris wheel?"

"Here it is," Mother said to Daddy, "here's your tie clasp. It was under your handkerchief. You ought to put things up where they belong. Then you could find them. Not have all this scramblin' around every time we start to go somewhere."

"Thank you, Little Shug," said Daddy meekly, smiling broadly. "I wouldn't take a pretty for you. You're my right arm."

"You're my true love," Mother said.

Finally we were all in the 1920 car except Daddy. He was in front of Henry Ford's invention, cranking the engine with the bent handle stuck in its hole. He turned and turned, and his face grew red before the Ford sputtered and jerked . . . and choked down. Again and again it happened. "Damn it," said Daddy.

Lucy sat on the back seat between Little Brother and me, her red arms around us holding us close to her muskrat, which smelled like kerosene. Mother sat on the front seat, frowning. "What's the matter with the car? Why won't it start? Does it have gas? We're already late. It'll be night by the time we get there."

Daddy cranked and cranked. He jumped up and down. "Damn it," he repeated.

"Damn it," said Little Brother. "Damn it," the little boy repeated and laughed, relishing the new word.

"Ah, Gainer, you ought not to lose your temper and say curse words. Now you've got Little Brother saying them."

At last the engine coughed to life. Daddy sprinted to the door and jumped onto the high leather seat, throwing the crank down on the floorboard, gunning the engine. With his strong left hand gripping the wheel, we lurched off.

"Thank the Lord," said Mother, "you finally got it started!"

And we were off, Daddy accelerating until we were going forty miles an hour west, to "town" and the fair. The engine was purring, the wind blowing through the open car like a hurricane.

"Oh, how nice to be going to ride after staying at home all week," said Mother, holding onto her red straw hat with both hands. As we passed the cotton gin and the cemetery, she turned around to adore her two little jewels. But her smile turned to a scowl. "Lord-a-mercy, I forgot my umbrella," said Mother as we passed Aunt Lou's cabin. "Gainer, I've got to have my umbrella. Turn around and go back, let me get my umbrella. It won't take but a minute."

But Daddy drove on, saying nothing. His hand was on the wheel, his eyes on the road. Clouds of dust followed the car. Daddy despised nothing more than being forced to return for something once he'd got the car started.

"It ain't goin' rain, Miss Lila. Sun shinin'."

"You never can tell what the weather's gonna do. Anyway, I need the umbrella to shade my face and neck from the sun. Don't wanna get sunburned. Gainer, we'll have to turn around and go back and get my umbrella. And make sure I locked the front door."

Suddenly, like a pop-the-whip, Daddy wheeled the Ford around in the middle of the road. We all squealed in surprise and fear. Mother's big black purse fell to the floor. Lucy and her muskrat tumbled over me. Brother piled on top of Lucy.

"Damn it!" said the exasperated driver, righting the Model-T with his hand and elbow and heading toward home. His face was as crimson as Mother's hat sitting askew upon her head. "I didn't wanna go on this trip anyway."

He halted the car abruptly at our mailbox, all our heads jerking backward. While Mother hurried through the gate, the yard, up the steps, into the house to fetch her scarlet parasol, Daddy leaned his head over the steering wheel. I could see his lips moving as he muttered a prayer of repentance.

We finally reached that place of enchantment, the county fair. But as exciting as the rides, the shows, and the crowds were, nothing could compare to Daddy's sudden U-turn in the middle of the Riddleville Road.

8 All Are Precious in His Sight

In our village the bells rang every Sunday from the Baptist belfry. Just beyond the schoolhouse, the Greek Revival church building sat well back from Sandersville Road and next to Mount Moriah Road. But our Baptist bells didn't ring in the morning. They sounded on Sunday afternoon, the only time we could get the Reverend Rivers,* who lived in the Davisboro pastorium and preached in their church on Sunday mornings.

Nor did the church bells ring for all to come and worship. They chimed for whites only. In Riddleville and all across the Southland, Sunday was the most segregated day of the week. Supposed to stand for love and brotherhood, the church was instead the most segregated spot in all of Christendom.

On this last Sunday in September a hush lay over the village. In the warm sun, Riddleville's three stores were closed tight, bars across their doors. Men slept late, and nobody worked.

Except the women.

The women, both black and white, were up early putting fires in Southern Comforts. They fried eggs and country ham, cooked grits, and made biscuits in old, hand-hewn dough bowls handed down from their grandmothers. After breakfast they drew water, washed dishes, and started big Sunday dinners.

While Daddy visited his widowed mother, Mary Bryan, then drove to Davisboro to get the *Macon Telegraph* and brought it home to read the news, Mother and all the other mothers in their respective homes prepared a country feast. After breakfast Mother went to the chicken coop, caught a reluctant Dominica by the feet, brought him back to the chopping block, and chopped his cackling head off with her hatchet and strong right arm. Then she pulled out all its gray-and-white barred plumage, set fire to a wad of newspapers, and singed off the tiny pin feathers embedded

*Not his real name.

60

in the skin. I stood nearby, revolted by the hiss and smell of burnt feathers and chicken flesh.

But I forgot my distaste of the slaughtering and singeing once Mother fried drumsticks, pulley-bone, and breasts to a crisp golden brown, once I saw them waiting upon the dining table laid with white linen. Today Daddy was there to ask the blessing. Mother shed no tears. We ate our fill of creamed corn, butter beans, hot biscuits, and chocolate meringue pie.

After she finished washing dishes, Mother slung the dishwater into the backyard. Taking a basin of clean, warm water to the bathing room, she said, "Y'all be still and quiet while I get ready for Sunday school," and she closed the three doors—one to the kitchen, one to the hallway, and one to the bed-sitting room.

I knew that, standing before the washstand, she was sponging off her pale, plump body, washing away the grease, grime, and sweat of wood-stove cooking. Then she would dry, powder, and perfume her five-foot-five-inch figure and put on her best dress, one that she had sewed herself of rose pink crepe de chine. It had short sleeves, ecru lace around neck and hem, and a black velvet tie at the throat. She brushed and shaped her dark hair into a neat coiffure and clasped a single strand of cultured pearls around her neck.

Turning her attention to her children, Mother buttoned a pongee suit consisting of shirt and short pants onto Little Brother. The unbleached silk of the suit was the color of beach sand. It sported a tie fashioned from a rectangle of beige-and-brown silk. While she struggled with his brown slippers and tied the shoestrings, she kept one eye on me. I stuffed my chubby body into the frilly frock she had fashioned from mauve crepe de chine, lace, and ribbons bought at the Union Dry Goods Company in Sandersville.

At 2:45 the bells began their ringing from the steeple of our church. I thrilled at the sound of the joyful bells. Like angels singing, they were ringing for me. I was allowed to respond to their summons, go to Sunday school, sit with Rachel.

Mother walked between Brother and me, clasping our hands as we approached the white-columned, clapboard church erected in 1859 by our great-grandfathers as a chapel for Mount Vernon Institute. Calling us her "jewels," she beseeched us to keep our clothes clean, to sit still and be reverent in God's house. At three o'clock we were climbing the steps when the bells rang again above our heads. Brother and I pulled away from Mother's grasp and clamped our hands over our ears.

Inside the little church Emma Lee began playing the upright piano for the opening of Sunday school. Holding an open hymnbook, Great-Uncle Tom Fulghum stood next to the piano. Grandma Mary Bryan's brother, he was a prosperous merchant-farmer and the leading deacon in our little church. Uncle Tom and Aunt Emma made wood fires in the heating stove in winter and opened windows to let in cooling breezes in summer. At his signal, everyone stood to sing the familiar chorus:

> Red and yellow, black and white;
> All are precious in His sight;
> Jesus loves the little children of the world.

While we lifted our voices in praise, I heard a wagon creak past the open window. Standing on tiptoe to get a glimpse through green shutters, I saw Lucy, her daughter Gozella, and Gozella's three-year-old daughter, Evalena, sitting upon a board placed across the wagon's sides. Willie held the reins of the mule, and Cleophas swung his legs off the rear of the wagon. They were headed for Evergreen Church, three miles out of town.

At the same time Aunt Lou and Nannie Lee walked along the sandy path on the other side of Sandersville Road. They would turn on the road just beyond Grandma's house to go to the African Methodist Church on Breezy Hill. There they would worship with Nannie and Dole and others of the community's colored people. Without benefit of a piano or organ, they would sing "All God's Chilluns Got Shoes," "Swing Low Sweet Chariot," and "I Must Tell Jesus" in their separate, and unequal, sanctuary.

At 3:45 Uncle Tom sounded a table bell to call children, teachers, and parents from classrooms to assembly. The folding doors were pushed back, and we children left our rooms to stand on the low platform and proudly recite to parents and teachers the memory verses we'd learned from the Bible: "God is love," "Love one another," "Love thy neighbor as thyself."

Then everybody except Rachel found a pew to squirm on for "preaching." Men sat on the left side of the sanctuary, women and children on the right. Rachel skipped out the door, down the street, and home to Grandma, who rarely went to church or anywhere else. Grandma always said she could worship the Lord at home in her rocking chair. When I saw Rachel go, my heart went too. I begged to go with her. But Mother's firm no and strong hand planted Little Buttermilk on the hard pew.

Meanwhile Uncle Tom pulled the bell rope again, calling parishioners to come to preaching. Through the open door and down the brown-sack carpeted aisle strode the Reverend Rivers. He shook a few hands to right and left and climbed the rostrum to the pulpit. Middle-aged and half-bald, he seldom smiled. Fearsome dark eyes behind horn-rimmed spectacles accented his stern demeanor. Of medium height, he looked well fed. His stomach protruded as though he had just swallowed a watermelon whole.

As he preached his hellfire sermon, he paraded up and down the rostrum, pounded the pulpit with his fist, wiped sweat from his face, plunked the handkerchief down on the pulpit. He was particularly opposed to dancing, card playing, and liquor. Today, with an uncharacteristic grin, he told a story to my parents, cousins, aunts, uncles, and neighbors who made up the congregation: "Once a pretty young girl tried to teach me how to dance. She guided me out to the polished dance floor, and she said: 'Put your right arm around my waist.' And I was happy, brothers and sisters, to do what she said. Then she said: 'Put your left arm around my neck.' And this command, dear friends, I was glad to obey."

Snickers erupted from the men's corner.

"Then she said, 'Hold me close and follow me.' And I said: 'Dear girl, this is good enough for me.'"

The people laughed. And the Reverend Rivers drove home the point of his antisex, antidance, antifun sermon.

"Brothers and sisters, if you don't repent and be saved . . ."—the fist pounded the pulpit—"you're going to burn in hell . . ."—the preacher marched back and forth—"in everlasting fires of damnation!"

The sermon sank as deep into my parents' consciences as a fence post into the ground. They nodded, determined that no one in their household would ever be allowed to go to a dance.

After the service ended, everyone lingered in the churchyard to chat with neighbors, cousins, and friends. While Daddy talked with the men, Mother, holding purse and parasol, stood in the circle of women. Surnamed Paradice, Fulghum, Page, Bryan, all wore felt cloches like bowls turned upside down on their heads.

Little Brother and I played with the other, short-haired, children, my long gold mane shining in the sunlight. Little Brother's candied-sweet-potato top glowed. Mother said little to the women. Her mind seemed constantly on her "jewels," her eyes following us everywhere as we romped in and out among the oak trees, buggies, Fords, and Chevrolets.

"Don't tear your dress," I could hear Mother admonish.

"When are you gonna bob Grace's hair?" asked one of the women. "I know that long hair makes her hot."

I so wanted to be like the other children! Delighting in this little moment of freedom, I frolicked with the white, giving no thought to the red and yellow, and especially the black, children who could not come partake of Jesus' love with us in our church.

I would soon enough begin to see for myself the poverty and the oppression of their existence.

The next Friday progressed as hundreds of others had for Lucy Riddle. Nothing stirred in the air to indicate that a piece of yellow paper would break Lucy's heart before the clock struck five.

The mulatto wore a faded cotton dress made of brown-checked gingham. Over this was a long apron splotched like a painter's smock with grease, pot likker, and dishwater. The ever-present snuff can bulged from an apron pocket. She wore saddle oxfords and brown cotton stockings. A rust-colored stocking cap was pulled down tightly over her ears.

At our cottage, Lucy picked up the "bresh broom" and went to work on the front yard. Fashioned of slender dogwood limbs stripped of their leaves, the broom's bony branches were tied together with strings of red polka-dotted fabric scraps left over from Mother's sewing.

Our fall rains had littered the grassless earth with needles and balls from the older cedars, planted decades before by Dole. Beneath them Lucy swept until the cement-colored earth of the front yard showed only the traces of the broom. With her brown fingers, Lucy scooped up trash from a pile and put it into an old rusty washtub. Mother emerged from the house to help. Little Brother left his spot on the front porch and followed. Mother gripping one washtub handle and Lucy the other, the two women carried tub after tub of sweepings and emptied them in the field beside the barn. Sweat trickled from brown and white faces as they worked together under the early October sun.

The screen door slammed behind Mother as she went back into the kitchen to wash dishes and clean the accumulation of soot from the stove.

Then she scrubbed the lamps, trimmed the wicks, and filled their glass bowls with kerosene poured from a can.

In the meantime, Lucy swept the backyard. I watched from the swing as dust flew up in white clouds and she piled up dead pecan leaves, dried chicken litter, bits of paper. Stooping to scoop up the mess, she spoke her thoughts out loud, "Wishen' I could hear from Claudia. Ain't heared from my baby since she left here two-three munt' ago. I don't know how long it been since I seen my baby, my pretty Claudia. I feared I never goin' see my baby no more."

The end-of-school bell rang. White children galloped down the steps, filled the street, climbed on buses. Suddenly Lucy's son Willie burst through the back gate, walking faster than I'd ever seen him, waving a yellow paper in his hand. "Mama, us done heared from Claudia. This here 'gram come from Dee-troit to Mist' Tom's store. He done read it to me, and it say Claudia dead. She been cre-cre-momate, somethin'-other."

Lucy clutched the bresh broom and shrieked, "Oh, no!"

"She dead, Ma, Claudia dead," Willie asserted. "It say so on this here 'gram what come from Dee-troit. She been cre-mo-nate!"

"She been what?"

"Cre-mo-nate. That mean burnt up."

"Oh, Gawd! Oh, my Gawd!" Lucy screamed. "Oh, Gawd, my baby dead. Claudia dead! They done kilt my baby, burnt her up, just like Li'l Cha'lie. I never see my baby no more. Never see my baby again."

Mother heard Lucy's screams and called from the back door, "What's the matter?"

I came running from the swing, scuffling through dead leaves. Next door, in the house just across Harrison Road, Aunt Clara, her straight black hair pulled back and knotted at the nape of her neck, crept to the edge of her back porch. She drank a dipper of water from her old oaken pail.

"My baby dead, Miss Lila. They done kilt Claudia, burnt her up. I never see my baby no more."

By this time we were all gathered around the stricken woman, all except Aunt Clara, who stared from across the street. Lucy threw the broom down. It fell on top of a pile of pecan leaves. "Lawd, Miss Lila, I gotta go home where's I kin cry loud as I wants to. They done kilt my baby. Claudia dead. Claudia dead!"

Mother patted Lucy on the shoulder with a kind hand. "I'm so sorry, Lucy, so sorry." Her voice was soothing, full of compassion. "Of course you have to go home. You just go right on home and lie down. I'll finish sweeping the yards. You lie down and rest. I'm so sorry, Lucy, so sorry about Claudia. How did it happen? Did they say how it happened?"

"I dunno how it happen. I cain't read this here 'gram, whatsomever 'tis," Lucy stammered between wails. Mother took the telegram and read it out loud:

REGRET TO INFORM YOU CLAUDIA RIDDLE DEAD.
BODY CREMATED.

"That all it say?" sobbed Lucy, wiping her eyes and blowing her nose with the bottom of her apron.

"That's all it says. Oh Lucy, I'm so sorry, so sorry."

I watched my nurse and Willie trudge out the side gate. Wiping her face with her apron, she bent nearly double in her grief. Her wails could be heard all up and down the main street. "My baby dead. They done kilt my Claudia and burnt her up. I ain't never goin' see my baby no more."

Black and white stood stock-still in front of J. Y. Bryan and Sons store, at Tom Fulghum's store, and Cudn Bill's store, and the icehouse, the filling station. They stared at and listened to the grieving widow. A horse and buggy stopped in the middle of the road, its driver mesmerized by the weeping and the wailing. Aunt Clara let the dipper sink into the water bucket.

But no one joined the heartbroken pair tramping home to their hut behind the white church where we sang about the love of God Sunday after Sunday.

"Poor Lucy!" Mother said as she scooped up the trash and put it in the tub. "Poor Claudia."

"Poor Wucy," mimicked Brother. Wearing a navy shirt with a sailor collar tucked into his first pair of blue denim overalls, he picked up a twig and tried to throw it over the edge of the tub.

"Poor Lucy." Mother said again. "Here, Grace, come and help me."

I grasped a handle of the tub, my heart breaking as my nurse's cries echoed through the town. Yet I felt a new strength inside, because I was needed at this critical moment.

"Poor Wucy!" Little Brother repeated, toddling behind us.

"Poor Lucy!" Mother said as we dumped the trash. She was sweating. "Poor Claudia. When I get through, I'll take a bath and put on a clean dress and we'll go over to Lucy's, take her something to eat."

"Poor Wucy."

"It sure is an awful thing. Makes me think of that lynching. Men tearing through town with guns poking from their cars. Burning up that boy."

I had to know. "Mother, what's a lynching?"

"They tied the boy to a tree and burned him up. They didn't even know he was the one that shot Mrs. Kitchens. Didn't even wait for a trial. Just took the law into their own hands. Colored folks left here in droves, they were so scared."

"Oh!" I squeaked.

"Don't ever tell anybody these things I tell you."

"No, ma'am."

After we were cleaned up, Mother was as good as her word. She, Little Brother, and I hurried past the town well, the schoolhouse, and the Baptist church. Since I had never been to a Negro's home before, I was filled with curiosity and eagerness and heartbreak as we approached the former slave cabin.

The sun was setting when Mother stood on the single stone step of the dwelling. She rapped on the hand-hewn door. Lucy let us in, her eyes red and swollen. She held her apron to her face and sobbed afresh. Willie, Cleophas, and Gozella sat in the shadows wailing. Three-year-old Evalena clung to Gozella.

Mother gave our black neighbor the food we had fetched along in a shoe box. "Lucy, here's chicken, potato salad, ham and biscuit, and a jar of blackberry jelly left from dinner."

"Lawd, Miss Lila," Lucy cried, "I cain't eat nothin'. I ain't never goin' eat nothin' no more. Just ain't hungry. Cain't do nothin' but cry, seem like. My mouth taste like salt."

"You will be hungry, though. You'll need something to eat. You'll get hungry after a while. You must eat to keep up your strength. And your children will need food. I know how you feel. That's the way I felt when my sister, Lucy Jackson, died. She was so fine, so smart and beautiful! And just twenty-six."

Lucy's sobs deepened into moans. She wept and she wailed.

I looked around. Lucy Riddle's hut consisted of two rooms, a bed–sitting room and a kitchen to the rear. There was a huge open fireplace, its brick and stone masonry whitewashed with kaolin clay. The ceiling was just the underside of the roof boards and under them the exposed pole beams. Newspaper and rotogravure sections of the Sunday *Macon Telegraph* lined the walls. In the front room were a wooden double bed with a feather mattress, a bureau with a cracked and mottled mirror hanging over it, and a few straight chairs.

Lucy took the shoebox to the kitchen and set it on the cold stove. "Have you got any food in the house?" asked Mother.

"Ain't got nothin' but a little fatback. But I cain't eat nothin' noways now."

Mother opened her purse and gave the grief-stricken woman fifty cents for sweeping the yards. "How old was Claudia?" Mother asked.

"I dunno, Miss Lila. You know us ain't never kep' up with our ages, such as that."

"She 'bout Miss Mary Lizzie's age," said Gozella. Mary Lizzie was my daddy's sister. "Miz Bryant give Mama Miss Mary Lizzie's old clothes for Claudia. She a little younger 'n Miss Mary Lizzie. She 'bout thirty, I believes. I twenty-six."

"Ah, Gozella, you ain't twenty-six. You twenty-seven," said Willie.

"I don't know how old she were," Lucy said. "I just know I never see my baby no more."

"Yes, you will, Lucy. You will see Claudia again. You will see your baby in heaven. We'll be reunited with our loved ones beyond the sunset. I'll see my daddy and my sister, and you will see your daughter."

These comforting words from Mother brought fresh tears. Lucy had cried so much her dress was wet. She kept wiping her eyes with her soggy apron and blowing her nose. Her children cried until the rafters shook. And I tasted salt on my tongue.

Mother wiped tears from her own big brown eyes. Putting a loving hand on Lucy's shoulder, she spoke for all of us. "I'm so sorry, Lucy, so sorry."

9 The Lone Eaglet

Lucy never heard any further word from Detroit. In October chrysanthemums bloomed yellow and bronze. First frost fell on Halloween morning, transforming turnip patches from emerald to icy white. Pecans and
walnuts lay scattered on fields, yards. A low fire burned in our fireplace
beneath the ticking clock.

Every time the grieving mother slipped in, she stared into the flames
and spoke of her lost daughter. Tears often stood in her dark eyes. But she
never learned any more about what happened to her loved one after she
left home. Neither funeral nor memorial service was ever held for one
Claudia Riddle of Riddleville, Georgia.

Christmas came with a new doll and doll carriage for me, a toy train for
Little Brother, ambrosia and fruitcake for all. At Grandma's, aunts laughed
and opened gifts, uncles gathered around the fireplace after dinner and
smoked fragrant cigars.

As the winter days of early 1926 grew longer and spring returned to the
village, the pear tree turned to white in the corn patch. Lucy gradually
became her old cheerful self. But never again did we hear her say: "Shoot,
I's goin' to Dee-troit myself." It was clear she had decided that the northern
city was no better for blacks than our southern village.

When the roses bloomed again on the picket fence and I'd had my sev-
enth birthday, Mother gave in to my pleas and to the harassment of the
village women to bob my hair. Daddy was home and had gone across the
street to The Store. Putting Little Brother in a corner with his teddy bear
and building blocks, Mother set the baby's high chair in the middle of The
Room. Then she grabbed the scissors from the drawer of the sewing machine. "I've decided to go ahead and cut your hair before you and other
people worry me to death."

I didn't know whether to be happy or sad as I climbed up and settled
into the oak chair. Excitement mingled with fear as my frowning mother
loomed over me with the scissors she used for cutting out our dresses and

Brother's pants. But first she wrapped Daddy's shirt around my shoulders and buttoned it at my neck. "It's nobody's business but mine how I wear my hair, how my little girl wears hers. It's my business. I don't have to be in style. 'It's the style, the style.' That's all I hear. I don't care what the style is. I don't have to be in style. Sit still now," she commanded, coming toward my left side with the sharp, cold scissors.

"Yes, ma'am."

"And don't ever tell anybody these things I'm telling you."

"No, ma'am."

"Little children are to be seen and not heard."

"Yes, ma'am."

Whack went the scissors just below my left ear. A honey-colored curl fell to the bare floor. Mother stooped and picked it up. It was seven inches long. She fondled the hair as if it were a gold medal. "It was so pretty," she said in a tearful voice. "Your hair was so pretty! You looked like a big doll." She laid the strands on white tissue paper, handling the curl carefully as though it were rolled-out pastry.

I didn't know whether to laugh or cry. I feared Mother would cry any minute. Then I visualized Rachel's curly top, and my heart leaped. But I pushed my thoughts deep down inside, afraid to speak. I might say the wrong thing.

Mother picked up the scissors again. "Have to go ahead with it now since I've started." Whack. Another seven-inch curl fell to the floor, then another and another. Mother and the scissors moved behind me and the chair until the last whack sounded and the last curl fell into Mother's open hand.

She picked up the other seven curls, one by one, put them on the tissue paper. Then she folded the paper carefully and wept, her tears falling onto the tissue. "I didn't want to cut your curls. But you just kept worrying me so." She found a box that had once held Christmas greeting cards, arranged the wrapped curls inside, and put the lid on. Wrapping the box with a length of pink satin ribbon, she tied it in a bow. Tears wet the bow. Then she tucked the ribboned box into a Union Dry Goods Company bag and placed it on a wardrobe shelf with her pink satin slips and teddies. Only after she put her treasure away did Mother look at her daughter.

She frowned. "Now your hair is bobbed! And I hope you're satisfied!"

She brushed it smooth, trimmed a little around the bottom. "It's as straight as a stick. Hasn't got a curl in it."

Then she burst into tears, clasping both hands to her face. Little Brother jumped to his feet, knocking over his tower of blocks, and clung to Mother's skirt.

My heart hurt for Mother. I actually enjoyed the pain, thinking I deserved it. *My mother is my best friend and I've made her cry, because I worried her until she cut my hair so I could be like Rachel. I'm going to be sorry when I see her cold, dead body, sorry I wanted to be like other girls.*

I yearned to feel my bobbed hair, see it in the mirror. But I was paralyzed. I couldn't lift hands to head, couldn't get out of the chair with Mother crying like that. *I'll just sit still and say nothing. Maybe then she'll quit crying and I can move.*

Finally Daddy strolled in from The Store. He'd been talking to his brothers as they sold cans of salmon and sardines, gasoline, mule collars, and chicken feed. He looked at Mother, and he looked at me. Then, in his characteristic southern drawl he said, "Well, Little Buttermilk, Mother has cut your hair." A smile split his face. "You look pretty, pretty as a picture, with short hair. Mother did a nice job, like she does everything."

Mother stopped crying and sputtered: "Ah, it's as straight as a stick. Hasn't got a curl in it. I didn't want to cut her hair. But every time I stepped out, people said, 'Why don't you bob Grace's hair, bob Grace's hair!' I just got tired of it."

"Well, it looks good to me, Little Shug. You did right, I think."

"Get down!" said Mother to me. "Let me clean up this mess. I got to get dressed. We're going to your grandma's for fish and oyster stew."

I jumped down and ran to the mirror while Mother went for the broom. What a shock! I didn't look like Rachel at all. I looked like a peeled onion. My hair was not curly like hers, but straight and flat. And my face was as round and fat as a full moon.

I was ashamed of myself.

Sixteen months later, in the year Charles Lindbergh electrified the world by flying solo across the Atlantic Ocean, and the year I was eight years old, I finally started to public school. At last Mother opened her wings a bit and let her lonely eaglet limp out into society.

On a cool, cloudy Monday morning in September, Mother and Little

Brother walked me to school that first day. But I would never go to the schoolhouse next door. The old rust red school was abandoned for a new building on the other side of the village, a quarter-mile away.

The sidewalk, an unpaved path lined with grass, sometimes became so narrow we had to walk one behind the other. An airplane droned overhead. We stopped, threw heads back, pointed skyward, exclaimed, "There goes an airplane! There goes Charles Lindbergh!"

We hurried past the weather-beaten Methodist church and a field of tall brown grasses, broom sedge, and briars before the new frame schoolhouse atop a hill came in sight. The first bell rang. My heart bounded like a doe in the forest. The bell was ringing for me.

The school was surrounded by noisy children dressed in faded overalls, ragged shirts, gingham dresses. Jacob Bryan presided over the water pump. Rachel, Jessie, Pauline, and Jack lined up for a drink. All the children were white. The school for blacks, two miles out of town on the Davisboro Road, wouldn't open until November, and it would close at the end of February so the colored children and teachers could work in the cotton fields.

Joyous anticipation mingled with fear as I climbed the steps. I could smell chalk and erasers, oiled floors, unkempt bodies. Little Brother and I followed Mother down the hall to the third and fourth grade. In the room, third-grade pupils sat in three rows of desks on the left, fourth in three rows on the right. Mother told Miss Johnson I knew the multiplication tables and was ready for fourth grade. When the second bell rang, Mother gave her little girl a long wistful look and departed with her boy.

Little did she realize how socially immature her child was. Conversation was rare in our home. When Daddy wasn't there, only Mother talked. We communicated by "uh-huh" or nodding for yes, and "ugh-un" or shaking our heads for no. Almost as silent as a Helen Keller, I became so isolated by the time I was eight that I preferred solitude to any company, even Rachel's.

Scared of the other children and terrified of the teacher, I found the worst thing was the way my voice behaved. As days and then weeks went by, my speech seemed to lie dead and buried deep inside somewhere. If Miss Johnson called my name and asked a question, I broke out in a cold sweat. Any answers I'd memorized fled like dead leaves in a November wind. When at last I reached into the dark depths and pulled up a sound, my answer would be so weak and wobbly I thought my voice must surely belong to someone else.

And I wished it did. The other children responded with curious eyes and giggles.

Rachel sat on the third-grade side beneath the windows. Jessie Hodges squirmed in the seat in front of her. Jack and Jacob wiggled behind them. They were in love with Rachel and Jessie. I loved all four of them and watched them constantly, yearning for their companionship, yet unable to reach out for that which I needed as desperately as a nonswimmer at Brooks' Springs needed a float. How could I keep my mind on arithmetic and geography? I was jealous, because everyone loved Rachel and no one loved me.

On the playground it was different. At recess time the lone eaglet became a celebrity. With my new cotton dress and bobbed hair and tight new shoes, I was singled out by the other girls for a place of honor. They held hands on a grassy knoll near the girl's privy, stretching their arms taut to form a long line.

"Red Rover, Red Rover," called the leader, Rachel, "let Grace come over."

Grace's heart danced and skipped. Her feet sprouted wings. She ran to break through the chain of girls' arms and join the human race. Her heart sang throughout the remainder of recess, English, spelling, geography, the walk home down the path to our white house at four o'clock. The words became a refrain, repeating and repeating themselves inside her head until she fell asleep that night: "Red Rover, Red Rover, let Grace come over."

The lyric was still in my head when I woke the next morning. I couldn't wait for recess to play again. "Red Rover, Red Rover, let Grace come over."

At Christmastime Eula Belle Johnson quit, and Mother was hired to teach our fourth grade. She arranged for Lucy to keep Brother, who was not yet six, at home for the rest of the school year. When I entered fifth grade, Little Brother, clad in blue denim overalls and red plaid shirt, trotted along behind us to his first grade. Somehow Mother managed to be promoted along with her growing daughter to fifth grade, then to sixth.

Daddy had graduated from Mercer University and secured a job with the Sunday School Department of the Georgia Baptist Convention. He traveled the hills and highways of Georgia, writing letters home postmarked with unusual and picturesque names of Georgia towns: Snapfinger, Crabapple, Happy Valley, Shady Dale, Dewey Rose, Flowery Branch, Ty Ty, Summerville, Winterville. Sometimes he took us with him to conventions and summer assemblies at Macon, Atlanta, Savannah, Gainesville, and even Washington, D.C. Mother had become adjusted to her husband's work, to being a part-time wife. She no longer cried about it and took pride in the position Gainer Bryan was earning for himself and his family.

In the meantime Little Buttermilk found herself the star of the student body. Because Mother was a member of the faculty, I shuddered in the spotlight. All I wanted to do was mesh with the crowd. I yearned to be free of Mother. But that was impossible. She who had hovered over me all my eight years in private now hovered over me in public. She paused by my seat during her rounds up and down the aisles, giving her child special instructions. Every letter had to be as perfect as the model, every test paper merit an A; I was required to be the best reader in the room.

At home she said, "I want you to be valedictorian of your class, like my sister Lucy," and "Study hard, like your cousin Charlotte." Never did she tell me to be myself. I should have been grateful for her demands for excellence. But what child wants to stick out? Like all children, I wanted to be popular with my peers. But they dubbed me "teacher's pet."

For my heart, heavy with conflicting emotions, or my brain, packed with problems to the point of stupor, I could find no relief. I had no one to talk to. And I hadn't learned to sing my troubles away, as Aunt Lou did.

Brother was as bright as a gold medal. During first, second, and third grades, he delighted us with the songs, words, and rhymes he learned. One night, in an effort to get Mother off my back, I said, "Mother, Brother will make you proud when he grows up. He's so smart, he'll be your valedictorian."

Mother smiled at her red-headed son and said, "Maybe so."

What a relief to have a brother to become Mother's pride!

But this reprieve from the weight of others' expectations did not lighten the burdens of growing up white and isolated in the segregated South.

10 Chart and Compass

Next to Christmas, the most exciting season in Riddleville was the first week of August. The Baptist church held its revival then. The first Sunday of the eighth month marked the annual Homecoming with dinner on the grounds. Leading the series of services were a visiting preacher and singer. Preacher Harvill spent the week in our home. Singer Sibley stayed at Aunt Emma's and Uncle Tom's.

All through revival week every white for miles around came to the meetings to hear the good-looking young preacher Daddy had discovered at Mercer and to join in the singing, listen to the choirs. They came on foot, by horse-drawn buggy, by Model-T Ford.

Every night at seven-thirty, every afternoon at three, we carried funeral-home fans to cool our heads and handkerchiefs to mop sweat from moist faces. The pews filled to the very front row; young men in shirt sleeves perched in the open windows. Stores closed for the afternoon services, reopened briefly, and closed early so merchants could go to the evening service. Women cooked big dinners for the visiting men and our own Rev. Rivers, and the preachers and singer ate at a different home every noon, every night. Friends and relatives were invited to feast at one another's boards, spreading a festival atmosphere throughout the village.

Tables were loaded with fried chicken, country fried ham, creamed corn, butter beans, black-eyed peas, string beans, sliced tomatoes, cakes, pies, and hand-churned peach ice cream. Lucy, Aunt Lou, and the sweating Nannie Lee helped with the corn shucking, pea shelling, chicken frying, and ice-cream freezing both morning and afternoon. Then, while we went to the church to sing "Jesus Is Calling" and "Whosoever Will May Come," the colored people remained in our steaming kitchens to wash and dry stacks of plates, bowls, glasses, silverware, pots, and frying pans. Lucy, Lou, Willie, and Cleophas knew all too well that "Whosoever will may come" meant "whites only" in the Jim Crow South, and they stayed "in their place."

This contradiction within our brand of Christianity troubled me. But no one else seemed to worry about the double standard, or anything else, during revival. Everyone seemed joyous. Her face free of frowns, Mother put up her hair every morning before breakfast and smiled and laughed during the first week of August more than at any other season of the year. Daddy canceled all his trips, stayed home the whole week, called himself "on vacation." At every service he sat on the front row, left foot propped on right knee, left hand cupping right elbow.

This week in 1929, family and guest Harvill ate breakfast in the dining room. Our round oak table was covered with a white linen cloth. Mother cooked and served sumptuous breakfasts: fried ham, scrambled eggs, grits, butter, biscuits made "from scratch," and preserves—peach, fig, and pear—plus sugarcane syrup. Serene and smiling, Mother sat down to eat her superb dishes with her children, Daddy, and the preacher.

Afterwards Lucy came and helped us draw water, wash dishes, feed chickens, bring in stove wood, and sweep floors, all for fifty cents and a pan of leftover "vittles" to take home to Cleophas and Evalena.

Every night the young preacher finished his sermon, took a handker-chief and mopped sweat from his glistening face, and announced: "The doors of the church are opened. We invite you who will to repent of your sins and come to Jesus and be saved from everlasting damnation."

While Emma Lee played the upright piano, choirs and congregation rested their fans and stood to sing the soul-stirring words of "Just As I Am." The first night nobody walked down the aisles, though we sang all six stanzas. Monday night one "lost" woman made her way forward and, tears glistening upon her cheeks, gave the preacher her hand.

Wednesday night Preacher Harvill stopped the music between the fifth and sixth stanzas to plead, "Come to Jesus, repent, confess your sins and be baptized! The angels in heaven will rejoice when even one lost soul comes to Jesus." When the singing started again two young people walked down each aisle, followed by two more. I watched and wondered.

Thursday morning after breakfast Daddy called to me from his office. He closed the door. Sitting at his desk, he instructed me to sit in the chair opposite him. His hair was thick and dark upon his head, his velvet brown eyes shone behind his glasses. His blue shirt was open at the throat. As usual, his right shirt sleeve was neatly folded back and secured with a rubber band.

Using a nickname referring to my love for fried chicken, he drawled, "Chick, do you know what it means to be saved?"

My heart fluttered. I shook my head. At ten years old, I had never "made a confession of faith."

Daddy, concerned for the soul of his suntanned daughter, insisted gently, "Let me explain it to you." Leaning forward, he opened his Bible with his left hand, held the page in place with his right elbow stump, and read in his gentle voice God's plan of salvation from John and Romans.

My heart thumped. Remembering how I'd worried Mother, lied, and hated, I was ashamed. *But I can't tell my father these things!* As usual, I was speechless.

Nevertheless, Daddy prayed for me. Then he opened the door and let me go. All day I thought about it. From the front porch swing I saw crape myrtle trees raise their watermelon-colored blossoms near the cedars. Zinnias and marigolds bloomed yellow and lavender in the sun. I smelled the late summer fragrances and thought about the words Daddy read to me, words I'd memorized long ago: "For God so loved the world that He gave . . ."

That night Preacher Harvill finished his sermon and the packed house stood to sing:

Just as I am, without one plea,
But that Thy blood was shed for me,
And that Thou bidd'st me come to Thee,
O Lamb of God, I come! I come!

My heart thumped and thumped; goose pimples rose on my limbs. People walked down all four aisles, shook the preacher's hand, sat down on the front pew. I saw tears on their faces. A shiver went through my young body. Preacher Harvill mopped his brow. They started the second stanza:

Just as I am, and waiting not
To rid my soul of one dark blot . . .

I glanced up at Mother singing beside me. She looked so pretty with her brown eyes following the words of the hymnal. Her "fixed-up" hair formed a dark cloud around her lovely face. She smelled of Coty powder.

"Mother, I want to go," I whispered, choked up.

"Go ahead," she said, for once giving me freedom to do as I wished.

And so I crept, trembling, down the brown-carpeted path and gave Pastor Rivers my hand while Tom Harvill watched.

"Bless you," Rivers said, his big, warm hand covering mine. "God bless you."

At home my father put his left arm around my shoulder and said, "You did the right thing, Little Chick."

On the third Sunday in August our family walked to church at the ringing of the bell for "The Baptizin'." Revival had ended with thirty-three converts. One by one we went into the baptismal, normally kept covered, at the front of the church. When my turn came, I too was lowered into the water, forgiven and cleansed to start life anew.

We dried off backstage and dressed in new white garments and combed our wet hair. Then we stood at the front, and members filed by to shake our hands and welcome us into the kingdom of God. The piano played and the congregation sang a sweet refrain even while edging by:

Happy day, happy day,
When Jesus washed my sins away!

As 1929 melted into 1930, I remained a very quiet girl, and I began looking for role models, for a grand purpose for my existence. Every morning on my way to school, I stared at a larger-than-life image of Jean Harlow plastered on the gray wood side of Cudn Bill's store. The only billboard in our village, it showed the Hollywood star wearing a low-cut white satin gown and platinum blonde hair. She held a cigarette between her manicured fingers.

I saw the glamorous movie queen again every afternoon as I ran to The Store to get Mother a loaf of light bread for tomato sandwiches. I gaped at Clark Gable's leading lady even while I trudged back across the sandy road with a block of ice, wrapped with cord and melting, dripping onto skirt, legs, and feet; a penny's worth would cool our iced tea. I dreamed while fetching the can of smelly kerosene with a red potato stuck onto the spout to prevent the oil from leaking: *When I grow up, I'm going to be a movie star like Jean Harlow.*

One night after I was in bed Mother was reading by the light of her kerosene lamp. Brother snoozed. Daddy was teaching in Woodland. House and village were as quiet as the cemetery. Suddenly Mother said. "Listen while I read you a poem. It's called 'Abou ben Adhem.'"

Fascinated by the words and images from James Henry Leigh Hunt, I lay still and quiet as Mother read. Abou instantly became one of my heroes, one who loved God most because he loved his fellow man. When I grow up, I thought, I will write poems and books for lonely boys and girls. And like Abou, I will write my name in the book of gold, whatever that is.

In the meantime I gorged myself on Mother's fried chicken, chocolate pie, hot rolls, corn bread. I grew a few inches taller and a lot fatter. Every week Daddy drove away—to Camilla, Fitzgerald, and Moultrie; to West Point, La Grange, and Manchester; to Calhoun, Adairsville, and Rome. Aunt Lou still drew water and washed every Monday in our backyard. Tuesdays she washed for the Bretts, Wednesdays for the Pages, Thursdays for Aunt Emma and Uncle Tom.

One August afternoon when I was twelve, a black runner came to the back door crying: "Aunt Lou's had a stroke. She's dying."

Taking me along, Mother hastened to Aunt Lou's two-room hut. As we trotted down the grassy path past Uncle Tom's house, I recalled the washerwoman's song: *I must tell Je-sus, I must tell Je-sus. I can-not bear my bur-den a-lone. . . .*

Mother stood beside the cot where Aunt Lou lay dying. Lou was wearing the blue cotton dress and white apron she'd worked in that day. Her bare feet were still at last and spread wide. Standing at the foot of her bed, I saw blood gush from the woman's mouth and nose as she breathed her last. I heard Nannie Lee wail, "O Mama, don't die. Don't leave me with all these chillun. Mama, Mama, don't, don't leave me. O Mama, Mama dead!"

A lump filled my throat. Tears pricked my eyes, slid down my cheeks. Mother took a handkerchief, wiped her eyes and blew her nose. I stepped down the rickety steps into the yard where Aunt Lou's frightened brown grandchildren clustered. Five pairs of big black eyes gaped at me in my white slippers and frilly pink dress. Their clothes were soiled and torn, their feet bare. The littlest boy wore nothing at all. So these were Aunt Lou's burdens!

Sorrow and shame mingled; that day Aunt Lou's burdens became mine.

As we returned home, Aunt Lou's spirit seemed to hover above our heads like a low-flying cloud. Deep inside me, a Voice whispered: *Grace, when you grow up, you will do something to help Lou's children.*

Precisely what it was I would do, I had no idea. But I'd do something, I vowed, as Mother and I retraced our steps along the path from the hut of former slaves to the house of former slave owners.

"Poor Aunt Lou," Mother said. "She just washed herself to death, trudging to this house and that, scrubbing for everybody in town. I sure will miss her. Don't know what I'll do without her. Maybe I can get Nannie Lee to wash my clothes if she can get away from them children."

I said nothing to my dark-haired mother. My thoughts were deep as daffodil bulbs. From my heavy heart I tried to lift up a prayer. *Dear God, I'll help Aunt Lou's children. Somehow, some way, when I grow up, I'll help Nannie Lee.*

But I couldn't speak these desires to Mother or Daddy, Rachel or Grandma, or any living soul.

A curious combination became chart and compass to my course: Jean Harlow, Abou ben Adhem, and Aunt Lou's children.

11 *Crying on the Doorstep*

Every day and in every way my maturing seemed to be different from that of other girls in my world. The aberration that hurt the most was social segregation.

In the summer of 1933, when we were fourteen, Rachel and the young people began having parties in their homes on summer nights, then into the autumn on Saturdays and Sundays. They met at the home of Jacob Bryan and his sister, Pauline, or at Christine Brett's, or at the house of newcomers to our town, Doris and Danny Cash.

One night Mother let me go to a candy-pulling at the Cash house. Neither she nor I knew there'd be dancing. But after the boiling of the syrup and the pulling of the sweet mass into amber sticks of candy, after eating amid gales of laughter, Doris yelled, "Let's dance!" Mr. and Mrs. Cash rolled the rug back to create a dance area on the bare pine flooring. Doris put a record on the Victrola, and as the orchestra played "Five Foot Two, Eyes of Blue, Has Anybody Seen My Gal," the boys chose partners.

Harry Paradice danced with Jessie; Jack Garrett swung Rachel around the room. And blue-eyed Danny Cash put his arms around me. Danny was five feet six inches tall, had blond hair. I leaned my head upon his shoulder and knew joy as we danced and swayed to the tunes "Baby Face," "Yes Sir, That's My Baby," "If You Knew Susie Like I Know Susie."

It was to be the first and last time I would ever indulge in the "sin" of dancing, and Danny Cash the only boy I would ever dance with. When Mother found out about the fox-trotting, she was half amused, half afraid. But soon she made up her mind and decreed that her daughter would dance no more with boys. She was genuinely afraid that the close body contact would lead to "other things." Mother couldn't bear the thought of her daughter losing her virginity before marriage.

I didn't want to lose my virginity. I only wanted to have fun, be accepted by the other kids. I spent summer nights crying on the doorstep. Down the street I could hear the music start, the saxophones moan, and I was so left out.

I could visualize the crowd pairing off, Jessie and Harry, Rachel and Jack, Danny and . . . Who? Who would dance with the one I yearned so hard would notice me? I whimpered until my eyes burned, my mouth tasted of salt, the front of my dress was wet with tears. But I refused to bother my parents anymore, to let them know how much I was hurting. I withdrew into myself, gave up to heartbreak, loneliness, despair.

Though I tried to muffle the crying, Mother and Daddy heard. They saw my swollen eyes. The next Friday night Daddy brought a radio home. He set it upon the parlor table and explained that it was powered by batteries. He'd traded in the Victrola to make the down payment. Our radio was the first one in the village. Now, while my parents spent summer evenings in rocking chairs on the porch, while other youngsters danced, I pressed my ear close to the radio listening to Ruth Etting sing from New York City, Bing Crosby croon from Hollywood, California. Tuned in to that other, faraway world, I dreamed of becoming a famous singer. *Never mind the dancing boys and girls down the street. Someday I will run away. I will sing and dance in New York City.*

To help assuage her daughter's grief, Mother started making yeast rolls. Hot, buttery, they were so yummy I just couldn't get enough. I ate four or five at a time until people were saying: "Grace, you're as fat as a butterball."

One day Uncle Amos came home from the navy. He'd been at Newport News, Virginia, a year. Rachel and I had written her brother every week, had loved getting his letters. We were ecstatic when he returned, our conquering hero, our Amos home from the sea. My first glimpse of Daddy's nineteen-year-old brother in white sailor suit came on a Saturday afternoon. The blue-eyed, curly-haired blond perched on the side of the town well, laughing and joking with Troy and Ralph. Rachel and I strolled by, arms around each other's waist. I waited for my good-looking uncle to speak first, my heart throbbing, yearning for his kind greeting.

What I received was not a caress, but a slap that would last a lifetime. "Grace, what's happened to you? You're as fat as Nellie!"

Nellie was the town ugly—ornery, overweight, shapeless as a barrel. My darling uncle had wounded his niece sorely. I went home, sat in a porch rocker alone, and sobbed, his words echoing around and around in my brain. Mother heard the crying, opened the screen door, sat in the rocker next to mine.

"What's the matter with you?" she said tenderly.

"Amos said I'm as fat as Nellie."

Mother chuckled briefly, then grew serious. "Well, I guess you've been eating too many yeast rolls. You know I started making those rolls this summer, and they're so good, you eat four or five at the time. Guess I'll have to quit making them."

I wailed when I thought of giving up those delicious rolls.

"Don't take it so hard. I'll help you lose weight. I need to lose some myself."

I determined to lose the fat. Although movie magazines were forbidden, I managed to slip a *Photoplay* into the house, and in The Room, while Mother and Nannie Lee pickled peaches and pears in the kitchen, I read how Jean Harlow, Joan Crawford, and Norma Shearer reduced. I began by walking down the Harrison Road a mile every day, cutting down on breads, cakes, chocolate candy.

It was agony. But high school lay just ahead, and I wanted to be ready.

Riddleville's school went only as far as ninth grade. I would take a major stride toward freedom when I could ride the bus every morning to Sandersville High for grades ten and eleven. In the thirties there was no grade twelve.

That first September morning the sun rose bright and hot through branches of cedars and oaks. A chubby fourteen with brown silky hair, I was dressed in a Singer-sewing-machine pink. With me were Rachel, Pauline, Jessie, and Jacob. I climbed aboard the yellow bus in front of The Store, my heart fluttering like a baby wren trying its wings. We left Mother standing on the front porch of the cottage in her red polka-dot dress and felt bedroom slippers.

The dirt road to our Washington County seat, bordered on both sides by gray Negro cabins and the white-painted houses of white farmers, was fringed by fading crape myrtles and patches of white cotton. As Cecil Hodges drove the ten miles I would travel every morning for two years, Mother's words echoed in my ears.

"Study hard. Listen to the teacher. Make As. Be the valedictorian of your class! You are very fortunate to be able to finish high school. I never did get my diploma. It hurt me so bad when Mama took me out of school and sent me away from home to teach when I was just sixteen."

Although I knew the answer, I had asked her again, "Why did she do that?"

"I was boarding in Tennille with Mrs. Fann. The principal was murdered one day on the streets of Tennille by the father of one of the students, and Mama got scared and made me come home."

"That's awful!"

Mother changed the subject. "Find out about the music teacher at Sandersville," she said. "I want you to take music so you can play the piano at church."

"Yes, ma'am."

Emmie Johnson became my piano teacher, and I learned well enough to play a solo for graduation.

But soon I feared I'd never be Mother's valedictorian. There were too many distractions at Sandersville High in the tenth and eleventh grades. Their names were Roy, Richard, Joe, William, Oscar, and Tarver Holmes.

And then there was Tarver's older brother, Tom.

12 The Tallest Boy

Tom Holmes was in the same grade as I. His desk was second from the front, mine near the back on the same row. He sat sideways, his long legs crossed and sticking out in the aisle, so he could see the blackboard and teacher on his right and fix his intense brown eyes on that new girl from Riddleville on his left. At five feet ten and still growing, the dentist's son was the tallest boy in tenth grade.

Tom was also the thinnest, weighing only 130 pounds, and the butt of other boys' jokes. In weekly English compositions they read aloud, fellow students wrote, "Tom Holmes has the longest legs, the biggest feet." He took the ribbing with good humor, his brown eyes crinkling at the corners as he laughed at himself along with everyone else—except me. I, who had known little laughter in my fourteen years, felt sorry for the guy.

The most exciting thing about Tom was that his dark eyes bored into mine whenever he could look my way, from nine in the morning until three in the afternoon. But Tom Holmes was not the first young man to write me a note or ask me for a date. In spite of the attentions of others, it was that tall, skinny dynamo with piercing eyes who undid me. Mother's Little Girl found herself falling in love with a fellow her opposite. The sixteen-year-old's face was long and thin; mine round and chubby. He had a heavy shock of black hair; mine glinted blonde amid the brown. When this center of attention stood, he towered over every other student in the room, certainly over me. And my pulse raced at the sight of that tower.

One day I received a note from Tom, written on notebook paper cunningly folded into a two-inch square, and passed from desk to desk to mine. Heart pounding, I devoured it. Then I took it home and read and reread the precious words.

Dear Grace,

I have something to tell you which will surprise you very much. It is that I love you. I expect many other boys have told you this. But none have meant it as much as I do. Please write and say that you love me.

Love,

Tom

I slept with the prize beneath my pillow night after night after night, even when I received notes from Roy and Oliver and Richard. I put Tom's note away among my treasures. And when he continued to lock his eyes on mine and wrote more letters of admiration, my heart thrilled.

One Sunday afternoon in May, Tom parked his father's squared green Studebaker in front of our house. He wore a white linen suit, a tie, and white shoes. To me he appeared as elegant and noble as Sir Galahad, his hair as thick, black, and beautiful as chocolate fudge.

We went for a walk down Sandersville Road, past the town well, the church, the cemetery. Roses and magnolias bloomed on bush and branch, filled the air with heady fragrance as we strolled toward Aunt Lou's old hut.

"Will you be glad when we're seniors?" Tom asked. I relished the resonance of his voice.

"Oh, yes!" I managed.

"How old will you be when we graduate?"

Somehow I thought he knew! "Sixteen. Sixteen next April."

"I will be eighteen on June first. I didn't start to first grade until I was seven."

"My mother wouldn't let me start until I was eight."

For an instant he looked befuddled. "Eight? Were you sick?"

"No. She taught me at home, and when she did let me go, she said I was ready for fourth grade."

"Why did she keep you at home?"

"She said I might get hurt at school, go wild at recess. Why did you?"

"I started late because I was sickly. And too thin. Had to take a lot of nasty medicine."

His confession made me want to confide in him. "When I did start, I was scared of the teacher, and the other pupils, and the sound of my own voice. It wobbled like a loose wheel on a wagon. It still does."

He took my hand. "I've noticed you don't say much in class. I know how it is to be afraid. The bigger boys picked on me. Every day I got into a fight at recess, and I always ended up whipped by the stronger boys. The teacher would paddle me for fighting, and when I got home, I got another paddling for getting one at school!"

"Poor Tom!" I was genuinely sorry, and genuinely happy to have my hand in his. The sidewalk narrowed to a pig path, and the scents of magnolia and roses vanished. Ragweed and thorny vines grew around us. Aunt Lou's cabin came into view.

The scene jolted my memory. I found myself telling Tom the secret that lay deep inside me. Pointing, I said, "Our washerwoman used to live there. I watched her die while her grandchildren stood outside in the dirt. The littlest one didn't even have any clothes. I said, 'When I grow up, I'm going to do something to help those people, help the Negroes.'"

"They need help. What are you going to do?"

"I don't know," I said. We turned to go back. "They don't have anything to eat but fatback and cornbread!"

"They have collards and sweet potatoes. Every Negro cabin has a collard patch close by," Tom said.

"They need more than just better food! They need nice houses and new clothes and so many things! They have to go around to white folks' back door and work in their back rooms and backyards, and take whatever we want to give them. I think it's unfair! Something about it stinks!"

Suddenly I was afraid I'd said too much and he would think I was a traitor to my upbringing.

But Tom said, "I feel the same way. Tom Biggins is my best friend. He saved my life once—killed a rattlesnake about to strike me. But he always has to come in the back door and eat leftovers in the kitchen.

"He helped me grow tomatoes and cantaloupes to sell in town so I could buy boxing gloves. Before I was twelve, he helped me build a little produce wagon from an old buggy, taught me to hitch up our blind mule, and rode with me on that jalopy to town to sell our produce for dimes and nickels. Finally I saved three dollars and ninety-five cents, enough to buy the gloves from Sears and Roebuck. Mama had taught Tom Biggins to read and write, so he helped me fill out the purchase form and buy a money order. Then, when my gloves came, he taught me how to fight. As soon as he thought

I was ready, I took the gloves to school. And gradually I whipped every boy who ever beat me up."

I grinned. "Even Danny Cash?"

"Especially Danny Cash!"

"You know, I danced with him once, before Mother and Daddy decided they wouldn't let me go to dances." I pushed my lip out in a pout. "Everybody goes to dances but me."

"Not everybody. I don't. I think dancing is silly."

"You do?" I was incredulous.

Tom squeezed my hand. "Yeah. It's silly!"

A shiver went up my spine. My cup overflowed; I'd found my soul mate!

Tom Holmes worked at Holmes Canning Company during the summer. He was assigned to his brother Ed's pea-shelling machinery. He sent me notes, carefully folded and smudged with black grease, by Jacob Bryan, who worked with him.

When school started again in September, Tom and I were seen together everywhere—in the halls, the library, at recess, in speech class, at parties. We ate lunch together every day, swapping sandwiches.

In December we courted in Mother's parlor on a Sunday afternoon. In the picture on the wall, horses galloped. Flames leaped on the red brick hearth. Our chairs were pulled close together, our hands touching. "What are you going to be when you get through school?" I asked.

"I'm going to be an orchestra leader."

"What a coincidence! I'm going to be a singer."

"I want you to be my wife."

Startled, thrilled, I could only manage to nod and squeeze his hand.

In March 1935 Mother received a letter from Tom's mother, Kate, inviting me to spend a Friday night in her home. A house party was being arranged, she explained, including Rachel and Carleton and Tarver and his friend, Vera. She assured Mother that she would take good care of her daughter.

Almost sixteen now, a senior, I was so excited, so in love. I couldn't wait for Friday night, March 21, the first day of spring. A new blue linen suit Mother had sewn on her Singer machine hung in the wardrobe. I'd put in the hems myself. The day before, I polished my brown-and-white saddle oxfords to look like new, using a wet rag to wash all brown polish off the white, all white off the brown.

"He won't notice that, Baby," Lucy said. "A li'l brown on the white won't hurt nothin'."

"You better be studying your history," Mother said, "and practicing your music instead of all that primping."

The next morning a high wind blew through branches of cedar trees, rattling the still-bare limbs of pecans and water oaks. But it was a warm wind, scented with hyacinths, daffodils, and narcissi. Our yellow school bus cruised along the flower-strewn countryside where peach and pear trees were in their glory, gowned in pink and purest white.

After an interminable day, the three o'clock bell rang at last, and the house-party crowd climbed into Dr. Holmes's green Studebaker for Tom to drive the five teenagers to his home. At his home purple wisteria bloomed all the way across the front porch trellis. A lily pool surrounded by stones graced the front lawn. Inside, on the country kitchen table, freshly baked lemon pie waited, sugary bubbles dotting oven-browned meringue.

"Yum-yum," said Rachel, and we all ate, laughing and chattering with youthful abandon.

Then Tom went for his guitar. I didn't know he played a musical instrument! We followed the tall, stringy guy outdoors in the afternoon sunshine. Leaning on the hood of his Studebaker, he strummed the strings and sang "Stars Fell on Alabama," "Whispering," and "Moonlight and Roses."

I hadn't known he could sing, either. But sing he did, crooning like Bing Crosby on the radio, and stared at me. My heart melted like peach ice cream left too long outside the churn. Later I could not remember what his mother served for supper, or even whether we ate. All I recollected was that after darkness fell, Tom whispered in my ear, "Come outside, I want to show you the lily pond."

While the others played a card game beside the leaping flames, we went out the front door. He took me by the hand and led me in the moonlight to the water. There he instructed me to sit upon a certain stone and pressed close to me on the same stone, his body touching mine. Pulling me against his lean, hard chest, he kissed Mother's Little Girl full on the mouth. And she kissed him back.

He whispered, "I love you, I love you! I'll always love you!"

"I love you too," I murmured.

"Thomas!" called Kate Holmes from the porch. "You'd better come in now. It's getting cold outside."

Hurriedly we left the stone and hastened into the lamp-lit, fire-lit house to party with the others. Hearts hammering, our eyes connected every few minutes throughout the electricity-charged evening.

Early in April Tom stunned the senior class. His thatch of black hair and serious eyes were etched in my memory as he stood before us to say, "I plan to enter Mercer University in September and study for the ministry. I've decided to be a preacher."

I didn't know, when I half-promised to be his wife, that I was half-promising to be a preacher's wife! One Sunday in church I'd sat next to our pastor's wife, who was cold, stuffy, pompous. And I decided I didn't want to be like her when I grew up—I'd *never* marry a preacher.

But from that day forward pupils regarded their class treasurer with awe. No more compositions were read about Tom's long legs and big feet. And it didn't take me long to reconsider. It wasn't just that nobody could say no to Tom Holmes, or when he set his mind on a thing or a person, the person might as well give in. It was that I didn't want to give him up. So I quickly decided I could be a preacher's wife, if Tom Holmes was the preacher.

Besides, Tom had not asked me how I felt about it, taking for granted that whatever he did would suit me. Anyway, after graduation we would both go to college. But not together.

13 Gainer Bryan's Daughter

For several years Gainer Bryan had yearned to move away from the village of his birth, but he couldn't talk my mother into leaving their families and friends, her mother and sisters, gardens and chickens. She was also loath to leave the fine old cottage with its high ceilings, wide-board floors, and colonial doors that formed a cross at the top and an open Bible at the bottom. She loved the white picket fence and the roses, wisteria, and jonquils she'd planted and nurtured.

But Gainer's work took him all over Georgia. If we moved to the middle of the state, he could get home more often and with fewer driving hours. The man whose motto was "For I have learned in whatsoever state I am, therewith to be content" never complained about driving with only one hand, although it must have been a strain.

My father longed to give his wife and children advantages we did not have in Riddleville. On his trips he enjoyed electric lights, indoor plumbing, flush toilets. He wanted his family to have these luxuries. It was increasingly difficult for the forty-one-year-old to return to the deprived village Saturday after Saturday, to walk among his kinsmen, whose attitudes were as primitive as their outdoor privies. Their opinions had changed little from when my father had first announced his intention to go to Mercer. "You're a bigger fool than I thought you were," his Uncle Pete had declared. And Cudn Nellie still called him "that religious Gainer Bryan." My father no longer felt at home in his own hometown. He had stretched his mind at the university, and now he prayed that his children might do the same.

So for my sake, Mother finally agreed to move to Forsyth, about seventy miles south of Atlanta. She knew it was the only way in those Depression years for her daughter, and later her son, to get the college education she was determined we should have. Mother would make any sacrifice for her girl and boy. We were her reason for being. Yet giving up the family's ancestral home was wrenching for the country-born-and-bred woman.

The villagers were sorry to see Lila and Gainer Bryan move. My father had brought interesting, helpful preachers to minister to the little church. In spite of their expressed disdain for his occupation, Gainer's homecomings were a source of excitement to the simple, isolated folk. Mother would be missed, too, for she had taught their children in both public and church school.

Tom Holmes was delighted. "Forsyth is only twenty-five miles north of Mercer. I'll come to see you every Saturday," he promised. "If I don't have train fare, I'll hitch a ride."

In these hungry years of the Great Depression—when jobless men sold apples on street corners in New York City and in Sandersville destitute farmers paid their dentist with pine knots for starting fires, sweet potatoes for baking, sugarcane syrup for pancakes—Dr. Holmes had no money to send his fifth son to college. By selling turkeys, chickens, eggs, Mrs. Holmes raised a little money to help him get started.

As soon as our class graduated from high school, Tom went to work at his brother's canning company again for the summer, and Mother began preparations for our move to Forsyth. She sold the cackling hens, the Rhode Island Red rooster, the chicken coops. Lucy and Nannie Lee helped us pack dishes, pots and pans, pictures, and all our possessions for the move from impoverished village to cultured college town in Monroe County.

Thrilled, I daydreamed through the preparations. *I will never have to clean out another chicken coop, pick potato bugs, empty the slop jar. Never have to draw another bucket of water from the well, or bring in stove wood; trim wicks, clean smutty chimneys of kerosene lamps. Never again go across the street to the icehouse to bring home a penny block of ice for tea or for a churn of ice cream.*

We'll have electric lights, running water, a bathroom! I'm going to get an A.B. degree at Bessie Tift College, learn to be a preacher's wife. I will be Mrs. Holmes, Mrs. Thomas J. Holmes. I will be Somebody, have my name written in the book of gold.

Dr. Aquilla Chamblee, venerable clergyman and president of Tift, found the Bryan family an apartment in the old Rushin House across the street from the campus. Because of his admiration for Gainer Bryan, the tall, white-haired Chamblee gave Bryan's daughter a scholarship, letting me go to college almost tuition-free. I would live at home and my father, whose salary was a meager $150 a month, could give his daughter a fine education.

And so on a hot September day in 1935 we moved away from the land between the rivers. The ancient board floors and walls were stripped and naked. Nothing was left in the bare rooms except the old wood stove, stark and lonely in the kitchen.

When we passed Aunt Lou's cabin, Nannie Lee and her children stood in the yard, their brown hands waving goodbye. I could not know three decades would pass before I'd see them again. But everywhere in this land of the free and home of the brave I would see the despairing dark eyes of Aunt Lou's children. I witnessed them waiting in stores until all white customers were served, waiting with dejected faces in back rooms of doctors' offices until whites in the front rooms received attention. I saw the disgraceful "White Only" signs at water fountains, restrooms.

Lucy and Lou's people were shoved like animals to the backs of buses so that other whites and I could ride in the front seats. And every time I accepted a privilege denied to people of color, I knew the shame of hypocrisy. I was a slave to a system I sensed was out of joint, incompatible with the ideals of America and Christianity.

The double standard made a heavy burden upon my back. But at sixteen I had neither the freedom nor the courage to do other than accept the suffocating system, go along with the herd. My vow to help Aunt Lou's children when I grew up was pushed back with the other childhood visions and dreams. They had to move over to make room for Chaucer, Shakespeare, and Dickens; Napoleon; biology and logarithms; Bach, Beethoven, and Brahms.

However, the vow waited to surface again, waited to call me to abandon hypocrisy. The girl is mother to the woman. And when God plants a seed in a human heart, it will bear fruit one day.

While Mother had stayed home tending children and chickens, her husband had become a famous man. Governor Eugene Talmadge said he wished he had as many friends as Gainer Bryan. During the next four years at the college later called Tift, I met students and teachers, preachers and parents from all over the Georgia who knew and loved my father.

"So you're Gainer Bryan's daughter," became the familiar greeting by folks from Fitzgerald, Duluth, Chipley, Atlanta, Macon, Columbus, Rome, Augusta, Plains. I wore the label "Gainer Bryan's daughter" with pride.

Brother enrolled in the eighth grade at Mary Persons High School in Forsyth. Mother cooked and kept the three-bedroom apartment. But I, fourth honor graduate of Sandersville High, Riddleville School, and Mother's Tutoring Service, was no match for college. During the first two years I flunked mathematics, biology, and French—more than once. Baffled, I listened carefully in every class, took notes, studied afternoons and evenings. But I seemed to be lost in a very dark tunnel while my classmates from Atlanta, Columbus, and Douglas breezed through logarithms and French as though they'd already mastered them.

I dreaded report-card days like a trip to the operating room. I made Cs, Ds, Fs, and had to repeat courses during regular terms. Since there was no summer school, Dean Plymale had me come for eight o'clock classes to make up the failed courses. One of his math courses I repeated twice. Gainer Bryan's daughter lived in humiliation.

Meanwhile, Tom came to see me on weekends. He seemed to master his college work with ease and, on June 25, 1936, at his home church, he was ordained to the ministry and called to pastor the Antioch church.

Every quarter I tried a little harder to improve my grades. By the spring of 1937, I thought I was passing until the fateful day they mailed out report cards. Mother met me at the front door, showed me the horrid credits I'd chalked up again. In shocked disbelief I stared at all those letters of the alphabet revealing my failure.

She didn't fuss at me about the awful card, simply went back to her new ironing board that could be folded and put away. But I heard her voice in my head anyway, echoing down through the years: "Study hard, have some ambition, be Somebody in the world. Be like Charlotte, who makes all As."

I laid my books down.

Finally she spoke, her voice weary. "Lord-a-mercy, I pray." I stumbled past her to the back porch, sat on the back doorstep, and sobbed. A soft spring rain fell upon colorful pansies our upstairs neighbor had planted. Their blue-and-yellow fragile beauty only increased my suffering.

Mother came out and dropped down beside her daughter. "What's the matter?" she said tenderly.

My tears fell afresh. "I thought I was working hard, and I just don't understand it. I can't do anything but flunk! I'm so ashamed to disappoint you and Daddy after all the sacrifices you've made for me to go to college."

"Well, don't cry," Mother said. "You're younger than the others in your class. Riddleville school only went eight months. You weren't as well prepared as you should have been. And you know all you did at Sandersville was court Tom Holmes. Maybe you'll catch on after a while. Don't give up. When a thing's hard, you have to work harder."

The next term, when I was eighteen and a junior, new determination gripped me. I rose every morning at five o'clock, put on a warm robe and carried history, Shakespeare, French texts downstairs to the kitchen, built a fire in the little wood stove connected to the water heater. In the two hours of blessed silence while Mother, Daddy, and Brother slept until seven, I put the books upon the kitchen table and huddled there close to the warm stove. An electric drop light above my head, I learned how to study. In the solitude I found I could concentrate.

Morning after morning I toiled, and night after night I labored in my room, at the desk or sitting in bed. Taking notes in the college library, I wrote papers. Finally, I passed tests, then whole courses with Bs and B-pluses.

Tom and I saw less and less of each other. He was busy with preaching. He bought a 1930 Chevrolet coupe and came to our home nearly every weekend, but he had to depart on Saturday night to drive to one of his churches at Antioch or Allentown to preach on Sunday mornings. When I could find time, I dated two other young men.

When I graduated with my class in May 1939, Dr. Davis, professor of education, told my father, "Your daughter has made the greatest progress of any student I've ever seen."

Perhaps Gainer Bryan's daughter had had the farthest to come.

Gainer Bryan had progressed also. His dream of the ultimate success was realized in the spring of '38, when he was forty-four. All over the Southland, the Baptist Young People's Union had mushroomed to include children and adults. The name was changed, and the one-armed runt from a little-known village was elected as Baptist Training Union secretary for the state of Georgia. Daddy was given a secretary and an office on Marietta Street at Five Points in the capital city. He talked of moving to Atlanta. But Mother was reluctant.

Tom received his A.B. degree from Mercer and was called to two half-time churches in west Georgia, Gay and Senoia. He accepted, deciding to let seminary wait, and moved into the rambling parsonage alone in September 1939. In college he'd grown six more inches, and at twenty-two he topped six-four. He wanted me to marry and move in with him.

But I had contracted to teach fourth grade in Adairsville, a small town in northwest Georgia near Rome. Besides, I'd met Solon, another young preacher, and I was wild about him. So I decided I should date other men before settling down. During the summer and fall of 1939, I dated Solon in Atlanta plus a banker and businessman in Adairsville.

But none of them had the dynamism of Tom Holmes. One night in November I summoned the courage to telephone Tom that now I was ready to marry him.

"You are?" he said. "Well, you're almost too late. I've been dating Vallie. She teaches in Atlanta, but she comes home every weekend to visit her parents, who live next door to me. She loves me, and we're talking about marriage."

My heart sank into my shoes, but I talked him into promising that he would come to Forsyth to see me on Thanksgiving Day.

BOOK TWO

When Christmas Comes

14 The Preacher's Wife

When I met Tom at the door of my parents' home and saw that beloved face smiling at me, brown eyes crinkling at the corners, dark head as tall as the doorframe, I knew instantly that I was his, and he mine. He took me into his arms and kissed me, and that day we set a springtime wedding date. In February Tom gave me a diamond ring, and I thrilled to its sparkle.

During late winter I gave in to a siege of measles, sinusitis, and earache. On March 21 I had a mastoidectomy and stayed at home with Mother to recuperate. The doctor prescribed a tonic to take before meals to build up my strength. Half the time I forgot to take the concoction, which was as black and syrupy as axle grease.

One April day, Tom sat at dinner with Mother, Daddy, and me. Suddenly he demanded, "Did you take your tonic?"

"No," I said, "I hate that foul-tasting stuff."

"Well," he barked like an army sergeant, "You get up right now and take it! Here's a spoon." He extended a huge tablespoon.

Swallowing my mouthful of delicious roast beef and potatoes, I got up and, as meekly as a child, went to get the medicine as my husband-to-be commanded.

Mother was outraged. "Grace, I wouldn't do it! Don't let him boss you!" But I did. I took the medicine.

The next day Mother said, "You should not marry him, Grace! He's too harsh and dictatorial. He'll crush you. He's just a bag of wind, like G. J., who married my sister. He was unfaithful to her, and two years after their marriage she died of a broken heart and meningitis."

While she worked on the wedding dress, she warned me with wry humor, "You'll lie up there and get pregnant the first night. I waited four years. It's better to wait a while. A baby will tie you down, be a worry for the rest of your life. You'll never be free again."

But I wouldn't turn from my dream of becoming Mrs. Thomas Holmes. June 4, 1940, was the most important day of my life. Tom and I were married in a church wedding in Forsyth. After a brief trip we settled into the parsonage next door to the church in Senoia. With his own hands the bridegroom had installed a bathroom in the Victorian white frame, planted blue hyacinths in the garden. Now Mother's Little Girl and Gainer Bryan's Daughter was The Preacher's Wife.

I still adored The Preacher. He was lovable and tender with me most of the time. But alas! Taking the medicine would not be the last time I'd be caught between domineering mother and domineering husband. Less than a year later, my anxiety mounted as Tom drove the '39 Ford from Senoia to Forsyth for one of our visits to my parents. It was May 1941. Tom puffed on his pipe, and I looked sideways at his handsome profile, trying to comfort myself.

He has been so sweet about it.

As if he heard my thoughts, he said, "What will Miss Lila say?"

"Oh, Lord, I don't know! At least she won't say I got caught the first night," I said.

"You're still scared of your mother," my husband said. The youthful pastor of Gay and Senoia pulled up in front of the two-story white frame house in Forsyth.

For answer I poked my lip out in a pout, my habit from childhood. He was right. I was afraid of my mother's tongue, afraid to talk back, say what I really thought. There was little fight in the twenty-one-year-old woman who'd married the champion fighter of Sandersville High School.

"If you don't pull in that lip, you're going to step on it," said Tom in a voice as sharp as a nurse's needle. Without meaning to, Tom could make me feel as helpless as Mother could.

"I wish you wouldn't say that! You're always saying that! Makes me want to cry!"

"I was only teasing. The trouble with you is you can't take teasing. You're supersensitive."

As I pulled myself from the car, my shoes seemed to be made of iron. I wore my favorite pink dress, one from the trousseau. It buttoned from neck to hemline and featured a narrow belt. To please Tom, my brown hair was pinned up in a bun. We proceeded up the concrete walk, my tread heavy.

Mother met us on the timbered porch. A true lady of the South, she wore white sandals and a cool lavender-and-white cotton dress with a ruffle around the scoop neckline, centered at the front with a bow made of the same fabric. Her dark hair had been combed and brushed, parted in the middle, and neatly pinned up in a French roll all around her face and head. Mother looked as pretty as Melanie Wilkes, but she was frowning at me with displeasure.

"Well, I see you've got your hair done up like an old woman."

I smiled to mask my real feelings. "Tom likes it this way," I said softly.

"I don't. I like it down."

I preferred my mane long, loose, and free. But Tom liked me to wear my hair like his mother's, pinned up into a bun on the back of the head. This little conflict between my mother and husband caused pains in my stomach.

Inside my old bedroom I stood before the long mirror on the bureau. And one by one I removed the pins from my hair, brushed the silken strands, and left them loose and flowing. I felt better until Tom looked up from the book he was reading in the living room and grimaced.

Daddy was away at Crabapple teaching a course. Mother had cooked one of her great suppers. As we sat down to the fried chicken, creamed corn, green beans, and peach pie spread upon the round oak table, I decided *I'll tell her after supper.* After we ate I said to myself, *I'll tell her after we wash dishes.* But when the plates were dried and put away on the cabinet shelves, I thought it would be better to wait until we'd rested on the porch for a while. *It will be easier there. Mother will be more serene and accepting while swaying back and forth in the old slatted swing with cool breezes bringing the fragrances of roses and honeysuckle.*

While Mother was hanging up the tea towels to dry, Tom strode into the kitchen. "Have you told her yet?"

"Told me what?" she demanded.

I began to cry. "I'm pregnant!" I said at last, sobbing as though I'd got that way out of wedlock. I leaned my head against the refrigerator, hoping for Mother's approval, fearing wrath.

"That's all right," she said, taking me into her arms. "Don't cry. That's all right. That's the way it is after you marry."

The child-woman dried her eyes, reprieved. She had her mother's permission to birth her own infant.

During the long, hot summer Tom and I discussed names. Of course we wanted to have a boy first and name him for his father. But indecisive

Grace could never settle on the perfect name if the boy turned out to be a girl.

"What about Lila Katherine, for her two grandmothers?" said Tom one August evening. He tamped Prince Albert into his pipe.

"But that's a long handle for a girl to bear all her life. Sounds so old-fashioned."

"We could call her Lila."

"But Mother has never liked her name. She hardly ever lets people call her by her Christian name. Only Daddy, her mother and sisters, and Daddy's family call her Lila. Everyone else calls her Mrs. Bryan."

"Well, we could call her Katherine for Mama."

"If we called her Katherine, that would hurt Mother's feelings. 'So, I see what you think about my name,' she would say. 'You think Mrs. Holmes's name is prettier than mine. Mine isn't good enough for your baby.'"

"Your mother can never be satisfied."

My sudden, open anger surprised me. "Don't criticize my mother!" I said, and I slapped his face.

Without a pause, he slapped me back. "Well, it's true!" he said. The light slap stung.

I sat down heavily, stuffing my anger deep inside. It was the first time my resentment of his remarks exploded into anger, and I was so shocked I could not recall later whether we ever talked about the incident. I remembered only that there was never another.

"If you don't pull in that lip, you're gonna step on it," he needled.

I gulped and did not bring up a name to him again. As the long summer dragged into a hot autumn, my body swelled to frightening proportions, my feet disappeared. I kept my dreams of a girl's name to myself. *How about Carol? It sounds so musical. Or Carole like Carole Lombard? Or Jean like Jean Harlow? How about Kathy or Cathy or Julie or June? Now, June is a romantic name.*

"I like Lila Katherine," Tom said again in October. He struck a match to light his pipe.

"No, it's too long. Why worry when it's going to be a boy anyway?"

"It better be a boy! If it's a girl, I'm gonna send it back," Tom said laughing, showing me the red and white baseball cap he'd bought for our boy.

Five days before Pearl Harbor, at Georgia Baptist Hospital on December 2, 1941, after twenty-seven hours of labor, the doctor put me to sleep and used forceps. Even though I was anesthetized, my screams rang through the corridors. The young father-to-be was so shaken he came close to fainting.

Finally it was over. I heard my baby's first cries. A beloved head bent close to my ear and whispered, "Grace, we've got a little girl."

"Oh," I sobbed, half-dead, "Tom wanted a boy."

"That's all right," he said, kissing me on the forehead. "That's all right, darling."

A nurse stood on my left, cradling our baby in her arms, a bundle wrapped in a pink blanket. She laid the treasure close to me, and I saw our creation for the first time. She was tiny, red, stretching and yawning. With my left arm I pulled her close to my side.

"My baby," I said. "My precious baby." I hugged and kissed her, love flowing out to our infant like the sea onto the shore at high tide.

Our daughter was returned to the nursery, and I went back to sleep. When I awoke, Mother and Tom huddled in a far corner of the room, their backs toward me, bent over a table. They whispered as they wrote.

"What are you doing?" I asked weakly.

"We're writing the announcement cards," said Tom.

"The announcement cards? But the baby hasn't been named yet."

"Oh, yes, she has been named," he said.

"What!! What is her name?"

"Lila Katherine," said my husband happily.

Mother and Tom have named my baby without waiting until I waked, without even consulting me! Hot tears coursed down my cheeks while they continued to write the name Lila Katherine on the cards I'd addressed to family members and friends before leaving home. Too exhausted to protest aloud, to risk wounding Mother's fragile feelings, I lay there and wept until I tasted salt upon my lips.

They never noticed.

Complications prolonged my stay at the hospital. *Lila Katherine sounds so old-fashioned,* I reasoned as the days dragged by while I recuperated on the narrow bed. *I want our daughter to have a name that rings with newness and spirit, like Kay or Kathy. That's it—Kathy!*

"Tom," I said the next morning when the tall man strode into my room. "Let's call her Kathy."

"That's fine with me, darling," he said. Tom's eyes crinkled at the corners. "Whatever you want is fine with me. You're always right, you know." He squeezed my hand, leaned his dark head close to mine, and kissed me. "Grace, I've been thinking about something."

"What?"

"I need to go to seminary and study for my master's."

"Oh, I wish you could. You certainly should. But how can we, without money? We'd have to give up our churches and the ninety dollars a month they pay, move to Louisville or Fort Worth."

"I don't know."

"How are we going to pay the hospital bill?" I was sure my long confinement had run up a large tab.

"I'm thinking I'll have to sell the car."

"Oh, no!"

But he did sell the Ford. After seventeen days, Mother and baby finally came home, six days before Christmas. Tom picked me up and carried me into our bedroom. Laying me upon the maple four-poster, with love and tenderness he put little Kathy into the blue-lined bassinet. When I first put feet to floor, they felt as if needles were sticking in them. Kathy was three weeks old.

Now the nation was at war. Cousins, brothers, and friends were enlisting, flying off to Texas, Europe, and the South Seas. Brother became a navy ensign; Tom's brother Henry, a lieutenant in the army air forces.

"I want to join the chaplaincy," said Tom, furrows between his brows.

"Oh, no! I need you to help me with the baby."

He went to Atlanta anyway one day in January 1942 to enlist. He was turned down because of his weight—at six-four, he weighed only a hundred forty. He came home disappointed. I was relieved.

Two months later the skinny preacher became a member of the National Guard, complete with soldier's uniform and maneuvers. But he was restless until we made the decision to go to graduate school.

15 Seminary Sojourn

On a sizzling summer morning in '43 we kissed Mother and Daddy good-bye for a planned three-year sojourn in Texas. My husband, our sixteen-month-old, and I drove away in the '37 Ford we'd acquired by borrowing a hundred dollars from a friend and selling our stove, refrigerator, dining-room suite, sofa, and chair. Tom was twenty-six, I twenty-four. And we were so excited to be leaving the Deep South, stepchild of the nation, to be going west toward the land of adventure and opportunity.

As we traveled, I dreamed of our future. *We'll stay long enough for Tom to get his master's and doctorate. Then, if he's offered a distinguished pulpit, we may settle forever in a romantic city like Carmel-by-the-Sea in California.*

Our blonde daughter slept in the back seat on her mattress placed on top of our bedding. The collapsed crib was tied on the top of the car. A thermos packed with ice and bottles of milk nestled at my feet. We drove three days from the hills of Georgia to the plains of Texas. When we reached Fort Worth, Tom located the three-room apartment he'd already rented. Carrying our things in, we settled for the night, thankful for a place of our own to call home, even though we had to share a bath with the landlady's daughter and the pinkish curtains were frayed and dingy, the furniture shabby.

Sitting on the side of the bed, Tom took out his wallet and counted his money. Nine dollars.

"I'll get a job tomorrow," he said. Filling his pipe with long, expert fingers, he fragranced our room with the smoke.

Early the next morning he walked to the campus of Southwestern Baptist Theological Seminary, where he met Dr. R. T. Daniel, professor of church history and native of our Washington County, Georgia. Coming home at noon, he burst into the kitchen, where I was struggling with the little gas stove, cooking corn bread and peas.

"I have a job!" he said, smiling.

"What doing?"

"Garbage collector on campus," he said with as much gusto as if he had just been appointed to President Roosevelt's cabinet. "And Dr. Daniel said he will help me get a church."

"Some job!" I managed, wondering how he could be so excited over such dirty work. What would our friends say? I certainly was glad we were far from home. Maybe no one would ever know.

Soon he was going to classes every morning, reveling in his study of the Scriptures at the feet of the scholars. But it was almost more than we could do to buy the necessities of life on his tiny salary.

Back in Forsyth, Mother labored over the sewing machine and mailed her handiwork to Texas. For Kathy she copied exquisite creations that she'd studied at Rich's and Davison's at prices only the rich could afford. And Kathy wore ruffled, lacy outfits befitting a princess.

In a couple of weeks Tom was going out on Sunday preaching missions that paid twenty-five dollars each. Since gasoline was only twenty cents a gallon, he gave up his job as collector of garbage. I felt a good deal more honorable, although not much richer.

We could not afford dry cleaning, so every Saturday found me cleaning and pressing Tom's navy blue pulpit suit, which was all the more trying because those long-legged pants were longer than the ironing board. And because we had no automatic washing machine, I had to do the family wash by hand. A set of tubs stood in the backyard, and on Mondays I labored over a scrub board just as Aunt Lou had done back in the village. The small pieces were easy; but when I got to the towels, shirts, and sheets, my tears flowed into the washtub and mingled with the suds. *So this is what I struggled through college for, made up courses for. So I could be a washerwoman like Aunt Lou!* I recollected how she sang as she labored, but there was no song in me.

Biting chiggers added to our misery. Bites clustered around my waist and legs, covered Kathy's head. She scratched, turning them to sores that made her cry. Finally our living situation became intolerable for all of us. At the close of the summer session, Tom decided to transfer to Southern Baptist Theological Seminary in Louisville, Kentucky.

There we rented furnished rooms from a widow who spent the winters in Florida. Tom found a job in a supermarket after school hours, but the pay was small. We would not have had enough to eat without help from his home church at Sandersville and an occasional check from his older brothers, Lee, Ed, and Henry.

It was here I learned God does not forsake his children.

Two days before Thanksgiving, I answered the doorbell's ring to face a smiling young man with a huge sack bulging with groceries. "Is this Mrs. Thomas Holmes?"

"Yes," I said, curious.

"Well, our church has chosen you and your family to be the recipients of our Thanksgiving offering this year." And he held out the bag toward me.

"But we are not that bad off!" I stammered, feeling my face turn crimson. "My goodness, I have never thought of us as being poor!"

"Think nothing of it. We give a love offering to a seminary student each year, and we just happened to draw your name this time."

"Thank you! Thank you very much!" I said, reaching for the brown bag. With Kathy at my heels, I carried the love gift to the kitchen table. Delighted, we unloaded celery, lettuce, cranberries, bananas, grapes, pecans, oranges, apples, coffee—and in the bottom of the bag, a big, fat hen.

At Louisville I did laundry indoors—on my knees at the bathtub. We enjoyed the snow, and I stopped cooking and cleaning to sit with Kathy at the window and watch the lovely white spray sift from the sky.

After Thanksgiving Tom began to get invitations to preach in the rural districts of Kentucky and Indiana. Farm people were generous with their produce but tight with their dollars. So Tom returned from these weekend missions with ten dollars and the car laden with pumpkins and food enough to last for a week.

Our days were filled with hard work and study from early morning until far into the night. And it was lonely, because we had little time and money for friends or recreation. Kathy caught measles, Louisville smoke and cold weather caused Tom a lot of suffering from sinus trouble, and I needed an operation.

The cruelest blow struck on the first of December. Tom rode the trolley to school, because he'd left our new secondhand Ford in a shop for repairs to the motor. As the trolley drew near the repair shop, Tom saw the garage going up in flames. Getting off the bus with other spectators, he watched his wheels go up in smoke, then sat on the curb and cried. It wasn't much of a car, but it was all we had. Having no insurance, all we could collect from this disaster was thirty-five dollars for the scrap metal.

Now it was truly winter, and snow, once lovely to look at, soaked through my husband's thin-soled shoes. Every dark morning Tom, like Dr. Zhivago, had to walk through slush to the trolley, change to another, and then walk through bitter cold to classes. After school the teetotaler stacked cases of beer at the supermarket. Then he trudged back home at dusk through falling snow, his pipe in his coat pocket. He could not buy tobacco anymore. Nights came early on those dark days. But in winter when the days are darkest, Christmas always comes. And when Christmas comes, miracles happen.

A fellow student from Georgia offered us a ride home for Christmas. At my parents' home, Kathy ran to her grandfather, calling him "Pa-Pa." Thereafter Daddy became Pa-Pa to the whole family.

On New Year's Eve, Dr. Faust, secretary of the Georgia Baptist Convention's Department of Evangelism, offered Tom a job as state evangelist at $330 a month. "I want a man," said Dr. Faust, "who can preach the gospel in any church in Georgia, go into the homes of rich and poor alike. And I believe you are that man."

This opportunity was too tempting. Our sojourns west and north convinced me that the red hills of Georgia were the warp and woof of my being, and I agreed with Tom that he could succeed without a complete seminary education. He accepted the job beginning at the end of the seminary year in April. Borrowing money to live on until then, Tom completed his year and left graduate school forever.

Or so we thought.

16 Merry Weather

We acquired a second-hand beige Studebaker and rented an apartment in Decatur, a suburb of Atlanta. Tom, the evangelist, traveled the highways of Georgia and preached in churches from the hills of Fannin County to the marshes of Glynn. He bought a Dr. Grabow pipe and a can of tobacco and enjoyed his smokes once again. Smoking was no problem to the Southern churches. Most of the deacons and many of the preachers smoked cigarettes, cigars, and pipes. Only women smoked behind closed doors.

Every congregation who heard Thomas Holmes was charmed by his charisma. Young, tall, and handsome as Gregory Peck, he spoke with the sincerity and authority of the Apostle Paul. Congregations without preachers invited him to stay, become their pastor. He turned down half a dozen offers. But when the gracious people of Manchester issued a call, we couldn't say no. "I believe God is guiding me to this church," Tom said.

On the last day of January 1945 we moved to the little mountain town about seventy-five miles southwest of Atlanta, in the far reaches of Meriwether County. The temperature was a bone-chilling thirty degrees that sunny noon as we drove to our new home in a one-seated 1938 Ford coupe. Our tiny three-year-old daughter crouched behind us on the back of the seat. She wore a scarlet wool coat and leggings, a matching bonnet, and stars in her big brown eyes. We were as excited as Princess Elizabeth riding to her wedding in the royal carriage.

From a damp basement apartment in Decatur to a fine new manse we rode. Tom would pastor a little church next door to our home on the hill. The church chimes rippled out every evening at sunset, wafting hymns of hope and devotion across the roofs of homes and shops of our members: "Rock of Ages," "The Old Rugged Cross," "Blessed Assurance."

We would hear them that first day, music floating over the red slate roof of Denham's Style Center, over jewelry stores, drug emporiums, groceries; across the red brick walls of the Bank of Manchester and the maintenance shops of the Alabama, Birmingham, and Coastline Railroad; across the tracks to Callaway Mills and beyond to the green valley, peach orchards, tree-topped hills of Pine Mountain.

This was the same county Franklin D. Roosevelt had adopted and called "Merry Weather" because of its mild winters, colorful Novembers, and glorious Aprils. "We will live only four miles from Warm Springs, vacation home of the president of the United States," said Tom, "practically next door to the Little White House!"

While our small car brought us ever closer to the brick bungalow, several deacons and women of the congregation readied the rooms for their new pastor and his family. In a jovial mood, they were as happy as a bride and her mother and maidens preparing for the arrival of the bridegroom and the celebration of a marriage.

Ruby Jackson, a devout, agreeable churchwoman, met us at the French door with the oval glass. Petite and forty-six, Ruby wore her hair short, gray, and over-permanented, and she had funny large ears. But she was as dear as a favorite aunt. "Come in out of the cold," she invited, her smile spreading across her face from one floppy ear to the other. Both her rayon print dress and small black pumps looked as though a saleslady had fitted Ruby while she was looking the other way, preoccupied with the needs of some homeless waif or widow. Her laughter rippled through the rooms of our new home and reflected the joy of pastor and people alike at our coming that day.

Henry Denham took our coats and hung them in a closet. Though I tried not to stare, I couldn't help noticing that the forefingers of both his hands ended at the second joint, a congenital deformity. The owner of the Style Center, leading department store in town, he'd left his buyer and stepdaughter, Dot Woods, in charge and come up the hill in the middle of the day to welcome us. Born to a poor family in Thomaston, the fifty-six-year-old merchant had worked his way through Martha Berry Schools at Rome. By Spartan living and ascetic control, he'd built a rocklike character and a thriving business. "I'm the deacon that won't deac," he said laughing, and everyone laughed with him.

My heart danced as I beheld the beauty of our new home. Walls glowed with fresh white paint. Oak floors shone from recent sandings. The humming of the automatic furnace throughout the seven rooms and two baths was as comfortable and warm as a mother's lullaby. My fingers and feet began to thaw, and in my nostrils was the smell of frying chicken and hot buttered rolls.

Ruth McDonnell, wife of the owner of the hardware store, appeared in the arched doorway leading to the hall and kitchen. Her beautiful thirty-year-old face was framed with wavy brown hair. Tall and slim, she wore fashionable clothes like those I wanted but knew we could never buy on a preacher's salary. "Come see what we have for you in the kitchen," she said. "You've enough food to last a month."

"You won't have to cook for a week," Ruby laughed.

Everyone moved toward the kitchen. My stomach gnawed with hunger pangs. The aroma of yeast-filled bread fragranced the air and mingled with the laughter of women who'd been stocking pantry shelves: Earline Brown, Lois Winslow, Ruth Robertson.

The Second World War raged in Europe and the Pacific Ocean. All across America sugar, meat, and butter were rationed; groceries were bought with government-issued stamps as well as cash. But in our new home, at our marriage with the Manchester flock, there was no rationing that day. Home-canned and store-bought peaches, pears, and figs lined the pantry. The shelves groaned under canned tomatoes, beans, and corn; sacks of flour, meal, and sugar; jars of plum sauce, blackberry jelly, and sugarcane syrup. In a corner of the kitchen a card table spilled over with more sugar, pecans, peanuts, coffee, tea, country butter, Irish potatoes, sweet potatoes, and ropes of country sausage. The flecks of red pepper and smell of sage in the sausage reminded me of those Grandma Sally once made and mother broiled on the Southern Comfort. Red-topped counters were spread with baked ham, fried chicken, deviled eggs, chocolate and coconut cakes, apple pie, hot pound cake, nut cookies, and pimento cheese sandwiches.

"We're giving a party for you Friday night," said Ruth McDonnell, "at Mr. Denham's house, a reception. Everyone in town's invited to meet the new preacher, people from Columbus and La Grange."

"I'll keep Kathy for you," said Ruby Jackson. "She won't be any trouble."

"Preacher," said Mr. Denham. "Mr. Copeland's brother died this morning."

Wrinkles crept between the new pastor's dark eyes, and compassion showed on his long, thin face. He started toward the coat closet to get his coat and hat. "I must go see him."

"No. He's not here. He's gone to Brunswick. The funeral will be at Brunswick tomorrow."

"Then I'll send a telegram after lunch."

"Yes, just send a telegram."

How lucky we were that late January day! To be young and loved, to have seminary behind us. Our faces were smooth and unlined by the ravages of time, hearts unbroken by sorrow, grief, or pain. Years stretched before us as clean sheets of paper ready to be inscribed like Abou Ben Adhem's book of gold.

"Oh, Tom!" At ten in the evening I looked about: furniture and clothing had been unloaded from the van and set in place, the pieces of our bed put together once more and spread with clean white sheets and white, plumped pillows. All the food was crammed away. Our new friends had departed, leaving only echoes of laughter. Our tiny daughter was asleep in her little crib across the hall, her blonde hair shining in a pool of moonlight. "This is just what I've always wanted: a beautiful house on a hill with a fireplace and an automatic furnace. Let's stay here ten years. Let's stay fifteen years!"

Kissing me, my tall, handsome husband replied with a lightheartedness to match the day. "Whatever you want, my darling. You're always right, you know." I knew he was teasing. Tom thought he was always right, and I thought so, too.

And so I went to sleep dreaming of a long, peaceful life among the affluent in "Merry Weather" County, disturbed by nothing more than a baby boy joining the family and growing up with his sister, successfully and happily as a prince and princess in Camelot.

I could hardly wait till Friday night, so excited was I to be given a party in our honor, to be treated like a celebrity in the Denham mansion. The little girl from Riddleville would wear sapphire velvet borrowed from Elizabeth Brantley, wife of our Decatur landlord and my college Shakespeare teacher. I'd had no evening gown of my own since graduating.

Finally the big night came. The red-brick Denham home was exquisitely appointed with cherished antiques, Chippendale and Queen Anne furniture, and thick beige wool carpeting in the drawing room. It spread down the hall and into the several rooms where crystal chandeliers sparkled and original paintings glowed. Porcelain vases and ornaments dazzled as though wearing a sign: DO NOT TOUCH. I felt like a child in a museum clinging to Mother's hand, afraid I'd knock over and break an expensive piece and then be unable to pay for it.

Amid the luxury and loveliness, the rooms hummed with laughter and conversation as the elite citizens of the little city greeted us with the Denhams in front of their marble fireplace. I stood, short and plump in long blue velvet, wishing I were tall and slim like Ruth McDonnell, who moved with grace and beauty among the guests. I yearned to be expert at making small talk like Carrie Denham and her sister Ruby Jackson.

Instead a pain lodged in the pit of my stomach. My cold hands trembled. I feared I'd swallow my tongue and be unable to utter a single clever word. Or I'd say the wrong thing, forget names. Or stumble and fall going into the dining room and spill punch on the borrowed dress, forever spotting the velvet and ruining the Denham carpeting.

My ebullient husband, receiving to my right, called every name, had an easy salutation for every man, woman and child.

"This is my wife, Grace," said Tom to Mrs. Winslow, a white-haired matron.

"How do you do?" I said.

"Is this the preacher's wife? She's so young." And her steel blue eyes glared at me appraisingly through round spectacles. Her black-feathered hat elevated her to six feet and reduced Mother's Little Girl to the stature of a dwarf.

Tom's voice pulled my attention from the dreadnought.

"This is my wife, Grace," he was saying to the next person.

"How do you do," I said, pushing my hand toward the owner of the jewelry store.

"I thought you were the preacher's daughter," he joked. "You're so young."

Again I heard Tom say, "This is my wife, Grace."

"How do you do," I said, wishing I could think of something else to say.

"You're the prettiest preacher's wife I ever saw," said the Methodist lawyer. He smiled and bowed.

My face turned crimson-hot. Of course he didn't mean it. How could I be the prettiest anything when I was only sixty-two inches tall in my stocking feet and weighed a hundred twenty pounds?

His gray-haired wife gently but firmly elbowed him into the chandelier-lit dining room to be served coffee from a gleaming silver service, tiny frosted cakes from silver trays, toasted pecans from a polished silver bowl.

"This is my wife, Grace," said Tom once more.

"How do you do," I said. Were there no other words in the English language?

"You're Gainer Bryan's daughter, aren't you?"

"Yes," I heard my voice say.

"I'm Mrs. Hendricks from Woodland. This is Mr. Hendricks. We love Dr. Bryan. He stayed in our home when he taught a study course in our church."

"Yes."

Only house and company were brilliant. I was not. But at least, when the evening ended, I had caused no disaster.

Sunday morning found the pastor's family at Sunday school at 9:30. I sat in a class for young adult women, next to Ruth McDonnell, who looked like a model for the cover of *Vogue*. She wore a luscious mauve suit. Her brown heels, three inches high, revealed shapely ankles. She sat crossing and uncrossing pretty legs stockinged in silk.

Eying Ruth, I felt as shabby as Little Orphan Annie. Until I sat next to the *Vogue* model, I thought the long sleeves and tiered skirt of last year's black rayon dress were stylish. And my thick black suede pumps made my feet look as big as boats. I tried to hide my size sevens under the chair.

On this first Sunday of February 1945, Carrie Denham stood teaching the class of the prosperous and near-prosperous young housewives. Her hair was silver, perfectly coiffured. She wore a pale green Hattie Carnegie suit and a sable stole around her shoulders, pearls around her neck, a John Frederics hat upon her head. In her hand was an open Bible. A dynamic person and an eloquent teacher, she bubbled with "thanksgiving to the Lord for bringing the remarkable young man to our church." And she urged her class to "support him and the Lord with prayers, money, and talents," so the church would prosper and reach more lost souls, and so that the membership, now numbering 310, would double or triple.

She inspired me to unearth my buried talent (if I had one) and put it to work in the church, to search until I found my lost coin to drop into the treasury. Her splendid clothes also motivated the poor pastor's wife to covet a sable stole for her own shoulders and a $70 hat for her head to replace the plain little black felt one that had cost $3.95 in Rich's basement. Here, in prosperous Manchester, I thought it might even be possible, even though Tom would earn only $3,000 a year.

I knew we had to buy a dining-room table, a sofa, chairs, and rugs for our bare floors. We would need a piano in a few years so Kathy could learn music. I needed to practice, too. How long had it been since I touched the keyboard? What if they asked me to play "Amazing Grace" when the organist and pianist were away? Would not my halting rhythms and missed notes be embarrassing in front of these, our adoring parishioners?

At fifteen minutes until eleven the little sanctuary was resplendent, its pale pink walls lit by sunshine streaming through stained-glass windows as the chattering congregation filed in through several doors and packed into their place of worship. They were merchants, bankers, and doctors; peach farmers, dairymen, and ABC Railroad engineers; housewives, secretaries, and public school teachers. Children were led by the hand; high school girls sat with their boyfriends.

Dorothy Woods seated herself at the organ and began to play a prelude. Her seven-year-old son, Stuart Woods, sat on the front pew. Chatterings lowered to whisperings. The deacon-who-wouldn't-deac, clad in a wine-colored jacket and carrying his black Bible, found his accustomed seat at the end of the front left pew near Stuart, his grandson.

Two rows behind them, Ruby Jackson sat beside her tall, white-haired husband. Wearing a navy wool coat and navy felt hat, she chose to be in the corner next to the wall where she could eye both pulpit and pew. From this vantage point she could observe the reaction of pew to pulpit, of people to pastor, often nodding her head in agreement when the preacher spoke a truth she yearned for the people to hear.

Mrs. Denham, in her pearls and sables, worshiped near the right aisle, halfway down, beside Mrs. Dunn. The latter, who was very rich, clothed her stout, short figure in expensive but unadorned black. Her husband, Byron Dunn, owned the Bank of Manchester and the telephone company and all the little Negro houses on Dunn Row. An ardent backer of the

Eugene Talmadge political machine, he sat at the back, his metal folding chair leaning against the wall.

After everyone else was seated, a fifty-year-old African American placed a chair in the vestibule. Jim Marshall, janitor of the church, was also building superintendent of the "Y" across town and assistant at a black funeral home. He and his wife, Fannie, were leaders in the black community. He rose before daybreak in his humble home on Dunn Row, where he lived with Fannie and two of their six children. The oldest son, James, served with the army in Europe. Daily the carless Jim walked the streets, climbing the hills from funeral home to "Y" to First Church to sweep floors, dust pews, build fires, stoke coal furnaces, and cook and serve suppers for the Kiwanis Club at the Community Building. Silently and unobtrusively, as befitting a man of his color, Jim now sat alone, separated from the whites, to hear the new preacher proclaim the gospel of love and brotherhood.

While Kathy played happily in the church nursery with the deacons' children, I walked alone down the crimson-carpeted aisle. I felt all eyes upon me, looking me up and down from nondescript hat to big shoes. "Our pastor's wife," as I'd been introduced on the street, in stores and homes, was expected to sit near the front. Everyone wanted to see and take pride in her as they would a shiny new automobile traded for the old.

I was eager to do everything right, to be a good pastor's wife so everyone would love us. *When we finish here, we will get promoted to a larger charge with a larger salary,* I reminded myself. Down to the front I went and found a corner seat on the second row. *Maybe we'll go to Brunswick or Newnan Central.*

Dot Woods wore a ruby-red choir robe, her face framed by a cloud of dark hair. I watched her skillful fingers moving up and down the keyboards in a Beethoven prelude, and I wished I could play like that. The twelve members of the choir filed into their seats behind the console. The tall preacher proceeded to the pulpit chair, sat, and crossed his long legs. A hush fell upon the assemblage from Janitor Marshall at the back door to Deacon Denham on the front pew.

The prelude finished, Dorothy played "chimes on the hour" in slow, measured cadence. In solitary silence. I counted eleven bells. Then we stood to sing "Praise God from Whom All Blessings Flow." After gracious words of greeting, Tom opened the big Bible his grandmother Beall had given him on her eightieth birthday, just before he left for college. He preached from it every Sunday. It was special to me for another reason. He carried my picture inside, the one he'd clipped from the *Atlanta Constitution* of that Sunday in April 1940 when our engagement was announced: *Mr. and Mrs. Gainer E. Bryan of Forsyth announce the engagement of their daughter, Grace, to the Reverend Thomas Joseph Holmes of Senoia and Gay.*

What pride I felt in knowing that he was mine. The handsome young man towering above the pulpit of Manchester Church, this promising youthful clergyman everyone adored, was *my* husband, *my* lover, *my* Apollo!

After the service all 310 members of the rejoicing flock lingered to shake our hands, kiss our cheeks.

Jim, the janitor, quietly folded his chair with his black, brawny hands. He nodded his head in greeting to one or two departing white men as he silently put the chair back where it belonged. But a black man didn't speak to a white woman in public in those days. And white women had been schooled since girlhood never to look a black man in the face.

As the building emptied, Jim was joined by the chocolate-colored Fannie, their teenage son, George, and twelve-year-old daughter, Rosie Mae. Together they put the sanctuary and Sunday school rooms in order for the night service. Quiet as squirrels gathering nuts, they moved between the pews, collecting leftover bulletins from seats and carpeted floors. They stacked them on the table in the foyer.

An industrious family, each child helping the others to get a college education, they lived for the day when James would get home from the war. He was sending money for George to go to college.

Their morning work finished, the Marshalls went home for dinner, then to Calvary Baptist Church in Greentown for what they considered true worship.

Wednesday night at 7:30 we crossed the lawn in a freezing rain to attend the midweek prayer meeting with the members of our little flock. Terror followed me. *Will I have to pray out loud? Will we all drop to our knees?*

The crowd was thin. In attendance were only the Denhams, Dunns, Brays, Browns, Smith sisters, and maybe a dozen more. Dorothy Woods was nowhere in sight. Looking around from my seat near the front, I wondered why she was late. Then I heard whispers behind me. "Who will play the piano? Dorothy has gone to New York."

My heart fluttered. I could feel my face growing red, and I began to pull at the loose hangnail on my little finger. My stomach hurt, my hands grew numb. I longed to get up and go back down the aisle, through the front door, and out into the rain, feel its icy fingers pricking my face as I ran across the wet grass to our house, slam the French door behind me, and hide in our bedroom on our four-poster.

The lady with the steel-blue eyes punched me in the back with a heavy finger. "Don't you play, Grace?" Tom approached me from the front, open hymnbook extended, face pleading and brown eyes appealing. "Play for us," he said softly. "Play 'Sweet Hour of Prayer.'"

I jerked out the hangnail, and the finger started to bleed. Blotting it on the skirt of my brown suit, I rose from the pew, stumbled to the piano bench, placed the book on the music rack, and reached for a closed hymnal to hold the opened pages in place. The heavy songbook slipped off the narrow ledge and hit the keyboard, giving off discordant notes. Then it fell to the floor, hitting the little toe on my right foot.

The gentleman with the nubby forefingers jumped up from his front seat, picked up the hymnal, put it securely in place.

Two sharps—F and C, I knew that much. I'd always found sharps difficult, if not impossible. D was the first note. I tried to play an introduction. My cold hands seemed disconnected from my body. Somehow I got through the first four measures and, trembling, went on with the first stanza, faltering at every note, hitting wrong ones, Tom and the congregation getting ahead of me. Finally I ended up playing with one finger, the soprano notes only.

The next morning I awoke feeling joyous about our new home and the beautiful people of Manchester. Then I remembered the previous night and my poor rendition of the hymn. *How could I ever face them again? Tom must be so embarrassed.*

But it was necessary to face them Sunday. And it was essential to start preparing today, Thursday. I had to finish unpacking, serve three meals, sweep floors, dust furniture, mop the kitchen. And I had to search for a washerwoman.

So I sprang out of bed and rushed to start coffee, bacon, and eggs. Earline Brown was coming at ten in her little black Ford to take me to Dunn Row to confer with a black woman there about doing the laundry. For in the South in 1945, African Americans were still the hewers of wood and drawers of water, as they'd been for almost two centuries. And it was black, brown, and beige hands that scrubbed shirts and sheets on an antique scrub board with Octagon soap stinging the flesh, their bodies bent over zinc tubs, just as in the twenties Lou Howard bent over Mother's tubs.

17   Friends and Supporters

One bright morning in March Tom stopped before the Denham Style Center. Knocking the tobacco out of his pipe, he put it in his pocket, opened the glass door, and entered Deacon Denham's clothing store. He removed his battered Sears and Roebuck felt from his head and flashed his winsome smile to right and left, greeting the customers shopping at racks, opening purses at counters. "Good morning, Mrs. Bray. Good morning, Mrs. Jackson. And how are you this fine, springlike morning?"

Men and women turned to stare at the most dynamic man in Manchester, forgetting both purchases and purses. The new preacher was more exciting than either one.

"That was a good sermon yesterday," said Faye Bray.

"Just what we needed," said Ruby Jackson.

Henry Denham tripped from his office in the back of the shop and extended his nubby right hand. "I told my wife last night," he said, "that our church will do great things under your leadership."

"Ah pshaw!" the preacher said, his eyes crinkling at the corners. "I'm just a country preacher."

Before Mr. Denham hurried on to his customer he said, "Preacher, I want to talk with you, if you have time."

"Preacher!" Ruby Jackson tilted her curly head to the right and looked up. "Do you have any life insurance on Grace?"

"No, Ruby, I don't. I've been intending to buy some, though."

"Well, you ought to have it," she said, lowering her voice to a whisper, her face growing serious. "Don't tell anybody, but I want to give you the first payment."

"That's mighty nice of you, Ruby."

Henry Denham returned and said, "Please come with me." In his tiny office at the back of his shop, he reached in his pocket, took out a roll of ten-dollar bills, counted out ten, and laid them in the empty palm of my husband, saying, "I don't want you to be worried about money. I want you to be free to preach the gospel. Use this to buy books to widen your horizon, deepen your knowledge of the Scriptures."

"But . . ." protested Tom.

"No buts," said the little man, looking above the horn-rimmed glasses on his pointed nose and tightening his receding but stubborn chin. "This money is free, from your Savior. The Lord has been good to me. I've got a good business here. Since the war started, business has boomed. Callaway Mills is running full time, and people have more money to spend. The Lord has blessed me, and He's told me to give you this hundred dollars."

What could my dumbfounded husband do but thank him and thank him and thank him?

"Don't thank me. Thank the Lord."

Tom put the money into his thin, worn wallet and placed the wallet in the pocket of his cheap, five-year-old pants.

But the deacon-who-wouldn't-deac wasn't finished yet. "Come up here," he said as he hastened to the rack of men's suits. Pulling out an eighty-dollar suit, he said with authority, "Try this on."

"Oh, I couldn't buy that," said the three-thousand-a-year preacher.

"You're not going to buy it. I'm going to give it to you."

"But . . . !"

"No buts about it. Try it on," said the man with the stubborn chin. His short finger unbuttoned the double-breasted navy blue coat. Jerking the extra-long trousers off the hanger, he headed for the men's fitting room.

Shortly Thomas Joseph Holmes stretched himself to his full six feet four inches and preened before the three-way lighted mirrors of the Style Center. His dark eyes wrinkled at the corners, his lips parted in a smile. Clad in the finest suit he'd ever draped over his thin frame in all his twenty-seven years, he was as handsome as Gary Cooper. The thatch of black hair glistened upon his head as he turned to right and left, examining the fit of double-breasted coat over broad shoulders, slightly stooped like his father's.

Meanwhile Mr. Denham, tape measure around his neck, stooped to turn up the cuffs of the pants. Then he whipped the tape off his collar to measure the young man's back for alterations. His defective fingers were as quick and skillful as any man's perfect ones.

"Now," said the amazing Mr. Denham, the fitting finished, "let's have a red plaid tie and a blue striped one to wear with your suit, and new shirts. Here are some Van Heusens just your size." Opening a new box, he selected four whites with starched collars and long, French-cuffed sleeves.

"Now you shall have new shoes for your feet," said the wonderful little man. He hopped around like a cricket from shirt to shoe department in his beautiful little business he'd built from scratch through hard work, sacrifice, and dedication.

Tom admired the shiny black shoes on his long narrow feet. He luxuriated in the warmth of new wool wrapped around his legs. Unaccustomed to being pampered, he felt like the prodigal son returned to his father from the far country.

Tom had never had a close relationship with his father. Dr. Holmes was fifty-three when his fifth son was born, and in 1942 he had died of a heart attack when Tom was only twenty-four. My husband's best male friends, it seemed, were usually those old enough to be his father.

Henry Denham now saw to it that his support of Tom included a hat to complete the costume. Leaving the store, the preacher climbed the hill to the parsonage carrying his treasures in a box beneath his arm and wearing upon his head the first Stetson chapeau he'd ever owned.

And it would not be the last. Every year Deacon Denham outfitted his pastor in a new suit, shirts, ties, shoes, and hats. And every year he also gave Tom a hundred dollars to buy books. Occasionally he even gave the pastor's wife a new suit or dress.

In the summer of '46 I rejoiced to find I was pregnant again. But there were complications, and the doctor put me to bed for three months. We hired Jim Marshall's wife, Fannie, to come three days a week to help with housekeeping for $3 a day, the going rate. Nine dollars a week was a big sum for a $240-a-month-preacher.

Every Monday, Wednesday, and Friday, Fannie Marshall, clad in a clean cotton dress and sensible black shoes, walked from Dunn Row to our hill and entered the door with a smile and a pair of willing hands. We had no money for a vacuum cleaner. But Fannie knew how to use a broom and wet mop, how to keep hardwood floors shiny and dust-free, even in the corners. Tall and strong, she possessed a sweet spirit and rare dignity. She knew so much more than I about human relations and everything domestic. Yet she was never bossy but always soft-spoken, gentle, kind.

I loved Fannie and trusted her. She was old enough to be my mother, yet it never occurred to me—then—that I should call her Mrs. Marshall.

Since church and parsonage formed a whole, Jim mowed the grass every week in summer. And every winter day, about noon, he scuffed through our kitchen door from the church, tipped his battered black felt hat, and said, "Howdy." He was too noble a man to treat like a nonperson; and I forgot Mother's admonition, looked him straight in the face, and said, "Good afternoon, Jim." His tread heavy, he would then descend the basement steps to stoke the coal furnace. He took out clinkers, put in fresh lumps of coal, and kept the pastor's heater humming day and night, warming our rooms, fingers, and feet.

I should have addressed him with the respectful "Mr. Marshall." But I had not progressed that far in my pilgrimage from racism. Not a day passed that I didn't hear Mother's voice speaking from the wells of my memory, her many teachings, admonitions, lamentations coming to mind in snatches. They came in letters, also, two or three times a week. Even when we visited at the home of Tom's mother, a letter from her awaited my arrival.

During those early summer months of pregnancy, I got out of bed to prepare meals. Putting on a cool cotton dress, I slipped bare, tanned feet into white sandals and padded to the spacious kitchen and its double windows over the sink. One July day as Fannie and I worked together, she started talking about the thing neither black nor white ever spoke of to one another. Pushing the iron over Tom's starched white shirt, she said, "They say some peoples tried to register yesterday to vote at the City Hall. But they couldn't answer the questions, couldn't qualify."

I was so startled that the no-no subject of unequal treatment should erupt in my kitchen that the tomato-peeling knife slipped, and I nicked a finger. "What questions?" I managed.

"They ask, 'What do adultery mean?'"

"Who asked *that?*"

"Them white mens."

"What did they ask that for? What's adultery got to do with voting?"

"They was askin' questions the peoples couldn't answer to keep from registerin' them to vote. They ask them to say the Declaration Independence and the voter's oath."

My heart went out to my troubled friend and to her people who'd been embarrassed and humiliated when they simply tried to exercise a right I'd taken for granted since turning twenty-one. The election of 1946, which named Eugene Talmadge governor of Georgia for a fourth term, was the first in which Georgia Negroes were allowed to vote in a primary. Since reconstruction, blacks had been kept from the polls in Georgia. But while Ellis Arnall was governor (1942–46), he abolished the poll tax, and some people of color had voted in general elections. But now the United States Supreme Court decreed that they must be allowed to vote also in the primaries. The matter had reached the Supreme Court through a case brought by Primus King, a Columbus Negro, in 1946. So, in the summer of '46, blacks got the ballot. But they were not organized, and few were allowed even to register.

Tom and I, in silent agreement with the Negroes, did not want Talmadge reelected. We loathed his campaign rhetoric, his waving the red flag of racism. Just the week before, he'd brought his redneck followers to Manchester, and his tobacco-spitting disciples filled up the park across from our house, spilled over into the paved street with their rally. Tom and I found the Talmadge assemblies intolerable. So we packed a lunch and little Kathy into our small Ford and drove to Copeland's Lake for the day.

Traditionally preachers did not, must not become involved in politics. To speak out for a certain candidate would please some but anger others. But Fannie had told me plainly how the rights of American citizens were being denied. Surely, I thought, the time comes when the preacher must speak and act. "That's awful!" I exclaimed. "Unfair! I was never asked questions like that when I registered to vote."

"I know," said Fannie.

"Something should be done about that," I declared. "I'm going to talk to Tom!" Tom was young and brave, I naive and trusting. I believed the tallest man in Manchester could do anything. And we would not sit like statues while some of God's children suffered injustice and oppression. "Fannie, I want you and your people to vote. I'm going to ask Tom to go to City Hall tomorrow to see what he can do."

I had no idea that the men in question might be from our church. The next morning, when a sprinkle of brave blacks tiptoed into City Hall to stand before the city manager and the lawyer he'd hired to "qualify to vote," a grim-faced preacher sat among observing, concerned citizens. Although Tom sat between two of his deacons, his concern, unknown to them, was different from theirs.

Thomas Holmes remained silent while the lawyer asked the ridiculous questions Fannie had quoted to the preacher's wife the day before. The lawyer, crippled by polio, had come to Warm Springs for treatment and opened a law office across the street from our house, only four miles from the warm waters where he could find relief from his physical sufferings. The malady had left him bitter, and he vented his hatred upon blacks. Yet he was dependent upon them. Every morning I watched his black chauffeur drive him to his office, lift his overweight body from the car, carry the man like a baby into his office. At home he couldn't even bathe and dress without the aid of his servant.

Tom listened with mounting anger at the injustice in the little room. Then Fannie and Jim Marshall and their son, James, crept in. The veteran stood before the crippled lawyer.

"You James Marshall?" asked the lawyer in a gruff voice.

"Yes, suh."

"I see here," said the lawyer, looking at the book in his hands, "that you tried to register to vote yesterday."

"Yes, suh."

"Did you take the voter's oath?"

"Yes, suh."

"Quote it to me, quote the voter's oath."

James stood still, silent. Observers snickered.

"So you don't know the voter's oath. How're you gonna know how to vote?"

Still the black veteran said nothing.

"Define adultery," said the indignant lawyer. "You niggers ought to know what that means."

White men guffawed and slapped their knees. Tom's outrage brought him to his feet as the lawyer began to declare the black man disqualified.

"Sir, may I speak a moment?" There was no reply so Tom continued. "I registered to vote here a few days ago. And these questions were not put to me. All I had to do was write my name and address. And I say to you that if James Marshall and these other people are disqualified to vote, then I am also. If you are really interested in following the letter of the law, then you must challenge my registration also."

The clergyman's words hit the little company like bombs on Normandy Beach. The lawyer's mouth flew open, but he couldn't speak a syllable. Closing his book like a pistol shot, he started wheeling his chair toward the door, declaring, "The session's adjourned for the day!"

The man's servant, peering at Tom out of the tail of his eye, hastened to lift the lawyer's bulk and move him from his wheelchair to his Cadillac. As the group dispersed, one big, burly deacon from Tom's church, a Ku Klux Klansman, spoke angrily to his pastor. "Talk about splittin' the church. You gonna split the church doin' things like you done here today. Man, you already split the church! Man, you'll make trouble talkin' the way you talked today!"

But the clergyman was neither afraid of his deacon's threats nor intimidated. He lit his pipe, set his Denham straw upon his head, and strode up the hill and into the church office, where he and Jim often prayed together, to prepare Sunday's sermon.

The next morning when Fanny came to work, she was still not registered to vote. But a big smile shone upon her face, and her eyes were lit with love. A new spirit of comradeship rose between us. My relief was so enormous that I forgot to worry about what Mother would say.

I never learned what else Tom said or did that kept the deacons at bay. He preached that next Sunday about the Good Samaritan, the story Christ told in answer to the question, "Who is my neighbor?" And I sensed the enormous respect, the admiration the men and their wives, indeed all of the townspeople, held for my tall, young, determined husband. Indeed, Tom's pronouncements at City Hall were not mentioned again, and the deacon who had threatened Tom became one of our best supporters.

18 Crying in the Kitchen

Although they finally got registered, Jim and Fannie did not get to vote that year. When the '46 primary was held on a sizzling Tuesday in August, it was rumored around town that the Ku Klux Klan had met on the mountain between Manchester and Warm Springs the night before. It was also whispered that they'd burned crosses in front of black homes on Dunn Row and sagging shacks on muddy side streets. Tom had left for Jasper on Sunday afternoon, because six months before he had promised to preach for a week's revival in the north Georgia town. So four-year-old Kathy and I were alone.

I'd adjusted to staying alone, as Mother had, because clergymen often must go away to preach in other towns, to attend conventions and conferences. With an active little girl around, I was not lonely through the day. There was work to do and books to read. And I was determined not to weep into my plate, not to cripple my child by my fears and sorrows.

That election morning I rose early and dressed in cool pink cotton shorts Mother had made. Though I was beginning to fatten around the waist, I could still button last summer's clothes. The suit consisted of a ruffled wrap-around skirt which I could grab if the doorbell rang. In the forties a married woman didn't "show her hind legs" in public. Carefully I brushed my long brown hair, applied face cream, powder, lipstick.

Then I dressed Kathy in a lovely little sundress Mother had made. Mother still kept the sewing machine humming at her home in Forsyth for Kathy and me. When Pa-Pa was away on trips, she'd sometimes pump the old pedal until three o'clock in the morning to finish a garment. The fifty-one-year-old Lila got carried away by beautiful cloth and stylish patterns. She'd buy and buy, cut and sew, embroider and trim to her heart's content. Sewing dresses was her art, the one she learned while growing up in Indian Hill at the turn of the century.

After breakfast this election day, I did dishes, made beds, and lay down on the guest bed in the cool, comfortable back room. Four open windows and an outside door created a breezeway across the bare floor where Kathy colored pictures with her Crayolas.

"See my picture, Mommy!" she beamed. She had Tom Holmes's pointed chin, his brown eyes, his enthusiasm.

"Yes, darling, your picture is pretty," I said and went back to reading Homer's *Odyssey*.

At nine o'clock I got up again, put the skirt over the shorts, tied the sash, buttoned the front. Donning sandals for my feet, I took Kathy by the hand and set out for the Community Building to vote. It was only a block down the hill, a paved sidewalk all the way. Chatting, we passed the church and the filling station.

"Where we going, Mommy?"

"We're going to the Community Building to vote, my precious."

"We goin' to Mukinty Buildin' to bote," she repeated.

I laughed. "Can't you say Community Building?"

"Mukinty Buildin'," she repeated.

Mother and daughter laughed together, walking down the sunlit sidewalk in Manchester. I didn't realize that scorching morning how lucky I was until we were back home. At eleven-thirty I'd just left the bed again and come into the kitchen to make a bowl of tuna-fish salad for lunch when Fannie and Jim appeared unexpectedly at my door. Fannie was sobbing. Jim's black face was grim.

"What's the matter?" I asked.

Fannie spoke between sobs. "They wouldn't let us vote. Little white boys was there throwin' rocks at us. And the po-lice just turn their heads. We couldn't get in the door." Fannie's shoulders shook. Jim turned his hat in his hand. Round and round went the battered straw through the nervous black fingers.

My pulse raced to see the dear woman crying. I remembered the way Lucy had wailed when she received the message that Claudia had died. "I'm so sorry, Fannie, and after all the trouble you went to to register! I'll see what I can do."

I thought of Mrs. D., president of the Woman's Missionary Society. Monday after Monday we met in the sanctuary to read about the wonderful work our missionaries were doing in Africa, China, South America. We were establishing schools, hospitals, orphanages in darkest Africa with money southern women contributed. I'd heard Mrs. D. pray for the blacks in Ghana. I'd eaten fried chicken and chocolate cake with her at the after-meeting luncheons on the Day of Prayer for Foreign Missions in December, the week of Home Missions in March, and State Missions in September.

"I'll call Mrs. D.," I said. "She will help me. Her husband is the city manager." I hurried to the black phone in the hall, picked up the receiver, waited, and waited.

Finally the operator said, "Number, please."

I gave the number, heard "Hello?"

"Mrs. D.," I said. "Fannie and Jim Marshall are here at my house, and they say they were not allowed to vote. You know the Marshalls. They work at the church. They are fine people and they are registered to vote."

"They can vote. All the nigras are voting today. Where'd they go?"

"Wait a minute. Where did you go, Fannie?"

"We went to the Community Building."

"They went to the Community Building."

"They went to the wrong place. Tell them to go to the 'Y' at Callaway Mills. They can vote. All the nigras are voting today."

"Thank you, thank you." That was a long walk in one-hundred-degree heat. They would have to go down the hill and across the bridge spanning the railroad tracks to the Mill Village.

"She said you went to the wrong place. Go to the 'Y' at the Mill Village. That's a long walk in this hot sun. If I had the car, I would carry you. I got my driver's license last week. But Tom drove the car to Jasper. If he were here, he would carry you himself."

"That's all right," said Fannie, wiping sweat and tears from her face. "We'll walk over there."

"We walk everywhere we go, anyways," said Jim, putting his hat upon his head.

They left and I returned to chopping celery, pickles, and tuna. But I was so shaken by Fannie's cries and the thought of white boys throwing rocks at them that I could hardly eat.

At four o'clock the two Marshalls stood in my kitchen again, Fannie sobbing, Jim turning his hat in his hands.

"They wouldn't let us in."

"They wouldn't let you vote there either?"

"Nome, they had li'l white boys throwin' rocks. And the po-lice just turn their heads." Fannie's voice wobbled with sobs. Her shoulders shook. Jim's hat went round and round in his hands. Fannie spoke between her sobs, "We don't want to go to school with white peoples. That's not what we want. We just want our children to have equal opportunities and a better life than we've had."

Fannie's words dispelled the refrain I'd heard all my life, that the Negro was satisfied with his lot. There it was before me—the naked truth suddenly laid bare. "You're right, Fannie, and that's what I want for you, too, and your people. I'll call Mrs. D. again."

"Ain't your niggers voted yet?" Mrs. D. spoke with contempt. Then I knew finally that even our lovely town and church were ruled not by the gospel of Christ but by the rule of white supremacy, the despicable Jim Crow laws. Like most churches across the South, ours had married the culture.

Alone, I couldn't fight them any more than the Marshalls could. Mrs. D.'s tone of disgust paralyzed me, and I hated myself for it.

"I'm sorry, Fannie. I'm sorry, Jim." My eyes misted, threatened to run over. "I wish I could help, but I don't know anything else to do."

"We understand," they said in unison. "You've did all you could," said Fannie, "and we thank you."

But had I really done all I could? There must be something more!

When Tom returned and heard their story, he spoke to Fannie and Jim: "If I had been here, I would have carried you myself. Don't be bitter. There's a God in heaven who sees and cares. He knows what you suffer. Don't give up hope. Just keep singing the Lord's song. And some day He will right all wrongs."

Eugene Talmadge was elected that day. But before he could take office, the news of his death was announced on the radio one frigid December morning. When Jim Marshall scuffed through the back door on his way to stoke the furnace, we were eating breakfast. Tom said, "Well, Jim, our 'esteemed' governor-elect has died."

"Yes, suh," Jim said. "The Lord takes care of the least of these, and I am one of the least." Without a break in his stride, the oppressed one proceeded down the basement steps, his face wearing a weak smile of hope and relief.

19 God's Peculiar People

"Grace, we've got a little boy," whispered the dark head hovering over mine.

It was February 7, 1947, at the old Piedmont Hospital in Atlanta, later the location of Fulton County Stadium, built for the Braves and Falcons. Still drugged by the anesthetic, I thought I was in heaven listening to an angel who spoke in a male voice. In that blissful moment, I opened my eyes to meet my husband's dark ones, crinkling at the corners. His breath hot against my face, he pressed his lips to my feverish forehead and whispered, "I love you."

"I love you, too, darling." Then I felt the terrible pain where the surgeon had made the incision for a Caesarean.

"What will we name him?" Tom asked.

"There's only one name for our boy—Thomas Joseph Holmes, Junior."

When we went home a week later, Fannie Marshall came every morning for a fortnight to cook our meals while a practical nurse tended the baby and me. When the nurse departed, Fannie worked day and night until I recovered from the surgery and five-year-old Kathy returned from her grandmother's.

The next four years seemed the happiest of our lives. Certainly they were years of growth, not just for our children but also for the church and the preacher as well. Dr. Jackson started giving Tom shots of Benadryl, vitamins, and proteins to combat allergies. Tom's allergic condition improved, and by the time he was thirty-four, his six-foot-four-inch form filled out to 190 pounds.

His energy and enthusiasm were boundless. He spent mornings in our home library studying the Scriptures, preparing sermons, reading books. Through Henry Denham's generosity, we were filling a whole wall of shelves. I answered the phone and kept the house quiet for my husband's cherished hours of study.

Search committees from pastorless churches came to hear the promising young preacher and invited him to move to West Point, Milledgeville, Sylvan Hills, Atlanta—even Etowah, Tennessee. Tom considered each one, accepting invitations to preach in their churches, talking to their committees, visiting in their homes.

One cold, cloudy, and windy morning in March 1951 I sat in the living room reading *War and Peace*. A hickory log simmered in the fireplace. The front door opened and Tom's frame filled the entrance, the top of his Stetson brushing the lintel. He slammed the door behind him against the wind, and the Venetian blind banged against it as he strode across the room, tossing his topcoat and hat toward one end of the couch. "It's cold outside," he said. "Looks like snow."

Then he knelt on the small oval rug before the hearth and carefully, with fragrant pine splinters and hickory logs, rebuilt the fire. Tongues of flame leaped up the chimney, bark crackled and popped. A spark flew onto the carpet. Brushing it back with a quick foot, he came to sit beside me on the sofa and took both my hands in his. His long fingers caressed mine as he spoke. "Grace, I've made my decision. I have to go to Lakewood Heights."

"Oh no, Tom, no!"

"I understand how women are about giving up the home they've loved. But you'll get used to the new one." He was being so gentle, so kind, his brown eyes searching mine for a glimmer of understanding, adjustment.

But I could not fathom why my husband wanted to leave this comfortable home in this lovely town, leave these precious people. I could never adjust to a horrid white frame on Jonesboro Road.

"I feel my work is finished here and God wants me in Atlanta to reach the unchurched. Don't you remember the day A. D. Kendall drove us to the top of the hill and let us look down on that new suburban development?" Tom pulled his pipe from his pocket.

I remembered all too well. Row upon row of small white houses stretched in the valley like little boxes fronted by wild onion lawns and scraggly trees. My mind a tumult, I struggled to keep back tears. *Why doesn't God let us live where we want to, where we're happiest? I know I shouldn't think this way. I so want to please my husband and God and go where they want me to go with a smile and a song as The Preacher's Wife is supposed to do. But why won't He let us stay here? This would be a good town for the children to grow up in.*

Four-year-old Tommy helped me pack one afternoon. As we wrapped the last Havilland china teacup with newspapers and sheltered its delicate pink blossoms underneath wads of printer's ink, I surveyed the bare shelves of the corner cupboards and collapsed into my son's tiny blue chair, tears streaming. His little-boy hands wiped them away. The son who bore his father's name and his mother's face, who in my dreams was going to grow up a prince, already was acquainted with grief, frustration, and in-security.

On the April moving day I woke early, before dawn, to find myself as miserable as though lying upon a bed of stones. I left stones and bedroom, trudged through hall and into silent living room. Picking my way through packed cartons in gray half-light, I gazed through curtainless windowpanes and grieved. *This day we go. It's unbearable, yet it must be borne. We will leave this land I love, the purple hills and green pines, the gentle, gracious people whom we've come to call our own, leave the little city that's been our home for six and a half years, exchange this neat brick bungalow for that white frame on Jonesboro Road.*

The salary will be only fifty dollars a month more. We still won't have enough money to buy rugs, tables, lamps, a vacuum cleaner, a piano. I can't see that we are improving our station in life. Now if we were going to the beautiful north side of Atlanta, I'd be happy. But who wants to live between the federal penitentiary and the Chevrolet plant?

This room held so many memories. Over there, in the corner by the triple windows, the Christmas tree always stood. I recalled Ruby Jackson, Aline Cook, and Carrie Denham slipping in on Christmas Eve to leave gifts beneath the tree. The funeral home always sent a lovely poinsettia, which I placed on the coffee table set on our one rug before the fireplace. *How sad to give up this cozy room, those friends! There will be no Henry Denham in Atlanta with a clothing store to give Tom a handsome new suit every year, hundred-dollar bills to buy books.*

Where will we put the Christmas tree next December in the house on Jonesboro Road? Where the tinseled tree had glowed on Christmas morn-ings, I saw only cold, naked windowpanes. Their flower-strewn draperies were packed in one of the pasteboard cartons, ready to be hung on win-dows they would not fit. I shuddered. When Fannie and I washed drapes, we always hurried to get them back in place the same day because I didn't want to greet a single sunrise through unadorned glass.

Unlocking the door, I went outside to cross the lawn and stroll in the garden one last time. The rising sun, a ribbon of pink, mauve, and rose red, backlit sparrows, robins, and mockingbirds chirping from tall pine branches. Irises sent up purple, yellow, white flags. I remembered how I dug the holes and planted the corms with my own hands. *There will be no blossoms where we're going.* Where one pitiful violet bloomed, I paused, sighed, and wondered why the clumps I'd transplanted had withered and died. *Perhaps I didn't work the soil enough.*

Not so for the rosebushes. They were in full blossom. *I waited five years for those Tiffanies. Only last February were we able to squeeze the money from our overworked budget.*

Here is the bed where I always planted nasturtiums. I heard again the children's voices calling to one another in their play while I knelt on the grass to plant the seed. Last year Tommy wanted to help. Thoughtfully, the three-year-old buried a seed with his chubby hands. Then he turned brown eyes toward mine and said, "Mama, what makes the flowers grow?"

"God makes the flowers grow, my son."

"Why? How does God make pretty flowers from this little seed?"

"Well," I said as I took another seed and buried it in the warm, pliable soil. "We put the seed into the ground. It dies. Then God sends sunshine and rain. And God says, 'Wake up, little seed. Wake up and live.' The seed bursts open and new life springs forth. A flower, many flowers, bloom to make the world beautiful. You see, my son, when we plant seed, we're working together with God to make the world beautiful."

"Working together with God." My own words echoed in my ears. *That's why you must move to Jonesboro Road. You can't be like other people. A minister and his wife demonstrate, "laborers together with God" and "God's peculiar people, chosen and precious."*

Have you forgotten the five other homes you've transformed? You have a genius for making ugly rooms beautiful. Anyway, Lakewood Heights is planning to build a new parsonage. Think what fun you'll have drawing plans, selecting paint, wallpaper, new curtains.

It was a long, hot, sad day. About four o'clock I walked over the bare hardwoods once more to survey the progress of the moving men, anxious to get the ordeal over. Our slim daughter stopped me in the hallway between the bedroom and kitchen doors. The nine-year-old wore a yellow-checked frock her grandmother had sewn. Kathy's hair, clipped short, was as brown as chestnuts. A fourth grader, she had taken piano lessons since second and practiced daily on the church piano. Her little arms went around my skirt. She turned sad brown eyes up to mine. "Mama," she said. Her voice quivered. "I've been over to the church and played all my pieces on the piano just one more time."

I was surprised to see tears slide down her cheek. This transfer was as difficult for her as it was for me. I hugged her thin body. "I know just how you feel, Kathy. For weeks I've been feasting my eyes on the mountain at sunrise, singing with the chimes at sunset. But I feel better. Do you know what we're going to do for you in Atlanta?"

"What?"

"We're going to buy you a piano so you can practice at home. Daddy will make more money, $400 a year more, $5,800 altogether!"

"He will?"

"Yes, isn't that wonderful? And they'll pay utilities too, lights, water, telephone." Our hearts grew joyous again.

At seven that evening our weary company reached the new home near a busy intersection in southwest Atlanta.

"Look, the van's already here," said Kathy.

Backed into the narrow driveway, its doors were barred like a Brinks truck, moving crew slouched on porch steps and smoking. Taking a long drag, the head mover came to meet the weary preacher. "We'll have to have the money before we kin unload," he said in a gruff voice, flicking ashes with greasy fingers.

"How much do you want?"

"All of it, $200," said the man, poking the cigarette back into his sullen mouth.

Tom frowned and said: "The church is going to pay you. Can't you start unloading while I go find Mr. Washington? It's nearly night. My wife's tired. The children are hungry."

"Nope," he said. "I cain't unload nothin' 'til I have the money." He threw his cigarette butt on the pavement, stamped a heavy brogan upon it for emphasis.

Frowns dug deeper between my husband's dark eyes. He had the key to the house. But there was not a chair or a table in it, and the phone was disconnected. Many city blocks stretched between him and the man with the money. Dusk crowded in, Mars glimmered in the western sky. Truck and automobile traffic whizzed by the congested intersection, screeched to a halt at the signal light, boomed off again.

"Daddy, I'm hungry," said Tommy.

"I wanna go to the bathroom," said Kathy.

With a quick, nervous jerk, Tom reached inside his coat pocket and withdrew his checkbook, saying, "Here, I'll write you a check. They can pay me back tomorrow."

I knew his bank balance was a mere $19.19 and wondered how in the name of thunder he could write a check for $200!

"We cain't take no check," said Mr. Burley. "We have to have cash." He was calm, adamant.

"You have to have cash!"

"Yep, two hundred dollars."

Since the preacher couldn't swear, he drew down his lips till they formed a thin, hard line and reached around for his wallet. Flipping it open, he counted out his sixteen dollars and thirty-three cents. It was only a stall while he decided he'd have to go to search for the man with the filthy lucre.

As he sped away, the porch light snapped on at the white frame next door. A giant of a woman lumbered through the opened screen door, her dark head brushing the lintel. It was the wife of one of our new church's deacons coming to our rescue.

"You're going to eat supper with me," she shouted.

She plunked us down at her table for a cold meal of deviled eggs, potato salad, and baked ham. Along with a paper plate, she handed me a job in the church.

"I'm superintendent of Vacation Bible School this summer," she bellowed, "and you're going to be head of the seven-year-olds. And the preacher is going to do the character stories."

Tommy began to cry. "Is this where we're going to live, Mama?"

"No, darling. We're going to live in the house next door."

It was dark when Tom returned with Mr. Washington. He was a barber with white hair and blue eyes, soft-spoken and genteel. He didn't carry much cash in his pockets, but he had a beautiful checkbook in his hand.

Now he tried to talk Mr. Burley into taking a check on the church, explaining, "It's night. Everything's closed, and it's hard to find two hundred dollars in cash."

"Nope. We have to have cash on the barrelhead. We cain't take no check."

"What's the matter?" said Mr. Washington with a smile. "Don't you trust the church?"

"We cain't take no check," said Mr. Burley.

Lakewood Heights was made up of blue-collar workers in the Chevrolet plant, the federal penitentiary, and other trades, such as barbers and trolley operators. Few of them carried more than ten or fifteen dollars on their persons, so it took ingenuity and legwork to rake up the needed dollars that night to get our beds and pillows in place for our weary heads.

But at last the mover had his two hundred in his pocket. He swung open the yellow doors of the truck. Wearily we looked for bedposts, springs, mattresses, pillows. Instead, boxes and bicycles, books and garden tools tumbled out. I groaned. *Why is it the last items you need are always the first to appear?*

Tom unlocked the front door of our new home. We trooped in, inhaling stale, musty air. While I tried to find a place to put my purse down, Kathy squealed with joy, "Mama, look! Look at this big window!"

Hair tousled, yellow dress as wrinkled as an old woman's face, eyes wide with excitement, our daughter restored my joy that April evening. "Mama, when Christmas comes, we can put the Christmas tree here!"

As most churches do, Lakewood had many problems. Tom was harassed by them day and night. We rarely saw him except at mealtimes. Mornings he spent in his church office in sermon preparation and church administration. Afternoons he visited parishioners in homes and hospitals, the latter scattered around the burgeoning city. Every weeknight at 7:30 there was a meeting: deacons on Monday, committees on Tuesday, prayer meeting Wednesday, Sunday school visitation Thursday, wedding rehearsals Friday. And at least one wedding on many Saturdays. Sunday morning we all had to be at Bible school by 9:15, stay through morning worship, return at 6:15 for Training Union and evening worship. In between, Tom spent numerous hours counseling with people about their problems.

When I awoke every morning in the little box on Jonesboro Road, my days were already planned by zealous, club-loving women. I was plunged deep into a society of aggressive ladies married to submissive men. To these frustrated females, the preacher's wife was a dandy young woman to be used as sponsor for every organization.

Racism was not an issue at Lakewood. The church, as well as the community around it, was all white. While we lived there, I rarely saw a black person at close range, so complete was segregation in Atlanta. Since we could not afford to hire help, I did my housework alone.

The dinner hour, which I had always tried to keep serene, became exasperating. One evening Tom rushed in at 6:00, his face tired, a sheaf of papers in hand. In the kitchen I hurried to get hash and grits on the table. As soon as food was into stomachs, I must get the dishes back into the kitchen and washed, the children and myself brushed and beautiful, and everyone ready to leave by 7:15 for the prayer meeting at seven-thirty.

The black phone in the dining room next to the preacher's chair rang. Kathy answered. "It's for you, Daddy."

He sat in the chair, took the phone. "Hello," he said. "Yes. I know the sanctuary needs redecorating, and I'm working on that now. Got to raise some money. Who do you think would be good on that committee?"

They settled that problem or shifted it to another day, and he replaced the phone in its cradle. It promptly rang again. "Hello." He listened patiently to a member complain that she had heard their adult Sunday school class would be reorganized by ages.

Then Tom dialed the number waiting for him beside the white phone. "Hello, how's the baby?" His face showed that the news was not good. "I'll come to the hospital right after prayer meeting," he said, replacing the phone, picking up his fork.

"Let's eat," he said with an urgency that sent us flying off in every direction.

"Wash your hands, children," I said. "Hurry up, it's already 6:30!"

Finally we were all in place in the ladderback chairs around the mahogany table, bowing heads for Tom to ask the blessing on our food.

"Hello," said the weary father.

We all raised our heads, looked at one another, and broke into a gale of laughter.

The church-owned parsonage was near an intersection where three thoroughfares crossed. A constant stream of traffic screeched to a halt at the signal light, roared off again. Our "castle" was right on the street and as hot as a furnace. There was no air conditioning, so we kept the windows open in hope of cooling breezes. Motorcycles and trucks sounded as if they were crashing through the front rooms.

Our nights were filled with insomnia. Anguished in the steamy darkness, my soul cried out, *What am I doing here? I love beauty, music, poetry, the quiet of open countryside. I was not born for this concrete wilderness!*

In August Tom and I managed to escape the city for three days of rest in the mountains of north Georgia. Kathy and Tommy had been packed off to Forsyth to visit their grandparents. We read books, took walks, and slumbered beneath the hand-hewn rafters of a charming rustic inn at Neel's Gap. The third afternoon as we relaxed on our single beds, Tom shattered my peace with a startling question. "Grace, do you know what I want to do?"

"What now?" I asked sleepily. His long frame stretched the whole length of the bed, and his feet hung off the edge.

"I want to teach."

"Teach who? Where?"

"I want to teach young men, student ministers. I believe they could benefit from what I've learned in the pastorate. I want to be a college or a seminary professor."

"Oh, Tom. That's what I've always wanted for us!" I visualized myself in the gracious role of professor's wife on some magnolia-shaded campus: Tom, tall, dignified, handsome, a prince in tuxedo with black tie; I, beside him, gowned in pink satin, face shining, hand extended to greet young people filing by.

"But I would have to go back to school," Tom said, "back to seminary to get a doctoral degree."

"Oh no!" I cried, pink gown and black tie vanishing. I knew he'd not even finished the work for his master's degree. I sat up, my book thudding to the floor. "Go back to school at our age? Give up the new house they're building, live in a shabby three-room apartment or shack? We have no money, no stove or refrigerator of our own."

"We'll get them," said my thirty-four-year-old bridegroom confidently.

"But what will people think if you leave Lakewood Heights so soon?

You've only been there a few months. Some gossips will say you had to go, that you were run off."

The woman who hadn't wanted to come to Atlanta now didn't want to leave, at least not to live in substandard housing. But a preacher's wife must not think of *things,* she must think of *souls.* Aloud, I said, "You haven't reached all the unchurched you were going to, remember? Nor redecorated the sanctuary."

"Oh, I wouldn't leave before next summer. In about a year we can afford it. It doesn't matter what people think."

As I lay upon my bed staring at the hand-hewn beams, I recollected those seminary days nine years before. The memory was a nightmare.

Lila Smith Bryan, age twenty, 1915

Gainer E. Bryan, age
twenty-one, 1915

Grace Bryan, age five, 1924

Grandma Mary Bryan
and Rachel, 1929

Wescoloski-Bryan
House, Riddleville

Aunt Lou's cabin,
Riddleville

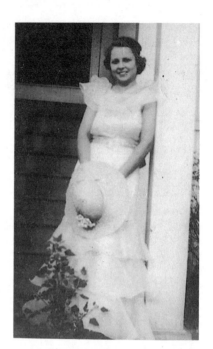

Grace Bryan, age seventeen, as a
sophomore at Tift College, 1936

Grace Bryan, age twenty, at the time
of her graduation from Tift College,
1939

Thomas Joseph Holmes, age twenty-two,
at the time of his graduation from
Mercer University, 1939

Wedding portrait, June 4, 1940, Forsyth, Georgia

Clockwise from upper left: Grace, Tom, Kathy, and Tommy Holmes, Manchester, Georgia, 1951

Grace Holmes teaching children at Lindsay Street Baptist Church, Atlanta, 1960. Used by permission of the North American Mission Board, Atlanta

Grace Holmes as the
wife of the pastor of
Tattnall Square
Baptist Church,
Macon, circa 1965

Dr. Tom Holmes as pastor
of Tattnall Square
Baptist Church,
Macon, circa 1965

Nannie Lee Daniel, Riddleville, 1968

Grace (right) and Tom with
Kathy (left) and her children,
Gay, Georgia, 1975

Grace and Tom Holmes on
their forty-second wedding
anniversary, 1982

20 *O Holy Night*

The next morning when the sun rose through the mist, we packed our clothes into Samsonite suitcases the congregation of Manchester had given us. I recalled once more how even the men had cried when Tom resigned, and the piqued committee in charge of a going-away present for us vetoed the usual silver service and gave us this set of suitcases instead.

Climbing into the car, we left the mountain resort and headed for Atlanta, exchanging green tranquility for the frenzy and concrete of city streets. At the wheel Tom puffed on his pipe, his eyes straight ahead. "I want to talk over this matter of returning to seminary with Dr. Black. Let's invite him to dinner tomorrow night. Then we'll take him to First Church, where he's teaching at seven-thirty.

"I hate to ask you to give up the new house, Grace," he said, stroking my knee. "But I believe it's God's will that I finish my education."

I succumbed to his charisma and agreed to invite the retired preacher and Greek scholar. Maybe our old friend could talk Tom out of this notion. But soon after the blessing over our food, little knots of fear began to form in my stomach.

"Dr. Black," said Tom, "I think God is calling me to return to seminary and get my master's and a doctorate so that I can teach seminary students. I want to talk to you about it."

Dr. Black paused in mid-bite. He laid down his knife and fork, fixed his eyes upon my husband, and said, "I've been praying for one whole year that you would decide to do just that. When I heard you teach at Mercer last summer, I knew you had the qualifications. Your experience as a pastor has equipped you to train young men for pastorates. It's a great life. As a teacher you multiply yourself many times." Turning to me he said, "It's a beautiful life, Grace."

He knew how to choose his words. What I wanted more than anything in the world was a beautiful life—house, car, clothes, children—and husband, elegant and educated.

"I have no money," Tom said. "It would mean giving up a good church, an ample salary, and a rising position with the Convention. And Grace would have to give up the new house."

"If God wants you to go, He will take care of you," the old preacher said.

Yes, God may keep us from starving. But I want to do more than just eke out an existence! Daddy went back to school after I was born, and he and Mother are only just now getting out of debt after twenty-five grueling years.

Of this much I am sure: I will not go back to any seminary unless Tom has respectable work and a decent house ready when we arrive. I will just be firm. I will stand on a stool so I can confront the towering male eyeball to eyeball.

Dr. Black's soft voice interrupted my resolves. "Grace, have you heard the call? I always tell my 'preacher boys' the wife should receive a call, too."

"No," I said, color rising to my face, displeased with his intrusion of my privacy. "I've never received any call." *I married that man because I love him, because he is handsome, tall and strong and enthusiastic. Because of those beguiling wrinkles in the corners of his eyes when he laughs. I never heard a "call" to be a preacher's wife!*

But now the Question rang in my ears like a ringing telephone in an empty house. "Grace, have you heard the call, the call, the call? Have you heard the call to leave everything, take up your cross and follow Jesus, as it says in the songs you've sung all your life?"

Maybe I have. Yes, I'm sure I've heard it. All my life. Sung about it in all the churches I've been a member of, from Riddleville to Lakewood. But so have all the other people in those churches. Nobody actually does what those songs say. And I've never wanted to be different from the crowd. I turn deaf ears to songs and sermons about surrender, tuck away in the farthest corner of my mind that business of taking up the cross daily. So has everyone else except Daddy and Mr. Black, and possibly Tom.

But that night those ideas refused to stay in their corner. I barely heard the men. Their voices dimmed as the Question grew louder, and my mind made a little rhyme: *Grace, have you heard the call, the call to surrender all?*

Somehow I served the apple pie, cleared and crumbed the table, and washed the plates. The Question burned in my brain while we drove downtown and parked at my dream church on Peachtree Street, a magnificent red-brick with towering white steeple. Separating, we went to different classes. I sat in a seminar for forty-five minutes and heard nothing but the questions beating against my brain.

Can you return to school, endure the sacrifices, give up the new house, nice salary, live on faith? Will you surrender your dreams of having a fine home, rose garden, carpeting, a piano, television set, stylish clothes, private schools for the children, summer camps, music and dancing and riding lessons?

I sat there, unable to answer. It was unfair! I had just given up one house and the garden I planted and nurtured. Already we had moved six times since our marriage eleven years before. I didn't want us to become rolling stones. Could such a life be good for growing children?

A murmur rose in the room. People stood, chatted with each other. Class was over. I stood too and followed them. Laughing and chattering, they moved out into the people-packed hallway, pushing me with the throng like a dumb, driven cow, not knowing where I was going, not caring.

We came to the sanctuary, cavernous, cream-colored, lovely. I heard music—two pianos, the pipe organ, trumpets—a familiar hymn by Mary Brown and Charles E. Pryor. Silently I sang it:

I'll go where you want me to go, dear Lord,
Over mountain or plain or sea;
I'll say what you want me to say, dear Lord,
I'll be what you want me to be.

Tears pricked my eyelids. I knew this song would be my undoing. On a crowded pew, I found myself alone. I didn't know where Tom and Dr. Black were. *I'll not try to find them. There must be a thousand here, or more.* Glancing to right and left, I saw no familiar faces, and I was grateful for the blessed isolation.

They were standing to sing. I stood, too, and held the hymnbook open in my hands. But I could not sing. Because if I opened my mouth, the dam would break, my tears would flow.

I watched young people sing the hymn I'd mouthed all my life without thinking about the meaning of the words. Now I knew. Tears streamed down my cheeks and made little puddles on the open hymnbook.

The song finished, and the music stopped. We all sat. A man in a dark suit on the platform half a mile away led a prayer. The organ and piano started again, and the congregation swung into the poem by Isaac Watts:

When I survey the wondrous cross
On which the Prince of glory died,
My richest gain I count but loss,
And pour contempt on all my pride.

Suddenly I saw a vision, the only way I could later describe the indescribable. I saw the cross, saw Christ suspended there before my startled eyes. He was high and lifted up above the rostrum, the pulpit, the head of the song leader. I saw His head, His hands, His feet, the blood trickling down, the whole cruel scene, all of it in one blinding flash.

In horror I knew it was I who put Him there. Because of my selfishness and rebellion, my humanity, He had suffered this humiliation and agony! And I'd always thought it was the Pharisees, the Roman soldiers who were responsible.

Then the still, small Voice said: *Grace! Take up your cross and follow Me.*
The congregation sang the last stanza:

Were the whole realm of nature mine,
That were a present far too small;
Love so amazing so divine
Demands my soul, my life, my all.

The song ended. Glancing from left to right, from right to left, I was astonished that no one else had seen the Sight, nor heard the Voice. Or had they?

No one seemed to notice.

When the sermon was over, I wove my way through the crowds, walked alone out into the night to wait for Tom on the columned portico in the cool evening air. I saw my father smiling his sweet smile as he greeted people with his left hand, right sleeve limp and empty. He was clad in a navy blue suit, white shirt, crimson tie. I wanted to rush to him and say, "Pa-Pa, something wonderful has happened to me, something tremendous." I opened my mouth, but could not utter a sound. So I stood detached, awestruck.

All up and down Peachtree lights glittered still, as though nothing unusual had happened. Automobiles whizzed by, stopping for signal lights and zooming off again, their occupants oblivious to the earthquake that had shaken me to the very foundation of my being. A light breeze brushed my damp hair, dried the sweat and tears.

I would never be the same again.

21 *Sacrifice and Song*

When Mary Magdalene saw Christ that first Easter morning, she ran to tell Peter and the other disciples, "I have seen the Lord, and He is risen as He said."

But when I saw Christ, I was struck dumb. Three months would pass before I could tell my husband my Good News, or even find a definition for that confrontation with Christ at the Cross. Nevertheless, a fire had been lit in my soul. A refiner's fire, it purged and purified.

The new parsonage was finished in October, and we moved into its spacious rooms with the church members assisting. The next morning, Indian summer sunshine filled the rooms with warm radiance as the family trooped downstairs for breakfast. It splashed painted walls of living and dining rooms and flooded cedar-paneled breakfast nook, where I served crisp bacon and buttered toast.

"I'll never get you off to seminary now," said Tom. "You'll never want to leave this new house, new draperies and all."

I recalled the miracle on Peachtree and my heart vaulted. *I've got to tell him! I've got to tell him that he's got a new wife too—that I'm trying not to become attached to this house and land, these ten rooms with their shiny hardwood floors, this brick and mortar and plaster.*

The telephone rang. As I spoke into the receiver, which hung on the cedar wall separating kitchen from dining-living room, I had no idea that the conversation would be the beginning of a lesson in prayer. It was Mother, in Atlanta for the day. She often rode up from Forsyth with Pa-Pa to shop. "What do you want for Christmas?" she said.

"Oh, Mother. I've been so busy with the moving and all, I haven't had time to think about Christmas."

"Well, I want you to have a piano. Kathy and Tommy should be taking lessons."

"Mother, I know, but we just don't have the money. I promised Kathy we'd buy her one, but we've been so busy."

"Well, I've got a hundred dollars I want you to have for a piano for Christmas. We've finally settled Mama's estate." Aged eighty-three, Grandma Sally had died in January 1948. "And I want to divide my portion with you and Brother."

"How good of you, Mother. A piano is exactly what I want for Christmas!" Heart merry at this unexpected good fortune, I returned to my cold coffee. "Mother wants to help us get a piano for Christmas. She has a hundred dollars she'll give us from Grandma's estate."

"I have fifty dollars saved," said Tom. "We probably could buy an old upright for a hundred and fifty. I've often said they have a better tone than the spinets. The strings are longer. We'll go to town and see what we can find." He folded his blue-checked napkin, rose from the captain's chair, and headed for his office.

On a cold, cloudy afternoon in November, we finally found time to drive downtown to Cable Piano. Inside the store we were met by a man in an immaculate gray suit. He whisked us by elevator to a vast room on the second floor filled with wall-to-wall spinets, consoles, baby and concert grands. Awed by their shining beauty, I wanted to touch the keys, ripple off a tune. Instead I buttoned and unbuttoned my brown jacket, feeling like Alice in Wonderland, dwarfed in this great hall of potential music.

Tom stroked the polished mahogany of a console model. "What's the price of this piano?"

"Twenty-one hundred dollars," said the man in gray without flinching.

"Do you have any used pianos?" Tom asked.

We followed the salesman to a side room where Victorian uprights stood stripped of their fronts, hammers, and strings, gaping like a senior citizen who'd lost his dentures. A blind man in baggy tweed and shirt sleeves cocked his ear to a tuning fork.

My timidity diminished. I played a few notes on each of the dilapidated instruments. All sounded harsh, brassy. We saw nothing we'd have. And even those were priced from two hundred dollars.

We left the store, poor in purse and spirit. Outside a cold rain fell. Dark-clad figures hurried up and down Peachtree Street, umbrellas raised, heads bent, each wrapped in his own worries. Dejected, we climbed into the car and headed home, Tom weaving his way through rush-hour traffic. I watched rain splash as the windshield wipers swished back and forth in metronome rhythm. We spoke not a word all the way back to Rhine-hill Road.

My brain was busy. *We just have to have a piano this Christmas. We've put it off long enough. We've always had to meet our needs without money, and surely there's a way to obtain this needed "luxury." Somewhere in this city of Atlanta in some shop or home, there must be a piano that can be had for a song and a prayer.* The idea of prayer struck like a thunderclap. I recalled a passage from the Bible: "If ye have faith as a grain of mustard seed . . . nothing shall be impossible unto you." My pulse raced. *Surely I have just one grain of faith!*

And so, while riding in the rain, I sent a petition heavenward in silence.

The next morning in the new split-level, I began a daily ritual that would instruct, inspire, and enrich me for the rest of my life. My Morning Quiet Time, begun in an effort to learn how to pray in faith, became as necessary as meals. It enabled me to go through the days with new confidence. I cleaned, cooked, mothered in quiet joy.

Every morning after breakfast and goodbye kisses, I ran back upstairs, cleaned bathrooms, made beds. Then, taking my Bible down from the shelf, I sat in the middle of our four-poster and searched the Scriptures as diligently as Forty-Niners panned for gold.

I read the Sermon on the Mount morning after morning for several days, savoring every morsel as a dieter devours a thick, juicy steak after a long fast on lettuce and cottage cheese. Then I found this gem in Hebrews 11:1. "Now faith is the substance of things hoped for, the evidence of things not seen." So each morning I closed the Bible and prayed with hope and faith and expectancy.

After that first prayer time, I jumped up from the bed and ran down the steps to the living-dining room. On the east end rose our mahogany table and six ladderback chairs. Along the inside wall sat the chintz-covered couch and a coffee table. Opposite these the picture window was framed by white draperies. On the west, at right angles to the window, was nothing but bare wall. Not even a painting punctuated its milky-white emptiness.

Ah! That's the spot for my mustard seed. I visualized a piano there, my brain conjuring up a mass of mahogany and ivory against a backdrop of bone white. And every day as I went into and out of the room, I *saw* it there, filling up the empty space. But I didn't tell a soul about my secret.

On the second day of December, Mother telephoned. "Grace, I'm at Rich's," she said above the clatter of Christmas shoppers and money changers. "There's a piano here I think you'll like. It's a used one but in pretty good shape. Costs three hundred dollars. Can you and Tom come down and look at it?"

"No, Mother. I'm sorry, we can't come today. Tom's out visiting the sick, and I've just put Kathy's birthday cake in the oven. You know Kathy's ten today, and she's having a party."

"Can you come Monday? Mr. Sims says he'll hold it for you."

"That's nice. Yes, we'll come Monday. First thing Monday morning. And thank you, Mother. Thank you."

But when Monday came, Tommy was sick with a sore throat, his temperature 102. I dared not leave him alone. While we ate bacon and eggs, I softly reminded Tom of the piano being held for us at Rich's. I wanted to tell him I'd prayed, but how could I when furrows were creeping between his brows?

He reached for a banana. "I won't have time to look at pianos today," he said while peeling the brown-flecked fruit. "I have to go to the Pastors' Conference, visit hospitals, oversee repairs at the church." He dropped the peel onto his plate, held the fruit ready to put into his mouth. The furrows deepened. "Got a lot of sick folks. And anyway, we can't buy a piano. We don't have the money."

"You said we had fifty dollars."

His brown eyes glared at me. "I'll need that for insurance. I've got to get off a check today."

"Don't we have thirty days' grace?"

His eyes became dark daggers. "I've already taken the thirty days' grace. The trouble with you is you want too much. You can't wait on things."

But we'd promised Mother. And the man had been holding the piano since Saturday. When he unfolded his seventy-six inches to tower over me, I stretched my sixty-two, stood on tiptoe, and glared back. Propping hands on hips, I said, "Now, listen here! We've waited long enough to get a piano. Kathy's ten years old. In six or seven years, she'll be leaving home. What we're going to do for her, we have to do now. I don't intend to have our children grow up without musical training. We *can* have a piano, and we will! Now, you'll just have to squeeze in enough time to go to Rich's today."

I fumbled with a pearl button, thinking that was quite a speech for Little Buttermilk to voice. She was not accustomed to giving orders to her husband. Nor was he to taking them.

But after the end of the banana disappeared into his mouth, Tom wiped his fingertips on his napkin, sighed, and said, "I will go."

On the way into Rich's he met Mr. Washington, who just happened to have the day off. "Good morning, Preacher, what are you doing downtown this morning?"

"I'm going to look at a piano, Deacon. My wife's decided we must have one for Christmas. Her mother has found a bargain here—and, well, you know how women are."

Mr. Washington nodded his head, smiled and asked, "How much is it?"

"Three hundred dollars."

"Three hundred dollars? I know where you can get one for forty dollars. My neighbor wants to sell his."

"Forty dollars. Is it any good?"

"Well, it's been abused. But it could be fixed up. Wouldn't cost much."

Tom's long face broke into a grin. His eyes crinkled at the corners. "I want to see your neighbor's piano. But first I must go look at the one Grace's mother picked out."

An hour later, Tom and Mr. Washington had whirled to the Southside home to appraise what had once been a fine instrument. A concert upright, it was fifty years old, scratched and scarred, and minus most of its ivories.

Tom decided to see how it sounded. So he sat on the round Victorian stool and played his one piece, all on the black keys as was his style: "Take Your Burden to the Lord and Leave It There." To his astonishment, the piano had an excellent voice, had held its pitch well. He went to the telephone and called a repairman, who agreed to come out immediately.

When Mr. Alverson had examined the wreck, he announced that he would put in new hammers and a new keyboard, get the case refinished, and tune it. He could have it as good as new by Christmas. And his price would be two hundred dollars.

Tom wrote a check to Mr. Washington's neighbor for forty. Then, before he began to ponder how he'd raise the hundred to add to Mother's Christmas gift, he phoned me and declared with love and enthusiasm,

"Mrs. Holmes, I've just bought you a piano. And you shall have it by Christmas."

"You have? Does it have a good tone?"

"Yes, and it will be even better when Mr. Alverson gets through with it."

I hung the phone on its hook, stood speechless and staring at the blank wall in the living room. *There is a God! He does answer prayer!*

When I told Mother she said, "Grace, do you mean you're buying a piano you haven't even seen?"

"Yes, Mother, I am. But don't worry. The piano is an answer to prayer. You see, Mother, I prayed for this piano."

Two weeks later, Mr. Alverson arrived with my "substance of things hoped for."

"Where do you want the piano?" he asked.

I pointed to the blank wall. Three muscular men bent and heaved under the weight of it. They lifted and pushed and shoved until it was centered against the bone-white space next to our sparkling Christmas tree.

Now for the first time I beheld what had grown from my mustard seed. Massive, Victorian, it was lovely. The mahogany had been refinished and polished till it shone like brown satin. Its ivories were as clean and white and perfect as a string of pearls. I yearned to bring them to life, but I was reticent.

The children bounced with excitement. Kathy played "Jingle Bells" with her right hand.

"Now you can practice at home," I said. "I'll find a teacher for you after Christmas."

Tommy banged "Chopsticks." "Mama, I want to take lessons too."

"Sure you can. I'll get you started when you're seven."

Tom strode in carrying his hat and a long white envelope. He hung up his Denham Stetson, and a smile split his face. "Let me show you something, Mrs. Holmes," he bubbled, pulling a check out of the envelope. "Here is a Christmas present from the church, one hundred dollars. With the hundred your mother gave us, we have just what we need to pay the piano repairman."

"Just exactly enough." Astonished, my heart again leapt for joy. "It's a miracle, Tom, an answer to prayer. I prayed for that piano."

"You did? You prayed?"

"Yes, darling. I asked God to give us a piano. And he did!"

"That's tremendous!" he said as he draped his long legs over the stool. Spreading his lengthy fingers over the black keys, he played his favorite hymn ceremoniously, a christening. This amazing man who never had a music lesson, who almost never touched a keyboard, played his one piece without missing a note.

In the days that followed, I couldn't wait to get to it. Now Quiet Time and Music Time flowed together like violins and woodwinds in a symphony orchestra. After breakfast dishes were washed, four-year-old Tommy and I spent mornings in the sun-splashed living room, I at the piano and Tommy on the oval rug nearby, where he played with his toy cars. Beds went unmade. Christmas shopping was postponed. Dust grew on furniture. I even skipped some of the missionary meetings while I feasted upon triumphant hymns of faith.

Old sheet music, frayed and yellowed, was moved from dark closet to music rack. I blundered through Bach, Beethoven, and Brahms with one hand, missing notes, skipping difficult passages. *If only I could interpret the Masters!*

Then I knew I'd never be satisfied until I could. I'd have to go back to school along with Tom and the children, to study music. I now understood Tom's need to return to graduate school. It no longer mattered what kind of house we would live in. When there was music in it, any dwelling would be a mansion. And if God could give us a piano, could He not provide us a home and a job also—plus money for lessons?

And yet every night as we lay down together upon our maple four-poster, I reveled in the beauty and serenity of our master bedroom. Something in me made me want to keep it forever—walls painted Wedgwood blue, windows opened to sighing pine branches and rustling oak leaves. One warm night after Christmas, when they furnished music to lull me to sleep, Thomas Holmes was listening to his distant drumbeat. In the darkness he said, "You know, darling, I just can't get this thing out of my mind."

"What thing?" My heart began to pound, for I knew what thing he meant.

"Returning to seminary. I believe that's what God wants me to do. And

I'll never be satisfied unless I finish the master's degree and get a Ph.D., because I want to teach, become a scholar. I hunger to delve deeper into the truths of the Bible, study Greek and Hebrew, learn all I can about God and His work."

"How long will all this take?" I asked, my heart hammering. *I've got to tell him!*

"Four years. I think you would like campus life. It would be easier for you than being a pastor's wife."

"That would be nice. But in the meantime what would we live on? Where would we get the money to buy food, clothing, shelter? Do you want to go back to the hot western winds and the treeless landscapes or to frigid Louisville?"

"No. I've decided I'd like to go to the new seminary in North Carolina. I think I'll be able to leave this church next summer, go to Wake Forest, and look for work."

"A home in Carolina might be nice."

"We will have to make sacrifices. I hate to ask you to move again. It will be hard on you and the children to give up this new home. But I'm sure I can get work. With my experience I should be able to get a good church."

Now is the time! "Tom," I said in a trembly voice. "I have something to tell you."

He lay very quiet. My heart hammered like a red-headed woodpecker in the pine forest. "Something wonderful has happened to me. Do you remember that night we took Dr. Black to the church on Peachtree?"

"Yes."

"Do you remember the question he asked me?"

"No . . ."

"He said, 'Grace have you heard the call?' Well, that night I heard it. All the way across town as we drove by the Capitol and up Peachtree Street, I heard it, repeating and repeating in my head. And I saw a vision of Jesus . . ."

When I'd finished telling of the incredible event, Tom turned on his side and covered my face with kisses. "That's wonderful," he said in a voice thick with emotion. "That changes everything. With your help, I know we can go! I'm so glad you told me." He sat up saying: "Let's pray about this."

So we got down on our knees together. "Dear God, if you would have us return to school," Tom said, "please open the right doors. We don't ask that you make the way easy, only that you make the way possible."

Almost immediately doors began to open. We embarked upon an adventure in faith that turned sacrificing into a song.

22 *Venture in Faith*

As soon as Tom arrived at his office next morning, he wrote a letter to the president of Southeastern Seminary. In a few days a reply came from Dr. Stealey granting us an interview for December 27.

Sharing Tom's excitement over this journey, I prayed every morning while I washed dishes. A double window over the white enamel sink allowed a view of a giant oak. Fixing my gaze on its winter-bare branches, I quoted verses I'd memorized about faith: "But seek ye first the kingdom of God, and his righteousness; and all these things shall be added unto you." Over dishwater I asked for a job near Wake Forest, a home, and the money to buy food, clothing, shelter, books, music lessons.

The after-Christmas conference went well. Early in March 1952 Tom received this letter from President Stealey: "I have wondered many times about you and have silently uttered a prayer that you may find a way to carry on your education according to your desire. . . . I believe that if you can make a *venture in faith* and move on up here, you will find the way open."

Venture in faith! To Mother's Little Girl and Gainer Bryan's Daughter, it seemed an exciting concept. But The Preacher, sole breadwinner, in the darkness of our bedroom said, "Perhaps we should give up this idea of going back to school and stay where we are. Here we have a nice home and enough money to live on. I've had no invitation to a church up there. And even if I get work as a student pastor, we wouldn't be half as well fixed financially as we are here."

But I'd changed. "I believe that if God wants us to go, He will care for us as he cares for the sparrows and the lilies. If He can give us a piano, He can give us a home, a job, our food and clothing."

Outside, rain pelted and fierce March wind whistled around the corner of our split-level. Bony branches of the water oak bumped above our room—thud, thud, thud. Inside, the house was cozy and comfortable. The sound of galloping rain on the roof wrapped me in security. I slept. But Tom, as turbulent as the weather, tossed until three in the morning.

Next morning sunlight flooded in. I padded to the window. Fresh green leaves budded on branch and stem. Daffodils bloomed across the street in a neighbor's garden. Perched on a limb, a male cardinal chirped and flew away in a flash of scarlet.

"Good morning," Tom said from the pillow. "Guess what I dreamed last night."

I turned to face his tousled head. "What?"

"I walked down a long corridor, came to a door, opened it, and inside stood Dr. R. T. Daniel holding out his hand to me. As we shook hands, he said, 'I'm so glad to see you back at seminary, Georgia Boy.' But Dr. Daniel teaches in Texas. And the door I saw in my dream was clearly a door I saw at Wake Forest when we were there last December!"

"All dreams are puzzling," I said, descending the stairs. At the kitchen sink I fixed my gaze upon the oak tree and prayed, "Dear God, please don't lead us back to the cow town, the prairie, and poverty!"

Five days later Tom lay in bed with a cold and sore throat. I was in the kitchen making him a bowl of chicken soup when he shouted downstairs, "Grace, guess what?"

I ran to the steps and looked up to see him towering at the top. Clad in blue cotton pajamas, dark hair rumpled, he smiled broadly. In his hand he held a copy of the *Christian Index*.

"What in the world?"

"Dr. Daniel is going to Wake Forest! I just read about it here in the *Index*. He's moving there in July to teach at Southeastern!"

The next Sunday, our friends drove up from Manchester. Unwilling to let Tom leave when he did, they often made opportunities to hear their favorite preacher "one more time." The three of them, Carrie and Henry Denham and Dot Woods, worshipped on the same pew with me. After we had uttered the last Amen and had greeted our parishioners, Henry drove us all downtown for lunch at the Chinese restaurant just off Peachtree. Oriental murals decorated walls; soft music relaxed diners. We sipped fragrant oolong tea and renewed relationships.

"We're going back to seminary," Tom announced.

"You are? When? Where?"

"Next fall. We believe God is guiding us." Then we told the Denhams and Dot about answered prayers, opened doors, Tom's dream.

The more we talked, the more their faces shone.

"As yet, I don't have the promise of work up there. But Dr. Stealey believes I'll get work once I'm on the field."

On the way out of Ding-Ho, Mr. Denham pulled Tom off to a corner and whispered, "You go ahead with your plans. Do what the Lord guides you to do. I will stand by you until you get work."

On the second Sunday in June, Tom read to the Lakewood congregation his letter of resignation, to take effect on the first of August. They were surprised, and some grieved. But it was not as it had been at Manchester, when grown men cried. At the age when most men are coming into their own, Thomas Holmes resigned the big city church with no place to go and no salary. He gave up a prominent place among Georgia preachers and then declined a larger position many ministers would have worked a lifetime to achieve—a call to the church at Brunswick.

It was not until one week before vacating our home that we knew where we'd live. But by the first day of summer, Tom had received eight invitations to conduct revival meetings. From these he earned almost a thousand dollars, paid our debts, and put some in savings. A trip to Manchester netted a new suit, shirts, shoes, and hat for the preacher-student, a red suit and a warm wool dress for the preacher's wife. Ruby Jackson responded to our venture in faith with "God has big plans for you two!" Cocking her curly head to one side, she offered, "I have a refrigerator you can have. It's old, but it still makes ice. And, Grace, I'll pay for your piano lessons. I'll send a check each month. Just let me know how much you need."

Mr. Washington helped us buy an automatic washing machine at wholesale price. Mother bought material, patterns, and thread. She pumped the old sewing machine all through the summer making dresses for Kathy and me.

In July we made another trip to North Carolina. A letter of introduction preceded us as we packed our apple green Kaiser and headed north. Our first stop in Raleigh was at the office of an important Carolina clergyman. We left there with another letter of recommendation, this one to Pat Purnell of Franklinton. "He's the key man in the church there. But I warn you," the clergyman said, "that churches in this area are not eager to have student pastors."

His warning did not quell the hallelujahs in our hearts. For had not God promised to go before us and prepare the way?

Just ahead of an afternoon shower, we drove into Franklinton, a sleepy town thirty miles south of the Virginia line and less than a hundred miles from Jamestown. At the Texaco station Tom strode inside and telephoned the "key man." Then we drove down a wide, shady street past a new school building and well-preserved antebellum homes, some dating back even to the eighteenth century. At a white stucco church with a steeple and stained-glass windows of deep colors, we paused. "Church needs painting," Tom said, as he put the car in gear to drive on.

At the large, dilapidated house next door, no curtains decorated the windows, no lilies bloomed in the garden, and the lawn was rife with weeds and wild onion spears. "That must be the parsonage. It would take a lot of money to fix that up," I sighed.

A block down the street we parked beside the Purnell house, a two-story brick shaded by tall oaks and magnolias. Remaining in the car, I waited and prayed in the ninety-degree heat as Tom got out and went to ring the doorbell. Tall crape myrtles bloomed above the green hood, a burst of hot pink beneath a cloudy sky. Their fragrant blossoms were rocked by a soft breeze so gently that even an approaching shower did not disturb their lazy swaying. Their scent brought memories of Mother and our myrtle trees in the village.

Tom returned, bringing Mr. Purnell with him. Of medium height and slender build, the white-haired gentleman was perhaps in his sixties. He was one of those rare persons who seem to be ageless, having the bearing of a young man, a sportsman. In his hand Mr. Pat held the letter we'd brought from Raleigh. I could tell by their smiles that he and Tom were friends already.

Big raindrops began to splash upon the roof of the car. The men crawled into the back seat. In my accustomed place in the front, I turned sideways to be introduced to the key man in Franklinton.

Something about him reminded me of the deacon-who-wouldn't-deac. Behind his gold-rimmed glasses Pat Purnell's blue eyes twinkled when he talked. At the same time they wore an expression of sorrow, and somehow I felt the Holy Spirit guiding us as He'd guided the Apostle Paul.

Tom was unaccustomed to this business of seeking a church. Churches had always sought him instead. But Mr. Pat put us at ease. "I think our church'll do well to get you, Mr. Holmes," he said in his slow drawl, turning the letter in gnarled hands. "I'm not a member of the search committee; but I'll talk with the chairman and get in touch with you, if you'll leave me your Raleigh phone number."

When we headed back toward Raleigh, I said, "Do you think we will ever hear from him again?"

"I don't know."

But we didn't know Pat Purnell. We didn't know we'd discovered our street called Straight, found our Ananias.

Pat Purnell once had a son named Tom. Mrs. Purnell and her cook were putting his eighteenth birthday dinner on the table when word came that her only son had been killed in an automobile accident. The mother's life stopped that noon as the tragic news was announced. She slipped into a deep depression. But Mr. Pat had learned to translate his grief into generosity. Had the boy lived, he would have been thirty-five now, the same age as my husband. The lonely old man loved Tom Holmes at first sight.

Mr. Pat arranged an interview, and three weeks later we knew we had a new home. Because the parsonage was in disrepair, the church rented for us five rooms in the mansion of a Methodist woman, Mrs. Rose. Almost hidden in a park of giant oaks and maples, the antebellum, three-story white house had formerly housed a millionaire's family and servants. In the middle of the front lawn a large magnolia displayed its perfectly shaped evergreen beauty.

Our new living room's simple elegance showed in pale pink papered walls, a fireplace with carved mantel, parquet flooring, and a bay window affording a leafy view of the park. I mentally placed the piano to the window's right, where there was plenty of light. And Kathy squealed, "Mama, when Christmas comes, we can put the Christmas tree here, in front of the windows!"

"That's the perfect place for the tree, Kathy," I said, happy to see our daughter dry-eyed, excited, and adjusting to the new home.

One year after Tom started talking about returning to seminary, we were settled in August 1952 in the fine old house just ten miles from Southeastern Seminary in Wake Forest. Upside-down moving cartons served as tables and apple boxes for bookshelves. We had barely enough dollars to buy milk and bread, tablets and pencils. Yet The Preacher's Wife was intoxicated, new wine bursting the old wineskins, happier than she'd ever been.

Tom started immediately on his pastoral duties and seminary studies, and I found my piano teacher—the wife of the Texas professor in Tom's dream! Days fell into a delightful pattern. I rose every morning at six-thirty, jumped into my clothes, brushed my hair, put on lipstick, cooked bacon, eggs, and toast, squeezed fresh orange juice. We ate breakfast around the kitchen table. As soon as Tom left for seminary and the children for school—Kathy in sixth grade and Tommy in kindergarten—I washed the dishes by hand and put a load of laundry into the washing machine. By nine o'clock I was at the piano.

As I hurried about, I found an hour here, a few minutes there for music. In the day's first hour of practicing, playing and singing great gospel hymns became my worship. Next I practiced scales, chords, finger exercises, followed by the works of Clementi, Mendelssohn, Mozart. After an hour with the great composers, I'd dash off to the kitchen, pull wet garments out of the washer, rush to the garden to hang them on the lines. This chore accomplished, I'd fly upstairs, make up beds, hang clothes in closets, sweep floors, clean tub and toilet. With music in my head, housework lost its drudgery. I became a liberated woman fifteen years before I ever heard of Betty Friedan.

I'd been liberated by Christ at the foot of his cross.

Here, as in Lakewood, racism was a nonissue. I did all my own housework and rarely saw a black person. The seeds of my vow lay dormant, waiting for another season.

One February day I picked up a pair of Tom's shoes where he'd left them the night before. Stopping in my tracks, I studied them. *Grace, you sure have changed. You're a new person. Here you stand dreamy-eyed over a pair of big black shoes you used to throw into the closet with a thud.*

But I love these shoes and him who wears them. And I love his mission! I carefully placed my sweetheart's shoes upon the closet floor.

With the arrival of spring our grounds exploded in color. Tulip trees bloomed pink and mauve, forsythia blossomed yellow, lilacs showed their lavender. When I bucketed into the garden to hang out the wash, squirrels and rabbits scampered to hiding places behind the hedge. One April day I noticed the ground was covered with a carpet of violets. I could not move without stepping on their tiny purple faces. I recollected the one pitiful violet at Manchester. For that one I'd sacrificed, I now had thousands.

I noticed another thing that spring. As I worked in the Eden-like garden, I began to pray and sing:

> Have thine own way, Lord, Have thine own way;
> Thou art the potter, I am the clay.

The rebellious woman had become putty in the Potter's hands.

Rhyming words bubbled into my brain. I flew in the back door to find pencil and paper. Sitting in the middle of the bed, I wrote my first poem. Within my soul was born the desire to write a whole book, telling how God guides.

Someday I will, I promised myself.

23 *When Christmas Comes*

Tom carried a heavy load at seminary our second year at Franklinton, for he wanted to finish in time to graduate with Southeastern's first class in April 1954. Four days a week he left home at 7:30 A.M., returning to Franklinton at 4 P.M. and stopping by the site of the new education building he'd encouraged the church to construct. Mondays and Saturdays he helped the volunteer crew. Any day of the week hospital visits had to be made in Durham and Raleigh, for there was no hospital in Franklinton.

Every night he studied for four hours, long legs stretched before crackling flames in the fireplace, feet propped upon an ottoman, books scattered on the floor. He mastered Greek and Hebrew. Across the hall, I practiced sonatas and sonatinas.

But in October Tom dropped the afternoon class of Greek to have more hours for visiting the sick. This meant he would have to postpone graduation. About the same time, he became aware of rapid heartbeats—paroxysmal tachycardia, the doctor called it—occasionally. These palpitations reminded him that his father died of a coronary at seventy-two, a cousin at forty. His mother survived a heart attack at age thirty-six. Tom was now thirty-six. The doctor told him to get more rest and recreation and to quit smoking.

As October's blue-and-gold days passed and the chilly November rains sent autumn leaves floating to the ground, Tom decided he wouldn't be able to continue the three more years necessary to earn a Ph.D. As we raked leaves and watched the children carry them off in zinc tubs, and when we chatted before the fire in the evenings, we reassessed our plans.

"I haven't received the slightest encouragement from any of my teachers to become a teacher when we get through here," he told me.

"And that's why we came here, that you might teach."

"I've received more encouragement to remain in the pastorate!"

In December of that second year at Southeastern, the washing machine, Tommy, and I fell sick in rapid succession. We got behind in the grocery, drug, and book bills and in our insurance payments. One morning after Tom and Kathy left for school, I went upstairs and knelt before the east window, using my college trunk for an altar, and prayed for help. Winter sunshine warmed my head. Six-year-old Tommy lay on a bed across the hall, his young heart damaged by rheumatic fever.

While I prayed, Tom telephoned Deacon Denham and asked for a loan. Less than a week later, Tommy was back in school, and Tom received this lovely letter:

> Dear Preacher:
> Yes, I love you as much as ever. . . . I had some money that belonged to the Lord, and I am now convinced that He had me to hold it back for this purpose. Don't send any note. This is FREE by your Savior. Just thank Him, as I always have told you. . . .
> "The deacon that won't deac"

Clipped to the letter was a check for two hundred dollars. We could not have been any more grateful had it been for two thousand.

On the Sunday night before Christmas week 1953, it seemed that the whole state of North Carolina celebrated. All up and down Highway 1 colored lights twinkled through windows of homes and crawled across rooftops of stores. Departing from the church immediately after the end of the candlelight carol service, we sped along the decorated highway, our eyes sparkling also. We were on our way to Georgia for Yuletide with families and friends, our ears still ringing with the sweet strains of "Silent Night, Holy Night" and the merry voices of our members shouting "Merry Christmas, Happy New Year!" "Safe trip to Georgia!"

All day our members had brought gifts to the apartment. Into our spacious kitchen they came clutching bags of fresh Florida oranges and grapefruit, Carolina pecans, a Smithfield ham. They brought golf balls for Tom, books for Kathy, toys for Tommy, and five-dollar bills for all of us. "For your trip to Georgia," the cards read.

We had planned to leave before sunrise Monday morning. But Tom and the children became so excited they persuaded me to get ready to go that night. So I was in a dither all day, packing suitcases, loading the car, answering the doorbell and the telephone, receiving callers, and practicing piano, because I was to play "O Come All Ye Faithful" and "Hark, The Herald Angels Sing" before the congregation.

Through the entire service I played like a pro! I could feel my fingertips caressing the cool ivories all the way to Charlotte, where we spent the night. The following afternoon, just as winter sunset glowed red in the western sky, we reached Forsyth. Parking in the backyard of my parent's home, we jumped out and rushed into the kitchen door. Mother's face was wreathed with smiles. The arrival of her children brought Christmas early for her, too.

Around Mother clung the delectable aromas of roasting ham and chicken, fruitcake, coconut cake, and divinity candy. In the living room a fresh pine permeated the air with its woodsy fragrance. Colored lights glowed. Gaily wrapped gifts nestled beneath green boughs. Mother started handing out presents to the children before we set our suitcases down. They ripped them open, squealing with joy.

Then she brought me a big box wrapped in wrinkled paper and ribbon she'd saved and used for several Christmases. Mother never discarded even a piece of string if it could be used again. "Open it," she said, her face beaming.

"You ought to save it until Christmas morning," Tom said.

"Open it now," Mother repeated. "See how it fits."

I obeyed. There beneath white tissue paper was a dress of crimson velveteen she'd sewed for her daughter.

"Mother, you made this for me!"

"Try it on," she sang. "Try it on now."

The dress fit perfectly. And while I was admiring it in front of the mirror of the old dresser, she slipped a small fur neckpiece around my shoulders.

"Mother, you shouldn't have!"

"It's mink," she said, her voice full of love.

"A preacher's wife can't wear mink," protested my husband.

"This one can," Mother said with authority. "Why not? The deacons' wives wear mink."

I pulled the tiny minks close around my neck and face, enjoying their luxurious warmth. By now the evening star was brilliant in the winter sky. Pa-Pa padded in from his Atlanta office, suitcase in his left hand, his right coat sleeve limp and empty.

"Pa-Pa!" chorused the children as each one grabbed a leg.

"Look what Mother gave me."

We all gave him a kiss, and he gave each of us a one-armed hug. "S-a-y, Thomas," Pa-Pa said in his sweet Southern drawl. "I had a long distance call today from Mr. Bryan Blackburn of Central Church, Newnan. Their pastor resigned last night, and he wanted to know when you will be finished at seminary. I didn't know what to tell him."

My heart skipped a beat. The richest church in Georgia was interested in my husband!

"Well, I won't finish in the spring as I'd hoped," said Tom. "I've had to drop Greek and church history. I was carrying such a heavy load with the building program at the church."

Dr. G. J. Davis called from Atlanta. "Tom, Sylvan Hills here in the city needs a preacher for next Sunday. I told them maybe you could come."

"Yes, Dr. Davis, I'll be happy to come."

"When will you finish seminary?"

"I'm not sure. I'd hoped to finish next spring, but I've had to drop some courses, take it easier."

"College Park has lost its pastor and I've recommended you. So you might have a search committee at Sylvan Hills Sunday."

"Well, I'll declare! I can't believe it. Two churches are thinking about me as pastor. And nobody has encouraged me to teach, which is why we returned to seminary."

"Well, maybe the Lord wants you to stay in the pulpit. We need good preachers like you, Tom."

Tom spoke three times at Atlanta's Sylvan Hills. Search committees from College Park and Newnan were at all three services. I wore the red velveteen with the tiny minks clasped at the throat. Tom was invited to speak also at Newnan Wednesday night and at College Park the next Sunday morning.

At Newnan we were entertained by Mr. and Mrs. Bryan Blackburn of R. D. Cole Manufacturing. While Mr. Blackburn drove Tom around the town to introduce him to deacons and other key men, Mrs. Blackburn drove me up and down one suburban street after another, showing off the homes of the members of Central. She pointed out new, sprawling palaces and antebellum Greek Revivals shaded by tall magnolias and oaks and accented by pyracanthas loaded with red berries. Manicured lawns as large as city parks surrounded the homes.

When we cruised past a two-story brick bungalow on Jackson Street, she pointed out a black Buick parked in the drive. "This is the preacher's house," she said. "We give our preacher a new Buick every year."

"That's nice," I murmured.

"Our preachers' wives always serve as president of the Woman's Missionary Society."

I felt like a ball and chain had just been clamped around my leg. Suddenly I was Little Buttermilk again, inadequate, intimidated, clumsy. Back in the Blackburn mansion, the four of us sat in the huge dining room under a sparkling chandelier, where a uniformed butler with impeccable manners served us a delicious meal. But for me, the richest church in Georgia was losing its glamour.

At 7:30 the splendid sanctuary was packed to hear Tom preach. Afterwards we stood at the front and greeted each person who filed by. Then Tom disappeared into a back room with Deacon Blackburn. When we were on the road beneath the moon and stars roaring toward Forsyth, Tom reached inside his coat pocket and pulled out a white envelope. He said, "Read it."

By the light of the dashboard, we beheld the first fifty-dollar bill either of us had ever seen.

"Well, I'll declare," said Tom. "We're leaving Newnan with fifty dollars in one pocket and a call to the church in the other. Quite a lot for a poor seminary student. Mr. Blackburn says they're ready to call me if I'll accept. But, Grace, I feel that's not the church for me."

"I feel the same way," I said, "I could never be the president of the WMS."

On Saturday evening we were entertained at dinner by the College Park committee and their spouses. Two dozen of us gathered around a rectangular table in the Empire Room of the Dobbs House at the nearby Atlanta airport. In a jovial mood, they treated us like Clark Gable and Vivien Leigh just flown in from Hollywood for the premiere of *Gone with the Wind*.

"Sit in the middle of the crowd," Lillian Ford laughed, "so we can all see you." We dined on oysters Rockefeller, charbroiled steaks, and black-bottom pie.

Sunday morning dawned sunny and cold. In our motel room we dressed carefully in our best old suits from the Style Center, departed at 10:30 for the short drive to the church. We went past the air terminal. Airplanes took off, came in for landings, thundering over our heads.

"There's the steeple to our church," said Tom.

I beheld the tall white spire in the distance rising above bare treetops and a silver airship flying over it. From my heart rose a fountain of prayer.

"Pete Ford told me last night they want me to come."

"He did?"

"Yes. I told him I couldn't come before the end of the school year in April. He said they would wait. It's a fine church, Grace, with a new building, new organ and pews, and a nice parsonage nearby, only eight years old."

"But you still won't have your master's. You lack four months."

"Perhaps I can work out something with them. I could fly back and forth to Raleigh-Durham, finish my studies, graduate next year. You see, darling, there's more than one way to skin a cat."

"Yes, I see."

"They have seventeen hundred members, and they pay twice as much as Franklinton." Tom parked the car, hastened inside to the pastor's study, his big black Bible in his hand. I waited outside for Mother and Pa-Pa, who were driving from Forsyth with Kathy and Tommy.

Standing alone, I looked up at the church at close range. It was red brick, of Colonial and Grecian architecture. From the steeple sacred music poured forth like great cathedral bells. Then I saw the people, hundreds coming and going from every direction. Men, women, boys, and girls shifted between Bible school rooms and the sanctuary for morning worship. My family arrived, and we all went inside.

I studied the shining interior. Walls and wood were new and white, even the pews and organ. The carpeting was wine red. From where I sat in the immense room, the pulpit looked far away. But everything I saw, I loved. As people assembled and the organ music crescendoed, my heart swelled, remained exultant throughout the service.

After the benediction, people closed around me, reaching from all sides to shake my hand, and smiling and saying, "Your husband's a good preacher." "We hope you'll come to us."

Pete Ford managed to inch his way through the throng to my proud parents and me. He, too, was smiling. "Come down front," said the big, tall deacon. "Come stand with your husband."

Finally we squeezed through the cheerful crowd, formed a receiving line in front of the pulpit and communion table, and shook a thousand hands, everyone talking at once.

"We like Reverend Holmes."

"We like you."

"Please do come and be our pastor."

After the last handshake we were taken out the back door to see the parsonage, a neat, one-story brick about fifty yards from the church. The chairman of the deacons and his wife proudly showed us through the rooms. We entered the kitchen, lemon yellow with a corner breakfast nook and cabinets all around. Across the front of the house were the living and dining rooms separated by an arch. Colorful draperies hung at windows; beneath our feet lay thick gray carpeting. In the living room were triple windows and a fireplace.

"Mama," chorused Kathy and Tommy, smiling in front of the windows, "when Christmas comes, we can put the Christmas tree here."

Finally, after we said goodbye to Mother and Daddy, we were on the highway to North Carolina. "I'll let you hear from me soon," Tom had promised Pete Ford and Billy Stephenson as we parted.

"Daddy, I don't see why you didn't tell them today you'd come," said Kathy.

Tom laughed. "I have to think about it and pray. Two churches have called me. I don't want to make a mistake."

Two weeks later he made his decision. For us Christmas had truly come. And what is Christmas but the coming of Christ?

But when Christ comes, can a cross be far behind?

24 *The Revolutions*

On the day the Supreme Court handed down its momentous decision outlawing segregation in public schools—May 17, 1954—we moved from North Carolina to an Atlanta suburb. Here Tom assumed the pastorate of the College Park church and its nearly two thousand members.

That same year another Georgia preacher, by the name of Martin Luther King Jr., moved with his wife, Coretta, to Alabama. King was a graduate of Morehouse College and Crozer Theological Seminary. He would receive his doctorate from Boston University in 1955. Rev. King became the pastor of Dexter Avenue Baptist Church in Montgomery, cradle of the Confederacy. The twenty-five-year-old black was destined to have a profound influence on our consciences and careers, even to change the course of our lives. But I'd never heard of Martin Luther King Jr. that Maytime of '54.

In high spirits, Kathy and Tommy, Tom, and I jumped from the Kaiser just as the yellow moving van lumbered to a halt in front of the brick bungalow. Jane, wife of the church organist, Frank Willingham, had promised to find us a maid. So Leila Howard, no relation to Aunt Lou, waited at the kitchen door. Plump and middle-aged, her face the color of toasted almonds, she wore a loose-fitting cotton dress, a checkered apron, and comfortable work shoes.

"You must be Leila," I said happily.

"I am," she replied, her almond cheeks dimpling. "Miz Willingham sent me to help you, you pretty thing." Since slavery blacks had found it expedient to ingratiate themselves to whites by flattery. Leila went to work unpacking our china while the moving men set up our furniture. Among them were the maple four-poster bedroom suite, the prayer piano, and some new pieces we had inherited—a bedroom suite and sterling silver flatware. They came to us after Mother Holmes died on March 10, and Tom and his brothers had met to divide their mother's things. Also there was the Pennsylvania Dutch cupboard handmade by "Father" Pat of solid walnut as a parting gift from the Franklinton flock.

More than a servant, Leila became my trusted friend. The widow, whose home was a three-room apartment beneath a small grocery in Colored Town, came three days a week to help me. I rose at five every morning to find two hours for precious "quiet time," when I read my Bible, meditated, and wrote. During this sweetest time of day, streets were silent, church doors locked, the family asleep. All I heard was bird song. Even so, that first hectic summer there was only time to write verse. Whenever I read the rhymes to Leila while she labored at sink or ironing board, her almond-brown face beamed. She'd laugh and say, "That's pretty, you pretty thing."

Our first summer at College Park was as enchanting as a Hawaiian honeymoon. Preacher and family were adored by the congregation and entertained at restaurant dinners, home dinners, progressive dinners. High above the parsonage at sunset we could hear the church chimes ring out sacred music to nourish the soul.

Jets took off from the Atlanta airport, two miles away. Roaring over our roof, they sounded as though they were stripping off the asphalt shingles. Neighbors complained, but the thunder of silver airships electrified me, lifting my spirit from the mundane to the magnificent. I had yet to take my first flight and often dreamed of jetting to New York for the publication of my first book.

Even missionary meetings seemed exciting. The first time I attended, Lillie Thomas pinned a large purple orchid on the shoulder of "Our Pastor's Wife." And Vacation Bible School, held for the children in hot and humid July, was the most exhausting week of the year. I played piano and told Bible stories to seven-year-olds every morning from nine to noon.

But all through the busy summer I yearned to get back to writing my book. I longed to tell others how to find the secret of true happiness, believing this to be the thing God was guiding Grace to do.

But Grace was not a whole person. At thirty-five, I was still too fragmented to listen to my inner voice and believe in that voice with authority. I was Child-Woman obeying Mother's voice and Preacher's Wife obeying the ninety-nine ladies in the Woman's Missionary Society. They were authoritative, aggressive women to each of whom my subconscious reacted as it did to Mother. Where I once had only one mother to cope with, now I had one hundred.

"We want you to work with the Girls' Auxiliary," said Ludie. "It meets twice a month."

"I'm afraid I won't have time. There's so much to do at home." I didn't want to tell anyone I was writing a book. That was my secret. Having a book is like having a baby; you don't show it until it's finished.

"Oh, but the preacher's wife always helps with the young people's organizations. Leila can do your housework."

And Mother's Little Girl wound up saying, "Yes, ma'am!"

"We want you to teach a class," said Jack, superintendent of the Sunday school.

"But I won't have time to prepare a Bible lesson week after week, visit absentees, and attend study courses twice a year—not with all the housework, my husband and children to care for."

"But we need you desperately to teach young mothers," Tom and Jack said.

"Yes, sir," said Gainer Bryan's Daughter.

"You must join the Woman's Club," said Eva. "It meets once a month at the clubhouse. I'll pick you up Tuesday at noon for your first meeting. We always have a luncheon."

I didn't want to join any club. But I had to, because I was the preacher's wife. The people paid our salary, seven thousand dollars a year, and furnished a home rent-free.

"If we succeed here," Tom whispered one day, "we can go anywhere."

Of course I wanted to help my husband succeed and fulfill his dreams! Believing I could be all things to all people, and apparently succeeding in the roles of wife, mother, and preacher's wife, I determined to succeed as a writer also.

At the same time, in our nation opposition grew to the struggles of Aunt Lou's children. Infuriated by the decision of the Supreme Court, white people of the South began to form lines of resistance beneath the magnolias that summer of '54. Public officials openly advocated defiance of the new law that had brought jubilation to the blacks. White Citizens' Councils sprang up in cities, towns, and hamlets, the first one in Mississippi in July. Old-fashioned demagogues became more vocal, stirred suspicions, inflamed tempers. Many folk who had once been willing to adjust to the inevitable developed a "Never! Never!" attitude.

On the other hand, the court's decision corroborated my gut feelings from childhood. I'd been wiser than I'd ever given myself credit for. Tom and I felt relief at the pronouncement that public schools must desegregate with "all deliberate speed." But soon we noticed with dismay that we'd have to do our rejoicing in the privacy of our home. The Christians in the church who provided our shelter and paid our salary greeted the news either with total silence or with plans of open defiance of the courts.

White churches, instead of leading the people to do the Christ-like thing, for the most part kept silent. Both ministers and members were entangled in the suffocating net. I was shocked and saddened by racist words spoken by churchwomen whom I had seen perform loving deeds of mercy to people in need. White women who rode unselfconsciously beside black maids as they drove them home from work showed a darker side of their natures at the idea of their children sitting next to black children in school.

"I guess you won't want to stay here long if 'they' make our children go to school with niggers," said a member to her preacher's wife. "If our children sit together in school, they'll fall in love and marry," said another woman. "How would you like your daughter to marry a nigger?"

No reasoning could allay their fears. It never occurred to many Southerners that marriage between persons of different color need not demean either. The very idea raised bile in the throats of most whites. Although Tom and I did not advocate intermarriage, I dared not even voice my belief that, if we treat people right today, we can trust God to take care of tomorrow.

At the very first deacons' meeting, Tom was asked to explain the Supreme Court's ruling. Standing before the body of two dozen leaders, Thomas Holmes knit his brows and chose words carefully. "This decision means that we are entering a new era, the era of the common man. It will be good if we can remember that God is a God of justice, and He is on the side of the man denied justice. This decision will affect every area of our lives here and around the globe. The freedom which has been denied can be denied no longer."

They just sat in somber silence.

Early in December, Christmas dinners commenced at the church behind our house. Every Sunday school department had a turkey dinner, program, and exchange of presents. The preacher and his wife were expected to attend every banquet. But children were not invited. We'd acquired our first television set, and Kathy and Tommy ate hastily prepared hot-dog-and-potato-chip suppers before the TV night after night while Tom and I feasted on turkey and dressing, cranberries, sweet potato soufflé, fruitcake, and ambrosia served on white linen–covered tables centered with holly, candles, and red berries.

Lillie Thomas, a white, middle-aged divorcée, was employed to supervise the kitchen. A member of our congregation, she became a generous friend to us. A black woman, Belle, who was a widow, was also hired to help. The two worked together in the church kitchen from nine in the morning until nine at night preparing luncheons, suppers, banquets. Slim, unsmiling, Belle was a marvelous cook. When she was not making yeast rolls at the church, she was whipping up chocolate layer cakes for the Willinghams and others. But, as was the custom, she did not worship with us.

New building custodians were needed in the fall of '54 to help with the Christmas festivities, to keep forty Sunday school rooms and the sanctuary clean, to put up tables for dinners and take them down for Sunday morning Bible school lessons. So one November morning, a big black man with a rubber face stood in the pastor's office, shifting from one foot to the other. His wife hunkered beside him, round and fat.

"Good morning," said clergyman Holmes, rising behind his desk to shake the hands of the applicants.

"This here George," said the Negro in a deep, gravelly voice. "I heared y'all need a janitor. This here Honey. She my wife. We come to 'ply for the job. Me an' Honey, we good workers."

Tom pumped Honey's hand, smiling and saying, "I'm glad to meet you, Mister . . . Mister . . . what is your last name?"

"Raven. George Washington Henry Lincoln Jefferson Raven. That's my full name."

"What's that again? I didn't quite get all that straight," Tom asked smiling.

"George Washington Henry Lincoln Jefferson Raven," repeated the man, grinning broadly. At five feet six and 220 pounds, he was shaped like a barrel.

"You were named for all the presidents, weren't you?"

"Yessuh, Boss. My mama, she done name me for the presidents." He broke into a laugh. Honey and Tom laughed with him.

"Jes' call me George."

"Who's the Henry for?"

"Pat-Pat-Patrick Henry."

"'Give me liberty, or give me death' Patrick Henry?"

"Yessuh, that'n."

Tom told me later, "Here is a man named for the fathers of American freedom, but he has never cast a vote in his life."

They were hired for two hundred dollars a month and went to work with brooms, mops, and dust rags. Since they lived in Buttermilk Bottom, in downtown Atlanta, they rode on the back seat of the segregated bus, arriving at the back door of the church at eight every morning. They caught the bus home in the starlight, after the suppers were finished and hundreds of dishes washed by hand. On the bus they had to squeeze through the packed front seats and standing whites to the very back, where a few seats were reserved for "colored." In accordance with an 1890 Georgia law, they often had to stand, swaying back and forth on sore feet, even when there were vacant seats up front.

"With all these Christmas dinners, we gonna work them pore ole niggers to death," the church secretary said, laughing, one December morning.

Her flippant statement set me to wondering as I wandered through the Lord's House that day. *Is this the right way to celebrate Christmas—leaving your children night after night, stuffing in more food than you need, working George and Honey to death? Is this what Christ hung on the cross for? Did He shed His blood that whites might feast and grow fat while poor blacks starve for justice and mercy?*

Is this the cause He meant for me to become involved in when He called me to take up my cross daily?

From the dining hall came the aromas of turkey and dressing roasting. I knew Mrs. Thomas and Belle were dicing oranges for ambrosia while George and Honey put up long tables, covered the tops with white linen cloths, fetched in folding chairs. George was dressed in baggy black pants and a dingy white shirt. Honey wore a loose-fitting cotton dress. Though the outside temperature was in the low forties, sweat rolled down their ebony faces as if it were August.

The next December, while banquet preparations were in full swing, a revolution erupted in Montgomery, Alabama. On December 1, 1955, a middle-aged seamstress, weary from her hard day's work and fed up with second-class citizenship, dared to break the law and take the first vacant bus seat she came to. Ordered by the white driver to vacate the seat for a white man, Mrs. Rosa Parks refused and was arrested. Her rebellion kicked off the civil rights movement that swept across the Southland like Sherman's army and made a hero of Martin Luther King Jr.

When Tom and I read about Rosa Parks's courage, we rejoiced. I lost half an ounce of Aunt Lou's burden I'd been carrying around all my life. But we couldn't talk about this explosive subject to anybody except each other, our children, and Leila.

Dr. King was pressed into leading the bus boycott for one day. For more than a year, Montgomery blacks continued to carpool or walk to their jobs, thankful for a leader at last to help them protest injustice and Jim Crow laws. Under the leadership of the young Dr. King, children of former slaves were throwing off crippling shackles, striding toward freedom.

And so was I. As blacks were revolting against racism, I revolted against "momism." For both, it was high time.

25 Losses and Gains

In 1956 Pa-Pa was sixty-two and still drove seventy miles to his office on Marietta Street from the Forsyth apartment. For eighteen years he and Mother had searched for a home in Atlanta. But Gainer Bryan's salary was too modest to buy a fine dwelling in beautiful Druid Hills, where dogwood trees lined the sidewalks.

Again and again we combed the area. Whenever Pa-Pa located a piece of real estate he could finance, it would be less than perfect to Mother. It didn't have dogwood trees or a fireplace or a front porch; or the ceilings were too low, steps too numerous, neighbors too close.

So they continued to drive back and forth between Forsyth and Atlanta. Their long trips after a day in the office and looking at homes taxed their strength. But when they relaxed in swing and rocking chair on the breeze-swept porch across from the quiet campus of Tift College, as they had for the past two decades, they forgot the inconvenience until Monday morning.

The quandary continued as they grew older and more weary. Now, following their sixty-ninth search, they came to our home one November night to sup and to sleep. After roast beef and potatoes, we gathered around the fireplace in the carpeted living room. The gas logs hissed and warmed our feet.

At sixty-one, Mother still had dark hair, but it was tinged with gray. Bifocals magnified her penetrating eyes, always fearsome to her timid daughter, making them doubly forbidding. But in the same room with her growing grandchildren, Kathy and Tommy, whom she adored, Mother's eyes lit up, tension lessened in her lovely mouth, and her sharp nose appeared more rounded. She even laughed. "When I'm with these children, I forget all my worries," she said.

Pa-Pa's hair, almost white, receded from his forehead. He wore rimless spectacles and a broad smile. Very patient, he would wait forever to move near his office, if it took his Little Shug that long to find what she wanted.

On the other hand, I yearned for them to live in Atlanta so he could cut out the long drives, have more time to rest at home. I began to pressure Mother to settle for a modest abode in a Decatur suburb of small new homes. Mother had often longed for a new house with new fixtures and clean new flooring.

But Mother disliked changes. Although she had complained countless times through the past nineteen years about the apartment, it was home, and, unknown to us, Mother had made up her mind to stay there. She who had grown up in the watermelon patches, apple orchards, and wide open spaces of the land between the rivers decided she would be too cramped on even a half acre in the city.

Not knowing, I dared to speak where angels fear to whisper and made a mistake no daughter should—I interfered with my parents' private business.

"Well, what did you find today?" I said.

"We found a nice house for six thousand dollars just fifteen minutes from the office," Pa-Pa said, his smile broad.

"Ah! It's got too many steps up the back. I might fall going up and down them steps. And the rooms are too little." Mother drew her lips into a narrow line.

Anger mounted in me, and I didn't let her magnified eyes stop me from speaking out this time. "Other people come to Atlanta and find a house in two days or two weeks. You have looked for eighteen years and found nothing to satisfy you."

Mother began to weep. I thought she was shocked that her daughter would dare to speak like a grown-up. "Take me, home, Gainer," she cried. "Take me home."

"Please don't go," I pled, feeling sudden weakness in my knees and pain in my stomach. But they left anyway.

"I'm proud of you," said Tom as I crawled into bed beside him at eleven o'clock. "You were right. They should go ahead and settle on something. Your daddy is getting old. He doesn't need those long drives."

But I lay rigid, scared Mother wouldn't forgive me. All that wretched night I slept little and determined never to cross her again. Yet my explosion turned out to be the catalyst that finally moved my parents to Toney Valley in Decatur, a month later. A week before the holiday, Bing Crosby's voice warbled "White Christmas" on the radio as Tom and I drove to their new house. Fetching mops, buckets, and wax, my husband and I waxed and polished the floors of the little house until its narrow oak boards shone.

The next day we helped them move in. Mother seemed so merry. She'd even stopped on the way to buy a Christmas tree. We helped her set it in a stand of water. She'd also ordered a mock fireplace with electric logs, and she instructed the delivery men to place it at "that end of the living room." As Mother joyfully told the movers where to set the round oak table and mirrored hall tree she and Pa-Pa bought in 1915, and where to put up beds and place chairs, I had no idea of the resentments she held.

For me she had given up two large houses she loved. I was to suffer for these losses on many a January, June, and July morning, night, and after-noon for three decades. But on this moving day I was happy for my parents. Mother had a clean, new house. Pa-Pa could get on I-20 and drive the little beige Studebaker to his office in only fifteen minutes.

That same December 1956, the bus boycott ended in Montgomery when the Supreme Court decision outlawed segregation on public vehicles. Re-verberations rolled like a tidal wave across other cities of the South. The next year, a group of black ministers violated the Georgia law of 1890, boarding a bus in Atlanta and riding unsegregated. They were arrested. This created a commotion among ordinary blacks, who were fearful of losing their jobs.

George waddled down to our door one morning, beads of perspiration standing upon his ebony face. "Boss," he said in his gravelly voice, "Me and Honey, we don't have nothin' to do wit' that there bus business. Us satisfied wit' things like they is."

Tom sought to comfort him. "Don't worry, George. I agree with the black preachers. You and Honey *should* be able to sit on any seat on the bus. You're as good as any white. We're all equal in the sight of God."

"Yessuh, Boss. Thank you, Boss."

26 *The Misfit*

The protesting preachers were never indicted. However, it would be 1959 before the buses in Atlanta were finally desegregated.

But by 1957 Mother's Little Girl found, to her horror, that she could not conform to the pattern cut out for The Preacher's Wife in a big city church. The first two years at College Park I thought I was managing very well, because I wrote as much as six hours a day, interrupting only to prepare meals, attend meetings, answer the telephone. The joy of words always in my brain, I sailed through dull meetings and troublesome chores with the ease of a sailboat gliding across a placid lake.

Except that our home was like a little mountain cabin leaning against a towering mountain peak, and meetings were held at the peak morning, noon, night. Members parked their cars in our carport and all around our dwelling. They peeped in our doors and windows as they trotted by.

Countless mornings the secretary rang up. "Put the coffee pot on," she'd say in her sugary voice. "I'm coming down for coffee at ten o'clock."

My God! I wanted to scream. *I haven't got time to serve coffee. I've got writing to do!* But The Preacher's Wife said, "All right," and interrupted her writing schedule. I served coffee to the secretary morning after morning after morning.

I mailed the finished manuscript to Macmillan Company in New York City. They kept it three months, while I watched every day for a letter or a telegram, dreaming of becoming famous and rich. I planned to buy a house in the country away from the big bustling church-club. My family and I needed a place of our own, so we could be independent of the people, find rest and solitude from the maddening crowds.

While I waited, frustrations snowballed. One bright morning the manuscript returned. Though it was accompanied by a two-page letter instead of the routine rejection slip, I was crushed and blinded with disappointment. The manuscript that once looked as beautiful as a newborn baby now appeared an idiot-child. I was so ashamed. I tossed it, still in its box wrapped with brown paper, into the trash can. I had bared my soul on those pages. When the august publisher rejected them, he rejected *me*.

My husband retrieved the box and put it away on a closet shelf, saying, "You're not going to throw this away. You're going to try again."

Mother telephoned. "What are you doing today?" she said.

I resented this intrusion into my privacy and melancholia. When I was down, the last person I wanted to talk to was my mother. Her anxiety would only multiply my troubles.

"My manuscript came back," I mumbled.

"I was afraid it would. Gainer's always sending a story off. But they always come back. You can't get anything published. Might as well quit trying." Her honeymoon with the new house had paled; its flaws were obnoxious; she was beyond disenchanted and began her litany of woes. "This house is too little. These rooms are too small, the ceilings too low. It's hot as pepper in this little box. I wish it would rain and cool off. The lawn needs mowing and your daddy can't run the lawn mower with one arm. I have to get out there and help him with the thing. I hold the cord while he runs it. All the neighbors are out planting dogwoods, redbuds, magnolias. I reckon we'll have to get out Saturday and plant some so we'll have a little shade next summer. They cut down every tree when they built these houses—just came through with a bulldozer. We haven't got a sign of a shade tree on this place. Your daddy can't dig a hole. I'll have to get out and dig holes. And my blood pressure is so high, I'm afraid I'll have a stroke."

"I'm sorry, Mother. I'm sorry. I hope you don't have a stroke. Maybe Tom and I can come help you."

"Ah, you can't do anything but go to church. You're gonna have a nervous breakdown if you don't quit going so much, get more rest."

Her tirades reduced me to a six-year-old who couldn't talk back, just as long ago in the village kitchen while she ironed by the old wood stove, hot iron hissing, blue pot boiling, the other children trotting off to school, when I could only listen and sympathize.

Besides my mother's disenchantment, my daughter, Kathy, was fifteen, and the usual anxieties that go with having a teenage daughter surfaced. My summer nights of 1957 were spent in a lounge chair on the screened porch grieving, worrying, trying to pray. There was no sleep in me, only consternation. My psalms turned into lamentations.

I went to see the family doctor. But he didn't have time to listen to frustrated women. He just wrote out a prescription for sleeping pills. The first few nights, the sleep capsule produced euphoria. I fell asleep feeling loved and adored, awoke at five in the morning exhilarated, energized, ready to write. I soon sent the manuscript off again. It was returned three months later with another two-page letter. "You certainly should be encouraged to write. You have talent, but . . ."

In September, weariness, despair, and confusion collided. Even with the pills, I couldn't sleep. I could no longer sit through a meeting. One day I squirmed in the chair through boring talks until I reached the point of panic. Before the end of the program, The Preacher's Wife got up and left.

How can I find time and temper to rewrite my book, look after the family, and go to all the meetings? How can I do the work God is guiding me to do and perform all the duties of the church-club? The telephone rang. I went to answer, but couldn't speak for sobbing. Tom returned from the hospitals, parked in the carport, strode into the kitchen. "Have there been any calls for me?"

Before that one, there had been half a dozen. When I began relaying the messages, my voice cracked, then collapsed into tears.

"What is the matter with you?" demanded the towering clergyman. His eyes seemed more piercing, his brow hugely wrinkled. Suddenly my darling looked as fearsome as Rev. Rivers.

"I don't know," I sobbed.

"You're supersensitive. You go around pouting. I've watched you lately. Everybody else is watching you. People can see your unhappiness."

"That's the trouble. Everybody's always watching me. But I'm a private person. I can't live in a fish bowl. I need some time alone, some solitude."

The tall man frowned. He walked up and down. Finally he said, "Would you like to go to Flowers Lake tomorrow?"

Warner Flowers, a deacon, had given us fishing privileges at his beautiful lake in the country near Red Oak.

"Yes," whimpered the woman who couldn't bait a hook, couldn't stand the feel of slimy worms in her hand.

"I'll get my fishing pole, and we'll go tomorrow after I visit hospitals."

I put my manuscript in a briefcase to take along. But once there, I wrote only rhymes while Tom baited and set his hooks. For three hectic years, I had tried to please husband, mother, and congregation. It was impossible. I ended up pleasing nobody, least of all myself.

I awoke morning after morning grieving about the sorry state of my life. Tears wet my pillow. But I couldn't speak of my hates, resentments, or guilt. After one restless night, Tom asked me again, "What's bothering you?" He took my hand. "Tell me," he said tenderly, "why can't you sleep?"

I began to cry.

"Tell me," he pleaded. "Tell me, darling."

"It's Mother," I blurted out between sobs. "She calls two or three times a day, rehearsing her problems, running Pa-Pa down. And I can't do anything but listen.

"If I try to cheer her up, it makes her mad. She faults me for not joining her in her judgments. But how can I help her criticize my own father? I love them both. I can't take sides.

"But I'm afraid if I don't agree with her, if I don't just listen, she'll get mad and not call at all, not speak to me. Once when I was at college, she got hurt about something and went a solid week without speaking.

"And she calls every day telling me what to do, how to manage our children. I don't want to do things the way my mother did!" Tears rolled down my checks. I began bawling too much to talk.

Holding my hand, Tom made a startling statement: "You are hostile toward your mother."

His words were like a sword to my sensitive soul. But after a few minutes to let the dagger dig in, I had to admit he was right. Never before in my thirty-seven years had I faced that awful truth. I was hostile toward my own mother, my best friend, who cooked and sewed for me, nursed me through pneumonia, fanned my face with her palmetto fan through many a sultry night!

We were alone in our bedroom, facing one another. Tom continued to hold my hands in his. "Just go ahead and talk," he said. "It's a sore that has to run."

"I feel like a traitor telling you all this. But the truth is I've never liked some of Mother's ways. I've always tried to do everything opposite from her. And now she's trying to talk me into restricting Kathy, as she did me. 'You better be careful how you let your daughter go on dates. She might get into trouble like that Smith girl did.'

"She never confided her troubles to anyone except me. She wouldn't talk to her sisters or neighbors, not even to tell them when she was pregnant, until it was evident to everyone. She just unloaded on me all her sad stories as a stepdaughter of a Civil War veteran. Ever since I can remember, I've listened to her lamentations. When I was little, and while she was ironing, cooking, canning, her mouth erupted trials and tribulations. Then she'd always say, 'Now don't tell anybody these things I'm telling you.' To this day I'm afraid to talk.

"I felt so sorry for her, my heart broke day after day, year after year. But there was nothing I could do except listen and sympathize and agonize."

"I'd no idea. Why haven't you ever told me your feelings about her before?"

"Because she always told me not to tell, and because I didn't want you to know what she's really like. I've always felt I had to protect her, throw a shield around her to keep neighbors, family, and friends from seeing the real Lila. I determined to be the opposite of her, just the opposite. And that's made me feel sinful, guilty. Because she's been so good to me, to us!"

"She's done no more than other mothers do for their children!" Tom declared.

"She's sacrificed herself countless times all through the years. She's sewn and sewn for Kathy and me until three in the morning. Even today she buys most of our clothes. We can't stop her. I know I shouldn't let her do so much. But we like pretty clothes, and I should be grateful."

"She has bought you. I didn't want you to accept so much from her. I've never liked that."

"Well, you've never had money for clothes."

He didn't take offense. "Smother love, that's what it is. Too much mother."

"She wouldn't let me go to dances with Rachel and the others. I sat on the doorstep and cried night after night while Rachel and the others had fun." Tears fell afresh. "I feel like a worm telling you all this about Mother, who's given us so much. I feel like I'm blaspheming God Almighty."

Now I was a wound-up machine that couldn't be stopped. "But she's not the only problem. This house is too close to the church. People pass here in droves every day. I have no privacy. The phone rings constantly. It's like living in a hotel lobby. And there are too many meetings to attend."

We had come back to the problem that precipitated my tears. Since he couldn't remove the church from me, Tom called our doctor. "Should I put her in the hospital?"

"No. Just get her away to some quiet place for two weeks' rest," said Dr. Hydrick. "Then get her out of that house. Ask the church to rent a house across town."

Tom arranged for me to go to the country. "You're going to Ed and Margaret's for a rest," he said.

"But I can't go," I protested tearfully. "Who will look after you and the children?" It was a Tuesday in September, and they had just started to school, Kathy in tenth grade, Tommy in fifth.

"Leave all that to me. Just get your things ready. You're leaving tonight on the six o'clock train."

A zombie, I obeyed and began to pack a suitcase while Tom called Mother to come and help with the children.

People were suspicious of anyone who admitted to a nervous breakdown or slipped into a depression. They feared the person would "wind up in Milledgeville"—at the state hospital. "What did you tell Mother? What did you tell Ed? What will people think? They'll think I've gone crazy and left you."

"Don't worry about what people think."

But I worried all through the steamy day as I washed and ironed the children's jeans, shorts, and dresses. I boiled beans, baked ham, prepared food enough to last a week. I feared my failures would not only hurt my family but also damage Tom's career.

In the muggy autumn evening, I took a train from Atlanta to Tennille, back to the land of my birth. My red, swollen eyes looked as though I'd cried for days. A tight brown-velvet turban covered my limp brown hair. I wore a cool beige cotton dress. Sinking deep into a corner seat as dusk settled outside, I stared into bleak buildings surrounding the Atlanta depot and waved goodbye to Tom. I didn't see anyone on the train who would recognize Gainer Bryan's Daughter, Tom Holmes's Wife. It was an enormous relief not to have to struggle to speak, smile, or pretend. At last I could escape the multitudes who'd torn me to pieces.

But was I losing my mind? How would I explain to Tom's brother and sister-in-law? I was so ashamed of myself, I longed for oblivion. Each revolution of locomotive wheels made me feel more worthless. After I met Christ at the foot of the cross, my life was supposed to be a lovely thing. It was going to sing. When I found God, I thought I could be both a good preacher's wife and a poet. But I was just a failure, a crybaby who'd run off the rails and had to be sent away.

When the train pulled into the Tennille station, I picked up my suitcase and stepped down into the sultry night. Ed and his wife, Margaret, stood waiting, compassion on their faces.

"Thank you for meeting me," I murmured. I yearned for the earth to open up. "I want to stay in the cabin by the lake, be alone. I can't talk to anyone. I can't explain this. I don't know what's wrong with me. I can't do anything but cry."

I, I, I. All I could talk about was I.

"Don't try to explain," said wise, dark-haired Margaret. "There's nothing to explain. Just rest. You'll be all right here. No one will bother you."

It was midnight and very dark. At the cabin there were no outside lights. But the darkness outside was no match for the darkness in my soul. Still, I welcomed the blessed solitude. Frogs croaked at the rim of the water, a clock ticked on the mantel above the brick fireplace.

I took a sleep capsule.

Just five miles down the road were the village and cottage where I grew up. *Oh, Mother, why did you cripple me? Segregate and overprotect me when I was young? Why didn't you let me run with the other children at school, at play; with other youths at dances; at college? You should have let me suffer the ordinary hurts of childhood and growing up. Surely those normal hurts would have been healthier than the abnormal ones.*

Now I can't run with anybody. I'm afraid of people. And as a preacher's wife, I cannot get away from them, not even in my dreams.

Is this eternal life? That I should snivel when I would sing? That I wail a melody of melancholia instead of conducting the symphony of everlasting vitality? Is this what it all was for, the driving, striving, searching, sacrificing? That I should wind up a broken reed in this pit of despair?

I repeated the Twenty-Third Psalm, but even those comforting words brought no peace into my pit. I quoted the Lord's Prayer, but it had a hollow ring. Every connecting link between earth and heaven seemed to have been severed. Once strong, my faith gave way to fear, hopelessness, chagrin.

"Oh, God, help me!" I cried aloud.

The clock struck one, one-thirty, two, two-thirty, three, three-thirty. Switching on the light, I opened my purse, searched for the sleeping capsules, and found a little pamphlet with Scripture verses. As I read, the clock struck four. I got up and took the second capsule. Will I wake tomorrow? Or will two pills put me to sleep forever? It didn't seem to matter.

Finally I found words of comfort. "Your heavenly father knoweth what you need before you know yourself." Still I did not sleep until after the clock struck five, and the morning star hung in the eastern sky.

At seven-thirty I woke, weeping. September sunlight flooded the cabin. Purple mist floated over the lake, machinery at Holmes Canning Company hummed, trucks arrived with bushels of yellow squash, black-eyed peas.

I walked the sandy path around the lake to Margaret's rustic country cottage for breakfast. Their Negro cook placed plates of honeydew melon, crisp bacon, and scrambled eggs on the maple country table, and their TV blared the *Today* show from New York City. As Margaret, Ed, and I sat down, awesome news split the morning air.

"Racial strife has erupted in Little Rock, Arkansas!"

Butterflies fluttered in my stomach.

Back at the cabin, I read and rested all day. That night I slept eight hours while the frogs croaked, the clock ticked, and trouble boiled in Arkansas.

The next morning we savored breakfast served again by the granddaughter of slaves, and the television blared more news: "President Eisenhower sends federal troops to Little Rock!" We saw black children escorted to school while a snarling white mob shouted insults. I yearned to go there and hold the hands of those brave children.

"Isn't that awful!" said my host.

"I don't see why the nigras want to go where they're not wanted," said my hostess. "I don't want to go where I'm not wanted."

The cook and I kept silent. I looked at her smooth coffee face. *She's churning inside, behind her mask, just as I am behind mine.*

Back home my husband called his deacons together. They loved their pastor and his family. Tom had ministered to the people in times of sickness and death, joys and sorrows, had baptized, married, counseled, preached. Now it was his turn to be ministered to. "My wife is sick," he explained with his accustomed charm and dignity. "She's gone to my brother's country place for a rest. The doctor says for us to get her out of that house. It's rather close to the church. We need a quieter place."

At once compassionate, the men decided to rent a house across town on a secluded street, where most of them lived. Tom telephoned the good news to me. Then he drove the hundred miles to see his wife. In the cabin, he sat on the sofa beside me, put his strong arms around my waist, held me close.

But when the deacons went home and told their wives, the women were not pleased. They conversed over telephones, typewriters, coffee cups. By the time I came home two weeks later, the deacons had reversed their decision. That house was good enough for the last preacher's wife, it was good enough for Mrs. Holmes.

No one came to visit, no one sent a flower or a card. I feared no one understood. Like Mother, I'd never had a confidante. I adhered to the unwritten rule: "The preacher's wife doesn't have close friends." That would make other women jealous. She never tells her private business, personal problems. She doesn't have frustrations; she's strong and unruffled and flawless. Moving with serenity among the members, she neither whines nor complains. She's a superwoman.

But, alas, I was given to human frailties. And I had reverted to Child-Woman. "I don't feel like going to church," I said that first Sunday morning in October.

"Oh, but you have to go," said the preacher.

I heard in my head another unwritten rule: "The preacher's wife shall not miss Sabbath services." In the pew at eleven o'clock I felt inner disintegration. As people assembled, chattering and giggling, the organ prelude started, but no one bowed his head in prayer. I sat throughout the service, unable to hear a word.

I wonder how I'll get through this throng when it's time to go. How will I walk the fifty yards home without coming unglued? What is my brokenness doing to my children, my husband's career? If only I could just slip away without shaking hands, or trying to smile at hundreds of grinning faces.

In spite of my fears, I managed, and no one asked me about my health.

Disappointed that his deacons had decided not to find us a more desirable place to live, Tom said that night as we lay down on the four poster, "I've been thinking. Since I've been pastor here these three years, I've worked day and night to build this church according to the plan of the Sunday School Board. I've visited, preached, and baptized. We've increased the membership rolls, built larger buildings and a library. But I can't see that the people are any more 'Christian' than they were to start with. They're still given to grumbling, gossiping, and backbiting. Deacons' meetings last until midnight because of wrangling. I wonder what kind of a church I am running here."

"Maybe, instead of 'running' your church according to the plan of the Sunday School Board, you should lead according to the plan of Christ: 'Proclaim liberty to the captives, and recovery of sight to the blind; set free the oppressed'*—including your wife!

"Tom," I went on, "I thought I was liberated, and here I am caught like a mouse in a trap. I don't have a real friend here. I wish we could move. If only we could buy our own house, a house in the country!"

He did not answer, only patted my hand.

I prayed silently. *Oh God, please help us move!*

*Isaiah 61:1, Luke 4:18

27 *New House, Old Misery*

I believed God heard my cries when, one month later, Northside Drive Church on the other side of Atlanta invited Thomas J. Holmes to lead their flock. Their chapel, started four years earlier as a mission, was situated on a twenty-three-acre green hill at the corner of Northside Drive and Northside Parkway. The congregation planned to build a sanctuary in a few years and start a parsonage this year. Although they had only five hundred members, they would pay a larger salary than we now earned.

I was eager to go. Tom was reluctant to leave College Park; he felt his work there was not finished. But since his wife was almost "finished," and the Northside flock was calling, he decided to consider. So, one Monday morning in October, their two deacons—Tom Jones and Albert Pirtle—took us on a tour of the ivory-carpeted chapel and a wooded acre fronting Moore's Mill Road where they planned to build the pastor's house.

The sun warm upon our backs, we inspected the building site just off West Paces Ferry Road. I was enchanted. To have a home on this pine-clad place, half a mile from the church, would bring healing to the broken spirit. To live and bring up our children here in Buckhead beneath the now scarlet-and-gold-leafed trees and surrounded on three sides by fine brick homes would make the years of struggle and sacrifice worthwhile.

But nowhere in the country could we ignore the nation's biggest problem—the poor and oppressed children of former slaves and the tensions created by two hundred years of bondage plus another hundred of segregation. Albert Pirtle pointed to a little gray shack on the opposite side of Moore's Mill. "A nigra woman lives there," he explained apologetically. "But this area is developing fast with fine homes—they're going to build the new governor's mansion not far away, on West Paces.

"Once all of these acres belonged to the Moore plantation. When the land was divided for building sites, Mr. Moore gave the family cook that house for the rest of her life. She was with the family thirty years. But she's getting old and that little hut'll soon be gone."

That little hut with the black cook in it doesn't bother me one bit! The prospect of a home here outweighed anything else. When I climbed back into the car, Mr. Pirtle laid blueprints on my lap. He said, "If you come to us, and I hope you will, this will be your house. And we hope you'll live in it a long, long time. If you want to make any changes, now's the time. Take the plans home and study them, and let us hear from you."

All the way back to College Park I studied those blueprints while Pirtle's words echoed through the corridors of my brain. I nipped the wide pages back and forth as Tom sped south on I-75.

"Does it have a study?" asked the husband.

"It will have a pine-paneled den with a fireplace and a kitchen adjoining."

"Does it have a study?"

"Let's see. It has a front porch with white columns."

"Does it have a study?"

"Oh, yes. Here! The study . . . downstairs . . . paneled walls, and a bath. Oh, Tom, this is my dream house, a brick colonial in Atlanta's loveliest suburb and a forest between the church and us! But you must not accept their pulpit just for me. The final decision must be between you and God."

Even as I spoke I knew that I couldn't bear it if he said no. The blueprints rolled together and slid to the floor as I leaned over and planted a kiss on that precious cheek.

On the first day of November 1957 we moved from "hotel lobby" to Thoreau-quiet woods surrounding the temporary home Northside had rented for us on Howell Mill Road. Leila Howard came with us to help with settling in at the temporary manse. I put her in our big antique bed in the guest room. She rewarded me with her busy hands, pretty brown smile, and flattering phrases. Leila cooked our breakfasts, unpacked boxes, and put away dishes, pots, pans, linens. She taught me how to use the automatic dishwasher and the garbage disposal.

Staring out the windows every morning at prayer time, I luxuriated in the loveliness, soaked up solitude, even planned to rewrite my book. Music coursed through my veins again.

But others in the family were not so serene. Tom was ailing. After the first Sunday morning service, he entered the hospital for hernia surgery.

Kathy and Tommy were unhappy about changing schools, losing friends. At fifteen and ten, they were too young to understand the reasons for their mother's collapse and her desperate need for change. When Leila returned to College Park, Mother came to help me with my sick husband and rebellious children.

Only four months after our last move, on the first day of spring 1958, we moved again, this time into the new manse on Moore's Mill. A light snow sprinkled our maple four-poster and prayer piano as khaki-clad men carried these treasures once more from moving van into a splendid new house that smelled of fresh paint and pine needles.

My days fell into a pleasant pattern. Waking early every morning in a pink bedroom, I padded barefoot down the hall over soft carpeting to the custom-crafted kitchen. While coffee perked, I pulled the cords of traverse rods in living and dining rooms to snap open draperies the color of vanilla ice cream next to matching walls. Reveling in the sheen the rising sun cast upon polished woods and original oil paintings, I whispered, "This house is almost as fine as Carrie Denham's. You've come a long way, girl, from a remote village to the fabulous north side of Georgia's capital city."

As I watched the sun rise over green treetops, I prayed, "Thank you, God. I'm going to hold onto this forever, never again ask you to help us find a home."

On an April afternoon when I was in the kitchen preparing dinner, there came a timid knock at the back door. A little brown woman stood there on crippled feet and carried a foil-wrapped package in her clove-colored hand. She wore a flowered kerchief knotted around her head, a faded cotton dress, and rag shoes on curiously twisted feet. A strange, filmy substance covered the pupils of her dark eyes.

"Miz Cook sent you a cake."

"Oh, thank you. Come in. What's your name?" I asked.

She smiled, childlike. "Flossie," she said softly.

"Flossie. I love that name. And where do you live?"

"I lives with Mr. and Miz Cook nex' door and they aunt, Aunt Carrie. I lives in they base-mint room. I takes care Aunt Carrie. She be's old and mos' always be's in the bed."

"Well, you're sweet to bring me a cake, and I thank you."

"Aunt Carrie wanted t' send a cake to the new preacher's wife."

"Sit down," I said, pulling out a chair, enjoying her company as we'd enjoyed Lucy's in the village. "Do you have any days off? I need someone to iron the preacher's shirts." I went back to breaking lettuce into a bowl, chopping tomatoes and green peppers, and tossing the salad.

"Yessum, I has Tuesdays off. I could help you on Tuesdays."

And so I hired the little lady who hobbled to work on misshapen feet. We became friends as Fannie and I, Leila and I had been friends.

"What happened to your feet, Flossie?" I asked one day.

"They was broke when I was a little girl. I was walkin' home from school, and a great stone was rolled over on both of 'em, and they was broke."

"I'm so sorry. Why weren't you taken to a doctor?"

"We lived so far away out in the country, and Papa didn't have any car, and anyway we didn't know they was broke. But I had to be carried a long time and set in a wheelchair, and I had to learn to walk all over again."

"Oh, Flossie, a doctor could have put your feet in casts and healed them. And you could have had strong, straight feet. How far did you have to walk to school?"

"Five miles."

"Didn't they have school buses then?"

"The whites rode buses. But us didn't have no buses. Us had to walk ever'wheres us went."

"Flossie, it hurts me to see you standing up ironing on your poor broken feet. Here, you sit down and peel these potatoes. I will iron the shirt. When I finish, I will read poems to you. Did you know that I'm a poet?"

Flossie brought back the sense of security I'd known when Lucy was my nurse. And I was content to enjoy the good life as days drifted by.

We were given memberships in the Atlanta Athletic Club and the East Lake Country Club, where we went for Sunday dinners. Wedding rehearsal dinners took us to the Biltmore Hotel, the Cherokee Town and Country Club, the Capital City Club. Tom played golf with his deacons and with other preachers at the Druid Hills Club. On Saturdays there were Sunday school suppers in the church dining hall and at luxurious homes of members. The menu was not the fried chicken and potato salad of former parishes, but charbroiled filet mignon and baked potatoes with sour cream and chives. Our cosmopolitan congregation rode in Cadillacs to church, sailed yachts on Lake Lanier, flew in jets to Europe. The people were considerate, leaving me to live in privacy.

By the time summer arrived, the house could not hold all the happiness. I carried cup and Bible to a clearing in the woods at the back door, where I'd arranged a little sitting room. All I could hear was wind whispering through pines and the music in me.

But it was not to last.

We were into our second summer at Northside when I detected misery in my husband's manner. Often cross with me and the children, Tom wore deep creases between his brows.

"Don't you like it here?" I said one July afternoon.

"Not much. I'm not doing what I really want to do."

"What is that?"

"I want to teach."

"Then why did you come here?"

"Because you wanted to."

"But I told you, remember, not to move for my sake. I never did tell you I wanted you to come to this church."

"You didn't have to tell me. And I consider it a failure that I left College Park the way I did. They were good to me there. The church even paid my airfare for four months while I flew back and forth between Atlanta and Raleigh-Durham."

I felt as though I'd been slapped in the face. Guilt boiled in my brain. I had ruined my husband's life.

As summer days sizzled on into August, depression returned with insomnia. I developed aches and pains in the joints, feared arthritis or some other disease.

"There's nothing wrong with you," the new doctor said after two days of tests and X rays.

"Then why do I have all these aches and pains? Why can't I sleep at night?"

"I don't know." He handed me a psychological test, four white pages of questions to answer about my inner life. Then he left me alone in the room, closing the door behind him.

When he returned to the tiny brown office, the doctor studied my answers. I waited helplessly. At last he spoke, choosing his words with care like a judge in black robes. "This shows insecurity, instability, a lack of self-confidence."

"I know. I'm afraid I'm going crazy."

"Are you having trouble at home?"

"Yes," I said. "I've had a hard time being a preacher's wife. There's never any privacy, and never enough money. And people expect you to conform to their pattern. There are so many meetings to attend, you don't have time for your family or yourself. It's easier at Northside, because the folk are fewer, and they leave me alone. But I failed at College Park. I failed my husband, failed the people. I couldn't cope, had a nervous breakdown, couldn't do anything but cry."

"Yes, it is a difficult life. But a great many women succeed at it."

Here was a successful man, son and grandson of achievers, telling me that many women succeed where I failed. It was as though he said, "I'm OK, but you're not OK." But I went on, "I have another problem, my mother. She tries to run my life as though I were six instead of thirty-six. Calls me every day two or three times, full of fears and worries about her problems, and tells me how I should handle mine. I try to be patient with her. . . . She's done this all my life. Didn't let me go to school with other children until I was in fourth grade."

"You hate your mother," he said.

I had to face that awful truth again. "Yes, I suppose I do. And I don't have much respect for my father. He's so gentle, he's always let her kick him around." I began to cry.

"You will have to take charge of your life, quit letting your mother control you. Don't have a big explosion. But let her see you are a grown woman now. And you're not going to stand for her domination anymore. The next time she makes you angry, hang up the phone and beat on the walls to let off tension."

When I gave Tom the doctor's report, he said, "I'm going to talk to your father." And he did. The next time Mother and Pa-Pa came to visit, Tom drove my father over to the church. Parking in the lot near the pine forest, my husband pled with my father to try to influence my mother to let their daughter go.

Although Pa-Pa was burdened for his daughter, every time he thought of bringing up the subject with Little Shug, he decided to put off the confrontation until a more appropriate time. The time never came.

One hot August morning Tom heard me beating on the wall, obeying the doctor's orders, and came running up the steps from his study to the kitchen where I fumed.

"What's the matter with you?"

"Mother's complaining is driving me wild. This is what the doctor told me to do," I said, pounding the wall with balled-up fists until the top of the teakettle rattled.

"If you can't tell your mother to get off your back, I can," he shouted. "I'm going right now and tell her she's got to leave you alone." He reached for his hat and headed for the car.

"Be gentle with Mother," I cried as he ran down the steps.

Tom found Mother and Daddy resting on the little porch of their house. Speaking with sharp courtesy, he said, "If you value your daughter's health, quit calling her every day, quit complaining to her, quit controlling her life. Let her grow up."

"It's not me who's driving her crazy. It's you, demanding that she go to all those meetings, move every whipstitch! Lord-a-mercy, after all I've done for her, for you and your children, you come over here and insult me! I've given up two houses for Grace, swapped houses I loved for this little hotbox. Now you're dumping me in my old age."

"We're not dumping you, Mother. We love you and appreciate all the things you've done."

Tom reported when he returned: "Your father sat there and listened and didn't say a word. I felt as though I was speaking words he never dared to utter."

Mother thought we were withdrawing our love. Her response was total silence. I wrote long letters trying to explain, but she was as mute as a sphinx.

My sorrow doubled. I had been her sole confidante for nearly forty years, her psychotherapist. How could she survive without me? She might even have a stroke and die. In trying to help, my husband had made the matter worse. I went to bed and cried, yearned for a wise friend or psychiatrist to talk to.

Kathy, packing to enter Mercer as a freshman, tried to console me. But it was not fair to do to her what my mother had done to me.

Then one day I heard about a free clinic. I set up an appointment with Dr. E. Augustus Verdery, who headed a team of pastoral counselors at Georgia Baptist Medical Center.

28 Buried Treasure

"You can tell me anything you want to," Gus Verdery said that September morning in 1958, "and I'll never tell anybody, not even my wife."

Those were the most consoling words I'd ever heard. At last I'd found a wise man who invited me to tell my secret hates and hurts, a friend who would listen and understand, a confidant who wouldn't tell Mother and the ninety-nine women in the church!

I cried. And the kind man with the soft voice showed no scorn or sympathy, only understanding. He shoved a box of tissues toward me. I pulled one out, wiped my face, blew my nose, then reached for another and another.

Behind the chaplain's chair the brown wall was lined with books. Up and down and across the shelves, I scanned mental health titles. Through the large window to my right, I could see a tall magnolia, green and glistening in September sunshine.

"What seems to be the problem?"

"Depression," I muttered finally between sobs.

"Oh?" he said. His quizzical look said, *Talk. I'm here to listen.* He reached for his pipe, leaned back in his swivel chair, touched the tobacco with the flame of his cigarette lighter. A man of medium height, slender build, and plain features, Dr. Verdery raised his eyebrows. They seemed to say, *Tell me all about it.*

His clock ticked away the hour. *Ten after eleven. He said I would have to go at twelve. I have to talk.*

"What's depressing you?"

"My mother. I've had a nervous breakdown. The doctor said I hate my mother." More tears spilled. My voice thickened.

Dr. Verdery just stared as though to say, *Go on. No matter what you say, I'll still like you. Tell me why you hate your mother.*

"I love her too. She's been so good to me. My brother says the word for what I feel is ambivalence.

"She tries to run my life by telephone. She calls two or three times every day, complaining. She berates my father and others in the family. She even berates my own husband. She's done this all my life. It's the same thing over and over and over.

"When I had the breakdown, I couldn't keep my eyes dry, couldn't sleep, couldn't sit through meetings.

"Tom got so fed up, he went to Mother and told her to leave me alone, to quit calling and complaining every day. Now she never calls at all. I've written letters trying to explain, and Tom has too. My brother's been to see her and tried to help her understand that a woman needs to sever the umbilical cord. But she got angry and accused him of taking my side against her.

"She won't speak to any of us now. Because Grandma Sally objected to her daughter—my mother—marrying a one-armed man, Mother now says to me, 'God is punishing me for marrying against Mama's advice.'"

"Isn't that pitiful?"

"Yes. I feel so bad to have caused all this trouble. It's like thorns pricking the flesh. I can find no peace, day or night. My condition is affecting our children."

"Of course it is. Don't blame yourself, Grace. Don't blame anybody. Who's to blame is not important. You and Tom did what you thought best at the time. The important thing now is to face your problem, which you're doing, then to work through it day by day."

"My husband and children need me to be strong, healthy, and whole."

"Of course they do."

"I advised Mother through my brother to see a therapist. But she was indignant. 'I'll never talk to anyone, outside of family,' she said. And I'm afraid she'll have a stroke. She's leaned on me all my life. I'm afraid she can't survive without me. And poor Daddy will have a heart attack or something without me to help him with Mother."

"Could be a good thing. Maybe they'll learn to depend on each other."

This was a new idea. "Oh, I wish they could! The very thought brings enormous relief. Tom tells me just to enjoy her silence. But I don't want total silence. I want a normal, adult relationship."

"Sure you do."

"But I feel so sorry for Mother. She's had a sad life. It caused her to be so afraid something awful would happen to me that she hardly let me go anywhere without her. I was like a prisoner. I yearned to be with other children, but I was segregated from them just as black children were from whites.

"For solace and companionship, I turned to our part-time servants, Aunt Lou, Nannie Lee, and Lucy. I loved and identified with these gentle women in the village. But I dared not speak about this love to any white. So love became a burden. I often thought I might as well be a Negro."

"You were very lonely, weren't you?"

"Oh yes, so lonely." I poured out my life story, and my mother's, to Dr. Verdery. At first I came for one-hour sessions every day. At the close of the third session he said, "You seem to have analyzed your problem. I don't think you need a psychiatrist. I think you and I can work it out. But you must keep coming, once a week if possible. It took you thirty-eight years to get the way you are today. You can't undo thirty-eight years overnight."

Monday morning became the most gracious time of each week. While I drove downtown to keep my eleven o'clock appointment, hands gripping the steering wheel, I rehearsed words I would speak. Once inside the halls of healing, I poured out bitter memories to Dr. Verdery. Resentment, fear, guilt, self-pity—the negative attitudes that had poisoned my life—ran like a river. Striving to prove that a person of value crouched inside the broken vessel, I often quoted from E. Stanley Jones, Shakespeare, my own verse.

Dr. Verdery puffed on his pipe and listened, concentrating, nodding his head like a caring father believing in his trusting child. Often he injected nuggets of wisdom, guidance, clarification. The more I talked, the more confident I became. If Dr. Verdery believed in me, then I could believe in myself.

"You must think of your mother as just another woman."

"That's very difficult. I keep hearing her voice in my head telling me what to do. One day in a restaurant, I saw a dark-haired woman who resembled Mother. I trembled, thinking, *Mother's caught up with me! She'll either ignore me, or she'll say, 'Grace, come on home where you belong and behave yourself.'*"

"You've got to quit letting your mother bully you. Listen to your own voice."

I worked very hard at this concept as months went by. One Monday after a year of therapy, I said, "Now I think I'm as smart as she, as capable as any person to control my life, plan my own days. 'To thine own self be true,' Shakespeare said."

"Right. I must be I."

"I must be I: I like that. Mother always said, 'Be like Charlotte, your cousin. She was valedictorian of her class.' But Jesus said, 'The kingdom of God is within you.' I've got to stop listening to Mother's voice, listen to God's voice."

"Right."

"But if only she could understand, and approve. She always said she was my best friend. Now it seems that my best friend has become my worst enemy."

"Did Jesus' mother understand Him?"

"No. I don't think so. His brothers thought he was crazy. He had to leave His mother to do His work. Once a disciple said to Jesus, 'Your mother and your brothers wait outside to see you.' He replied, 'My mother and my brothers are those who do the will of God.'"

He nodded. "So?"

"I must leave my mother. But I continue to feel sorry for her, to feel a tugging back toward her."

"Toward infancy."

"I don't want infancy. I want maturity. But failure to effect a reconciliation with my parents is a daily sword in the flesh. I am caught in this awful conflict between bondage and freedom, guilt and grace, darkness and light. I know I must continue on the course of separation I've started toward wholeness. I would love to do this with their understanding and approval. But continue I must, even without it."

"You've no alternative."

"Now I know why I've always empathized with black persons. In a way my plight has been the same as theirs. We both struggle from bondage toward freedom—and few masters *give* you your freedom. You've got to fight for it!

"I saw my father last Monday as I was driving away from the hospital. His back was toward me as he paced down Boulevard wearing his over-sized gray overcoat that comes almost to his ankles. He looked so dear and familiar with the white of his hair visible between coat collar and hat brim, his right coat sleeve limp and empty.

"I was so relieved to see he wasn't dead that I yearned to park the car, run to him, throw my arms around his neck, say 'I love you, I love you, Daddy.'"

"Why didn't you?'

"Well, both the congested traffic and my conflicting emotions—guilt, grief, gladness—restrained me like the giant hands of some Goliath."

"You might yet need to have a confrontation with your father, Grace."

"The very thought fills me with trepidation. I talked little to him, and he to me. But I can see my brokenness was perhaps not all Mother's fault. Had he been a strong father and husband, had he given Mother more support, she might have been happier, less domineering. He just rode away every week and abandoned me to a woman he couldn't handle."

"It's a pity he never learned to stand up to her. Your father had his limitations, Grace."

"Yes, I understand, and I must forgive. I have limitations too. We all do."

One day a thunderbolt of illumination hit me. "*I am responsible for the attitudes I formed, not Mother, not Pa-Pa!* Each person is responsible for his own thinking patterns. So I can't blame my parents, or hate them."

Inch by inch, I unlearned negative patterns, cleaned out hate and guilt from the tubes of my thinking as a plumber pushes grease and grime from water conduits. Fresh, positive attitudes flowed through whistle-clean pipes. Day by day, personhood grew stronger. By the end of '59, my self-esteem flowered.

With the catharsis came shedding of shame. Layers of pretense were cut away, much as a gardener prunes dead wood from rosebushes in late winter, until nothing is left but green stems ready for springtime blossoming. Then an extraordinary thing happened. I reached the bottom of memory's chamber and found a treasure chest.

"I went on a journey today, walked down a wondrous old road," I told Tom that evening.

"A journey? Where did you go?" said Tom, who always wanted to hear about my sessions with the therapist. Every Monday evening as we sat together on the red brocade sofa, I repeated the dialogue with Dr. Verdery. To my astonishment, Tom always agreed with my conclusions. The more

I talked, the higher rose my self-esteem. I no longer felt like a wilted petunia, but like a tall rose tree. Becoming increasingly assertive, by January 1960 I could speak words to the big man I never dared utter before. He didn't frown or shout. We'd laugh together and end up in each other's arms, equals at last.

Tonight I said, "I took a trip back, way back into my memories. I found the little girl I used to be, and I found her dreams, a treasure chest full.

"I hid them, hid my fantasies lest she discover the real me and laugh, frown, or scold. My dreams lay buried for many years covered with layers of rust and grit. But now the chest has been cleaned off and opened up. Inside I found beautiful jewels, sparkling like diamonds, rubies, sapphires, pearls—the visions, vows, and hopes inspired by my parents, grandparents, and teachers; by Rachel, my playmate and aunt; and by my black nurse, Lucy, and the washerwoman, Aunt Lou.

"I see my young mother again, and she was lovely.

"I see my father in a new light. He was wonderful!

"I remember Grandpa Jordan's parting words every time I left him and Grandma Sally at Indian Hill. Holding my young hand in his gnarled old one, he would say 'Study hard, and when you grow up, this hand will do fine, noble deeds that will live on, long after I am gone, long after you are gone.'

"I found the seed of what I dreamed but never dared to do. I wanted to love the oppressed black illiterates who served us. Instead, we paid them with a fifty-cent piece, a can of snuff, our old ragged clothes."

Tom nodded his dark head, now graying at the temples and thinning on top. "I remember what you said about Aunt Lou and her 'children.' And I remember Tom Biggins. He taught me many lessons while we plowed the fields. Although he was like a loving, older brother to me, we treated him as a lesser individual."

"That's right. But I saw their humiliation. It seemed I was the only white in my world who saw, and I hid my shameful love. Ours was a sick society, Tom."

"It still is."

"Yes. This wall of segregation runs through our very souls. It made a very confusing world for a child.

"Now I see: that little child fresh from the Kingdom of God was right and 'they' were wrong. It's God who tells you to love. Everywhere we've lived, and especially in our churches, I've seen people wanting to love, but afraid."

"Afraid to love," he said. "May God help us!"

On the first Monday in February 1960 I sat once more across the polished desk from Dr. Verdery. Two years of Monday mornings had found me here in this room of healing. Now as I looked into the face of the chaplain, it dawned on me like a sunburst: *Here I've been on holy ground, in the very presence of God. I've told this ordained minister all my ugliness, revealing all my rottenness, bottled-up hate, and rebellion. And he has listened hour after hour, caring for me as though he saw only beauty in the brokenness.*

Quick as a breeze blowing, I recalled one hot August afternoon in the village when I discovered the magic circle. Perching on the edge of my chair, I related the story: "One afternoon when I was six, Uncle Frank took Rachel, Brother, and me for a trip in his red pickup. He drove down Harrison Road alongside our house and a mile through the countryside until he came to Paradice Road. Then the seventeen-year-old turned right, drove half a mile and stopped at the weather-beaten Paradice house to pick up a sack of sweet potatoes to sell in The Store.

"This route to Cousin Gussie Paradice's was as familiar to me as Mother's face. We'd visited here many times, eaten grapes at her arbor. What happened next was as new as next year.

"Uncle Frank returned to the truck, dumped the potatoes in the back, got behind the wheel. But instead of turning around and going back the way we'd come, he traveled on down the Paradice Road half a mile, turned right again, drove another mile on Mount Moriah Road, where I'd never been before.

"I was scared we were lost. We'd never see Mother and home again. Though I was terrified, I couldn't open my mouth. We went past cotton patches and crumbling cabins.

"Suddenly I saw familiar homes of relatives. We had returned to the village via a road on the *other* side of home and church.

"'Rachel,' I said when our feet touched the ground in front of our house, 'it's round!'

"'What's round?'

"'The way to Cousin Gussie's and back, stupid. Come on, I'll show you.'

"Grabbing Rachel's and Little Brother's hands, we retraced our trip on foot. We ran, walked, crept—barefooted and bareheaded—under the sizzling sun. With childish abandon we covered the three miles, growing hot, exhausted, blistered. Little Brother cried, 'I'm hot. I'm as sweating as I can be.'

"Why did the trip take so long on foot, I wondered, when it seemed only minutes by motor?

"Finally, when the sun was a ball of fire in the west, we saw the church steeple again and the six columns of home. Mother and Grandma Mary were out in the middle of the street crying for their lost children; the whole town was alarmed! I was so weary, I couldn't define what it was I'd discovered, what had sent me on the expedition."

"You had found a new way home," said the chaplain, "a new road to peace, security, and comfort."

"Yes, that's what it was!" I said, excitement mounting.

"Isn't that the same thing you're looking for today, thirty years later?"

"Yes, and I've found it here in this room."

"You've found it in yourself."

"Found it in myself. Yes, now I believe in me." My heart swelled to bursting, tears pricked my eyelids. I jumped from the chair, swung around the room. "But I must keep walking on the new road, go on thinking the new way, be the new person. I must be *I*—no longer Mother's Little Girl, Gainer Bryan's Daughter, The Preacher's Wife—but Grace!"

At high noon that day, feeling as tall as Mount Everest, I decided to hurry to Mother. Getting into our white Buick with black top, I headed for Toney Valley.

Many months had passed since I'd heard from Mother and Pa-Pa. How would they receive their "prodigal" daughter? Palms damp on the black steering wheel, I rehearsed what I would say: "Everything's all right now. I love you. Let's be friends. I thank you for a beautiful childhood, thank you for everything. Please understand and love this mature, separated daughter."

But when I got to their little white house, the Studebaker was not in the carport. Doors and windows were locked as tight as a bank at midnight. Both devastated and relieved, I wondered where they had gone. To Possum Trot or Dalton or Hazlehurst? There was no one in sight to hear my declarations of love. My heart ached for the accepting smiles of my precious parents. Beside the carport a single red camellia waved in the winter wind, seeming to say, "You're too late. They're dead, and you'll never see them again."

When I returned to our Moore's Mill Road home, I dialed their number. The phone rang and rang. The next morning I dialed again, heard the phone ringing while Mother's words echoed in my head, repeating and repeating. "You're going to be sorry. You're going to be sorry when you see my cold, dead body. You'll be sorry you left me."

Am I healed and whole after all? Will I ever be? No, I will never be completely whole. I waited too long to break the chains of bondage. I will always need crutches.

29 *Nincompoop and the Grown-Up*

I continued to write to my parents every week, receiving an occasional answer from Pa-Pa. But he could not outrage "Little Shug" by telephoning or visiting this strange new person their daughter had turned out to be. As spring progressed, the tall wisteria at the corner of our yard turned lavender, its blossoms cascading like thousands of baby orchids. Closer inspection revealed that the wisteria had wrapped replica vines tightly around the trunk of a pine tree. They'd grown larger, stronger, tighter each year, until they'd choked all life from the pine.

Oh, Mother, please try to understand that if I had not wrested your loving ropes from around my neck, I would have choked to death like the wisteria-wrapped pine.

Now, after gaining a measure of freedom from the snare of my mother's love, and after twenty years as a preacher's wife, an opportunity arose to do something significant, go from the sunny side to the slum side of the city I love.

On the fifteenth of March, a high wind blew through treetops and scudded white clouds across the sky as Morelle, Jane, and I motored to Magnolia Street Mission. Emissaries of the Women's Missionary Society, we were taking our turn to carry cookies and cans of orange juice to African American children in the mission nursery school. Their mothers worked as maids in white homes, offices, hospitals.

By now the sit-in movement had spread to Atlanta. On the nightly news we saw thousands of student demonstrators. A picket line of people encircled the city. The racial revolution was like a river rolling over its banks.

At the mission, several five- and six-year-olds sat at a table drawing pictures with colored crayons. As I entered the room, a little boy with curly black hair pulled at my skirt and announced exuberantly, "I know the Twenty-Third Psalm. I can say the Twenty-Third Psalm."

I smiled into his black and white eyes and said, "You do? How nice! What is your name?"

"My name's Nincompoop."

"He calls himself that," explained Freddie Mae, the director. "But he really has a nice name."

Mesmerized, I watched him. Why did the boy zero in on me? Other white women from other white churches entered the day care center at the same time. But the child didn't speak to them—he spoke to me. His cheery greeting eased my entrance into the black community as I settled into a cane-bottomed chair, trying to repress feelings that had begun to creep into my thoughts the moment Jane's shiny new car had turned off Northside Drive into shabby Magnolia Street.

The room was clean, neat. A gas heater hissing a little to the right of center provided heat, but not quite enough. As I waited with the women, I could hear the door hinges creak, creak, creak every time a timid child passed through on his way to and from the bathroom as the little people prepared for their program. A tacky upright piano stood against the concrete block wall, its keyboard closed for lack of someone to play it.

Then the children formed a line and stood before the women. The boys' hair was black and curly and close-cropped. They wore blue jeans and plaid shirts. The girls' hair was done in pigtails with hair ribbons to match their colorful cotton dresses. The children sang "Jesus Loves Me" a capella, their voices joyous and tension-free.

Nincompoop recited his beloved psalm. I could not take my eyes off that boy as he quoted the sacred words I'd memorized at Mother's knee and which now connected the little boy to me.

Later Freddie Mae explained, "This child comes from a tragic home. He has two brothers in a juvenile detention home, and another brother tried to commit suicide recently. Finally we were able to get this little one into our nursery school. And how he loves it! He's here every morning at ten when our door opens, and every time we meet on the street, he asks, 'Is it ten o'clock?' Since we taught him the Twenty-Third Psalm, he says it to anyone who will listen. We hope eventually we'll be able to get into his home and reach his family.

"We don't have a church in this area, but we need one so desperately. There's so much wickedness here, so much misery and poverty. The people simply do not have money to build, do not feel the need. But you, can you not do something to help us?"

"Wasn't she nice?" Jane said, as we retraced our steps toward her car, careful not to muddy our stylish heels on the unpaved walk. "Freddie Mae, I mean. So well educated, so much devotion for the children! I have some clothes I could bring here, some my children have outgrown. I didn't know the needs were so great. I didn't know there was an area in the Bible Belt where people don't have easy access to a church!"

The streets were strewn with empty beer cans and broken bottles. We hurried past an unpainted corner store where idle, ill-clad men stared in mute perplexity. Their wooden faces seemed to say, "What are you doing here?" I shivered. *What will happen if the nonviolent revolution becomes violent?*

Although I could leave Nincompoop and Magnolia Street, I knew they would never leave me as long as I lived.

A week later, I lay on Kathy's bed in the apricot-colored room, recuperating from a bout with flu. Sheer white curtains billowed out the window opened to the woods. Soft spring breezes swished through green pines. All morning I'd been reading and writing, and now a confusion of books and papers cluttered the bedspread crocheted by Grandma Mary. Kathy's Manchester dog, Sandy, curled up in a corner close by the bed snoozing the days away until his mistress returned from Mercer. After lunch I dozed and caught a dream that startled me wide awake. Stretching across the oak floor at the foot of the walnut bed, a line of Negro children, including Nincompoop, were saying, "I know the Twenty-Third Psalm." "Is it ten o'clock?"

I sat up, thinking, *It's way past ten o'clock. And I want to do more for those children than go to the mission once a year carrying crackers and juice. I want to go every day, play that piano, teach them the songs about Christ. I want to help hurting humanity.*

But what will people say? Mother, Daddy, Tom, our children might be embarrassed. I'll be called a "nigger lover," a "white nigger." We could lose our home and job, all our friends; have all our windows knocked out; have to flee in the night, leave the South. Think of the humiliation!

No, I can't bring that on my family. No, I can't do it! I can't, I can't!

When the first rosy fingers of dawn appeared in the eastern sky next morning and I sat up with two pillows comforting my back, the boy from the tragic home returned with those dark-headed children asking, "Is it ten o'clock?"

Tears burned my eyelids, slid down my cheeks. *Little black boy, go away, go back to Magnolia Street and take your friends with you. Go away from my bed and leave me in peace in my comfortable room in my columned home on Atlanta's fashionable Northside. Go back to your slums. Don't you know you'll ruin me? Can't you see what a long way I've come, what a hard climb it's been up this ladder?*

You with the foolish name, Nincompoop, can't you see what you'll do to me if you don't go away? You'll pull me down off my privileged place on the top rung of this ladder, way down to the bottom. You with the black face and nappy hair and haunting eyes of the despised and rejected race from darkest Africa, go away. Brought to this country in chains to be my slave, what right have you to become my conscience?

Or perhaps this is what you've come for. To prick my conscience, challenge my Christianity, turn my cushion into a cross.

Pulling on brown slacks, beige sweater, and sturdy shoes, I closed the back door softly and headed for the forest. The rising sun sifted down through misty spaces, turning the wood into a cathedral. When I paused in the hush to pray, those black children surrounded me. There was no getting away from them.

Their song began to awake another lost memory of those long-ago Mondays when a little white girl stopped her play to listen to the aria of the washerwoman. Slowly, painfully, as the crucial month of March 1960 hurried to its finale, I struggled to unravel tangled strands of the precepts of racism that had been our southern heritage, to separate the true from the false, "our sacred way of life" from God's way, love from hate. I wrestled until the strands of those thinking patterns were untwisted, loose and lovely like a young woman's mane washed, dried, and brushed, flying in the wind, shining in the sun.

Perhaps this is the reason for my long battle. Hearing you sing your hymn, Nincompoop, makes the long years of struggle seem but a song. I can find no peace at the top knowing you're down there in the degradation.

To hell with what people think! I will gather you up into my arms and love you, little black boy with the haunting eyes and voice of music. And I will love your friends and take you by the hand and help you climb the ladder. And we will not be afraid, for God is with us.

What men will not do with the laws, we will do with love.

Early next morning I awakened to a spring symphony. Opening the draperies, I saw emerald grass erupted from the earth, tulips risen from dark, narrow graves, their golden-throated trumpets swelling the jubilation. A mockingbird trilled from the tallest tree as I pulled back the dining-room curtains for the first time in two years. To my shame, I had not wanted any reminders of my roots, and those draperies screened out our view of the cook's hut Albert Pirtle had said would soon disappear.

The mockingbird soared on white wings over the gray hut like a seagull wheeling over seawater. For the first time, I really looked at that little dwelling, glad it was still there. Winter rains, March winds, and summer suns had transformed the batten boards to a pewter patina just like the old well and Abe's cabin back home. Dogwood blossoms spread above the roof.

Why, it's lovely! Funny I've never seen the beauty before.

Suddenly I was twelve again, standing in the yard of that other gray cabin on a hot August afternoon in Riddleville. Aunt Lou is dying; Nannie Lee wails; ragged children stare with curious, despairing eyes at my pale skin, frilly pink dress, and white shoes. A soft Voice speaks inside my head. "When you grow up, you must do something to help black people." *The burden has grown heavier with the passing years, like Christian's in* Pilgrim's Progress, *until now every wronged black I see becomes one of Aunt Lou's children.*

Grown up at last, I will seize every opportunity to break down the barriers between us, starting this very day!

That afternoon I crossed Moore's Mill Road, climbed the broken steps, skirted the hole in the porch, and knocked on the door of the weathered cabin. I could hear someone moving about, a scraping of feet on bare floorboards. A bronze woman in her late seventies, white hair on her head, peered through the screen door. She waited, uncertainty upon her strong, wrinkled face, groping for words as though saying, "What are *you* doing at my door? What do *you* want?"

"I'm your neighbor from across the street. May I come in?" *Please let me come in. Help me to lose some of my burden.*

"Yes," she said, opening the screen. "I know who you is. I seen you goin' to church and back. You the preacher's wife, ain't you? I know your husband. I seen him workin' in the yard. He speaks to me. He a nice man."

"I've lived here two years and don't even know your name. I decided it was time I get acquainted with my neighbors."

"My name's Sarah, Sarah Simpson."

"I'm happy to know you, Mrs. Simpson." For the first time in my life I dared to call a black woman "Mrs." "May I sit down?"

The surprised woman pulled out a straight chair in her plain but neat living room. I dropped down and she, sitting across from me, picked up an aluminum bowl and resumed her potato peeling.

"My son'll be home at five-thirty for dinner."

"Where does he work?"

"He a janitor at that big Methodist church downtown. My husband dead. Jus' me and my son live here. I got two daughters in New York. My husband left me this house. He was a yardman, and I was a cook for more than thirty years. We worked hard, sent our children to school. My son's been through college."

"Your son has a college education?"

"Yes."

"Then why does he work as a janitor?"

"I don't know. He won't try to do nothin' else. I think he tried one time. He jus' sets when he at home. Guess he's tired."

When I got back into my beautiful kitchen and started preparing flounder fillets to broil, Flossie knocked at the back door. I'd told the little lady to use the front door, but lifetime habits are hard to change. As she hobbled in, she was close to tears.

"What's the matter, Flossie?"

"Aunt Carrie dead," she said and began to cry.

"I didn't know. When did she die?"

"In the night. When her husban' went in her room this mornin', he foun' her dead in bed. And he so broken up, and her daughter, she been cryin' all day, and their preacher, he come to see 'em. I loved her so much. She was so good to me."

I led the little woman to the living room, and we sat down upon the red sofa. She put her face in her hands, and the tears dropped through her clove-colored fingers.

"Why did you come to me?"

"I had to have somebody to talk to. I'm so sad."

"When their preacher came, didn't he say anything to you?"

"Not a word."

"He came to comfort the sad, but he didn't see that you were sad?"

"I'm jus' a pore ole nigger," Flossie wailed, rolling her head back. "They don' pay no 'tention to me. But Aunt Carrie was always so kine. Now she gone, and I never see her again."

"You're not 'just a pore ole nigger,' Flossie," I said, putting my arm around her sweatered shoulder. "You're a child of the King. God loves you, and so do I. He sent His son into the world to die for you. I will comfort you, Flossie." Remembering how she'd sat beside my bed, her quiet presence consoling me when I'd been sick with flu, I said, "Would you like me to read you something from the Bible?"

"Yessum."

"My husband, the preacher, does this when he visits the sick and sorrowful." Flipping through my Bible, I found the fourteenth chapter of John. "They always read this at funerals: 'Let not your heart be troubled: ye believe in God, believe also in me. In my Father's house are many mansions; if it were not so, I would have told you. I go to prepare a place for you. . . . I will come again and receive you unto myself; that where I am, there ye may be also.'"

I paused and looked at Flossie, and I saw not a glimmer of recognition or understanding in her filmy black eyes.

"You've heard this before, haven't you?"

"Nome, I ain't neve' heared it befo'."

"Why, I have heard this at hundreds of funerals! But you never heard these wonderful words before? You've never read them?"

"I cain't read."

"Oh, Flossie! You didn't know God prepares a home for us in heaven? Do you know we can have eternal life? That our loved ones who've died already are there, and we will see them again?"

When I saw that Flossie's eyes were blank, I perceived that the unlettered woman didn't even know what the words meant.

"You go to church, don't you? I see you walk by here on your way to church every Sunday. What do you do there? What does your preacher say?"

"He reads the Bible, but I don' understan' what he reads."

"Wait a minute." Going to my writing table, I selected one of my poems and read it to her.

> Lord,
> Into your hand
>   I commit this grief
> I do not understand.
> For You can take
>   the vilest wrong
> And turn it into
>   sweetest song.

As I read, I saw illumination and serenity creep into Flossie's eyes. And the black woman was not the only person in that room to receive illumination. *So this is what my brokenness was for, that I might help to heal the brokenhearted!*

I was back in the kitchen broiling the fish when Tom's little green Chevrolet passed the window and stopped on the paved driveway behind the house. Standing on tiptoe to kiss my husband when he entered the paneled kitchen, I said, "Are you going anywhere tonight? I have a thing to tell you."

"No, I'm going to stay home tonight."

"I'll tell you after dinner. I want to be free when I tell you, free of everything except my idea."

Finally dinner and dishes were out of the way, and I joined Tom in the living room. He laid down the *Atlanta Journal* and said, "What did you want to tell me?"

"I'm going to be a missionary." The words hung in the air for a moment. "Now don't say I'm too old or that it's impossible. I'm not too old, and you yourself have said many times that nothing is impossible with God."

"I haven't said it's impossible," he smiled. His eyes wrinkled at the corners.

"I'm going to be a missionary to Africa, not Africa across the ocean, but Africa here at home, in Atlanta. Did I tell you about my visit to the nursery? Did I tell you about Nincompoop and the children?"

"You told me."

"I can't forget those children. They haunt me day and night. I love them, and I've wanted to go back ever since I left. I want to go every day and take them more than a can of juice and a box of crackers. I want to give them love, acceptance, opportunity, equality." My eyes filled with tears. "I don't know where all of this will end up. Whites may call me a nigger lover. Perhaps they'll throw bricks and knock all the windows out. We may lose everything—house and church. But I know where I can start. I can start this summer with Vacation Bible Schools. First I'll train in our church as a teacher of seven-year-olds when our Bible school meets in June. Then I'll be ready to go across town, open that piano, play, and teach."

"I will not let you go alone. It's a dangerous area. I've been there, seen those winos hanging around the stores."

"I'm not afraid."

"Well, perhaps I can help. I'm a member of an interracial committee, you know."

"What is the committee doing?"

"Not much. The work is almost at a standstill because of all this trouble between the races, the student sit-ins, Martin Luther King and his movement. Tension and resentment are so high." Deep furrows crept into his brow.

"Almost at a standstill!" I said. "At the very time when our churches should show love."

"I led our church to send twenty-five dollars for the operation of a Sunday school at Magnolia Mission, and one of my deacons got mad. Said he didn't want any of his money going to 'niggers.' Now he won't come to church. We're building an athletic field for our already overprivileged boys, spending two thousand dollars on lights alone, and yet we can't give but twenty-five to poor blacks who have nowhere to go to worship!"

"No wonder they live in such misery, their children in juvenile detention homes, attempting suicide, while we sit in our splendid sanctuaries and piously pray, 'Thy kingdom come, Thy will be done.' Heaven help us when His will is done! We wouldn't recognize Him if we met Him in the street." I was wound up now. "I'm sorry, Tom, but I cannot spend the rest of my life sitting in meetings. For twenty years I sat and listened. Now I've got to get up, go myself, and do something for suffering humanity."

The tallest man rose from his chair, put his arm around my shoulders, and with his handkerchief wiped away my tears. "I'm very proud of you," he whispered, his breath warm on my cheek. "I always knew you had more to give than you were giving. That's why I loved you and married you. I saw your heart—the real person underneath the mask. I'd begun to despair that you would ever realize your great talents for loving and come into possession of your own powers."

"How did you put up with me so long, my blundering, rebellious ways?"

"I loved you. Now I love you more than ever!"

"And I thought you would be ashamed of me," I laughed. "I was afraid to tell you."

"When will you stop being afraid of me?" he asked, pulling me close into the circle of his arms.

"I'm sorry. I keep forgetting that we're equals now, man and woman, no longer father and child. It takes time to change my thinking patterns, to think like a giant, when for so long I've thought like a caged grasshopper in a world of Goliaths."

It had taken two decades of marriage before the split personality could know who she was, remove the shackles, become her own person. And the approval of my husband made it all the sweeter.

So, on a blistering day in July when John F. Kennedy was campaigning for the presidency, Tom and I became missionaries to blacks in Atlanta.

We worked with the Reverend H. M. Alexander, pastor of Lindsay Street Church, and his wife in conducting a Bible school for children of their congregation.

But we did not go alone. Kathy and Tommy volunteered, as did sixteen other white persons from Northside Drive. Wives of executives and the mother of a debutante left air-conditioned comfort to commute through sizzling city streets and sweat to an ill-equipped basement room. Young whites bored by too many privileges dared to do the dangerous thing, the thing from which they'd been sheltered. I wanted to sing hosannas. Instead of scorning me, family and friends joined in a six-car caravan every morning and motored from our fashionable north side to the Vine City neighborhood.

Tom assisted the pastor as principal. Harry Chafin, Northside Drive's associate pastor, conducted the music. Eighteen-year-old Kathy worked with four- and five-year-olds, and thirteen-year-old Tommy assisted me with sevens and eights.

Blacks and whites, teachers and children, lined up on the sidewalk in front of the red-brick building with stained-glass windows. Up the steps we processed, led by three older boys carrying the American and Christian flags and a Bible. Inside the sanctuary we remained standing, right hands over hearts, and pledged allegiance to each of the flags and then to the Bible. When I heard the victims of segregation shouting the words "with liberty and justice for all," tears started in my eyes and gooseflesh tingled my arms. In my heart I pledged anew to do everything I could to make the words come true for these trusting children.

Like the children at Magnolia Street, these wore a clean, scrubbed look and starched cotton dresses or clean, pressed shirts, boys' hair neat and close-cropped, girls' in tight pigtails tied with hair ribbons to match their dresses. On their feet each child wore polished shoes.

Downstairs in the crude basement room with its exposed pipes, broken plaster, and concrete-block walls, the seven- and eight-year-olds crowded around Tommy and me. A boy named Stephan rose to read the memory verse from the big Bible: "What time I am afraid I will put my trust in thee." His high-pitched voice, soft and sweet, was like water rippling over rocks. Then each child held the Bible and read the same verse.

When they filed outside in the scorching sunshine for recess, cold lemonade, and cookies, Stephan soon came back in through the side door followed by the other boys and girls. The schoolroom, its plastered walls lined with pictures of Christ helping the children, seemed more attractive to them than the grassless playground, and Bible stories more exciting than recess.

When it was time for the handwork, white women and teenagers helped the two black women direct the children. All over the building, I watched the women working joyfully, heard their happy voices. And once I'd been afraid that these same women would hate me when they learned of my love for African American children! Instead of hating, they helped as though they'd been waiting for someone to lead them into doing the thing they wanted to do.

This is the cross God is preparing me to carry. It's not a burden, but a joy. I can't stop with one school. I must help with another and another. In this way perhaps I can fulfill my vow, build bridges between the races.

Before we knew it, it was twelve o'clock and the first day was over. As the children lined the sidewalk and yelled good-bye, the missionaries climbed into their Buicks and Oldsmobiles and headed home. During this hottest time of day, steam rose from the city pavement. My nostrils filled with odors of second-class citizenship—cooking cabbage, burning fatback grease, foul garbage.

Suddenly I felt dirty, hot, sweaty. "I can't wait to get home to wash my hands!" I said.

"It's because you've been working with blacks this morning," Tom replied. "You've probably always associated them with dirtiness."

Back home on beautiful Moore's Mill, I hurried through our cool, carpeted house into the bathroom with its shuttered windows. I turned on the cold water faucet, luxuriating in the flow of cool water over warm hands. *My hands don't look dirty!*

It's not your hands that are dirty. It's your heart and your head. There's prejudice in your heart still and tangled thoughts in your weary head. You cannot by only an act of your will untangle in a day what it took centuries to knot.

A curse, born even before America was young and when democracy was but a dream, has come full-grown to dirty up our hearts, our heads, our hands. It soils the face of Atlanta and the lovely South, and all America in the eyes of the world. Making our vaunted freedom a farce, the curse of imagined white superiority also nails Christ again on the cross. Ingrained untruth is the rotten fruit of slavery, the ragged flower of segregation. I prayed for cleansing from this curse.

The next day I returned, renewed and expectant, to Lindsay Street. Twice young white men stopped and yelled at us: "Go home where you belong!" We ignored their taunts.

Every day more children enrolled. More Caucasians came from the north side, more African American workers from Lindsay Street. At first newcomers were hesitant, suspicious; but soon our enthusiasm swept away their fears. We taught, sang, and prayed together, sat down and ate together, and knew not that we were black or white. For a miracle had happened on Lindsay Street. People had become color-blind.

31   *Beautiful Horses Running Wild*

On Friday afternoon after the last session, Dr. Rufus Carrollton Harris, thirty years the president of Tulane and recently elected president of Mercer University, knocked on the door of the luxurious home I was planning to keep for the rest of our lives. In less than an hour, Dr. Harris talked Tom and me into moving to Macon. Tom would be director of development and alumni relations and would teach in the Department of Christianity for his alma mater. "And you'll be in line to succeed me as president of Mercer," Dr. Harris said.

Within a month we had rented Mrs. Barnett's cherished old homeplace on Rivoli Drive near the campus of Wesleyan College. "Woodlawn" was cool and green even when the September sun sizzled. No longer a pastor's family with free housing, we now paid rent for huge rooms with high ceilings that reminded me of the Wescoloski-Bryan house and of Mrs. Rose's Carolina mansion. I loved the terraced lawns and ancient trees with ivy vines trailing and drifting in the breeze. It was a place for dreaming, and more like home than any residence I'd had since leaving the village at sixteen.

From the upstairs windows I gazed at stately magnolias and cedars, remembering my first home and my last visit to Toney Valley. A sharp pain reminded me that I was still estranged from my parents. I had not seen them for many months, though I'd written letters once a week and Pa-Pa would sometimes write. But Mother never answered her daughter's letters. I went to see her on her birthday and Christmas Day. But she looked the other way and refused to talk to the strange new woman that wore her daughter's face.

Yet in my heart I knew I was following the course she had taught me. I continued to hear her admonition in my head: "Always be like Jesus."

Neither did I understand why God guided us to Macon just as I was beginning His work in Atlanta with so much success! I searched for an answer, for something I could do.

While I waited, my days fell again into a delightful pattern. I had hours to myself in the big, old, silent white-frame to write. Using Mrs. Barnett's huge desk, I set about the task of rewriting my book under the guidance of a Mercer professor of English.

A black woman, Mattie Mae, came twice a week to help with house-keeping. Released from burdensome church work, I joined only two organizations. One was the Mercer Faculty Wives' Club, whose members studied great books by Faulkner and Dostoevsky and T. S. Eliot, and Vineville Church, where I taught a Bible class on Sunday mornings. Enjoying more freedom than I'd ever had in all my forty-one years, I could now spend my days guided by God instead of the organized, segregated church.

Tom and I chose to join Vineville because it was nearer our home than the Tattnall Square Church on the Mercer campus. Tom served as supply or interim pastor for vacant pulpits, preaching almost every Sunday, at Wrightsville and Milledgeville in Georgia, Jacksonville in Florida.

All summer the student movement continued across the southern states. Daily we read about brave young blacks and the sit-ins, wade-ins, kneel-ins. We saw pictures of hundreds of black and white youths being herded into paddy wagons and jails singing "We Shall Overcome," praying, quoting Christ and Gandhi. They actively rejected the idea that they must eat leftovers at the back door rather than partake of full servings at the family table.

It was an agonizing, wonderful time to be alive, and each new report of the black uprising inspired me to get into the fray.

"But what can I do?" I whispered one morning at prayer time on Wood-lawn's breeze-swept porch.

In my lap, my Bible lay open to Genesis, where it told how God had spoken to Moses eons ago: "What is that in thine hand?"

A pen.

"Cast it down and write."

I obeyed. Gradually a poem about freedom emerged, inspired by that picture on Mother's parlor wall—horses galloping, free of riders, bridles, and bars. "Beautiful Horses Running Wild" would later win first prize in a national contest and be published and spoken in many places.

Meanwhile, in October 1960, Dr. Martin Luther King Jr. was pressed into a demonstration in Atlanta. For trying to dine at Rich's Magnolia Room, he was arrested and jailed in Reidsville State Prison. John and Robert Kennedy intervened, telephoned a Georgia judge, telephoned

Mrs. King. King was released. And Kennedy was elected president of the United States in November.

I wrote a story about Nincompoop and our Bible school. When it was published with a picture of the author teaching the black children in *Home Missions* in June 1961, no one called me a "nigger lover," nor did the sky fall in. However, in Atlanta my father read the story and wrote a congratulatory letter.

But there was total silence from my first teacher. I feared she thought her daughter had gone too far.

In the fall of 1961, I had to have a hysterectomy. I wrote to Mother and Daddy about the surgery in one of my routine letters. Remembering how I had waited on her while she recovered from the same operation almost twenty years earlier, Mother at last forgave me. She and Daddy came to visit me at the hospital.

It had been two years since I'd laid eyes on those precious faces. Only now both of theirs were lit with love for me. Although they looked a little grayer, their daughter's maturation had not killed them after all. Instead, they glowed in the joy of having rediscovered each other. In my room smelling of antiseptic and rubbing alcohol, I was so glad to see them, I cried. Sitting up on the side of the bed to embrace them both, I said. "I love you. I'm so sorry about what happened, and so glad it's over."

When I was able to travel again, Tom and I went to Decatur to visit my aging parents every week or two; and all through the sixties and seventies, I drove them on trips back to Riddleville, to the ancient cottage where Grandma and Uncle Herbert now lived. When bankruptcy had claimed The Store in the late thirties, Grandma had sold her house and moved into ours, which had been her birthplace.

I continued the struggle to change my thinking patterns, overcome a heritage of defeatism. Tom encouraged me all the way. After our move to Macon, he even went with me several times back to Atlanta to see Dr. Verdery. I changed and matured so much that Tom needed counseling also to help him adjust to the new woman his wife had become.

One day Verdery said a priceless thing to Tom in my presence that confirmed my sense of self: "Grace doesn't need you to analyze her. She needs your support."

Turning to me, eyes lit with pride and love, Tom affirmed, "I always wanted my wife to be a strong woman."

32 *Tattnall Square*

In the early 1960s the whirlwind sweeping across the Southland re-
volved into Macon, Georgia, and onto the green campus of all-white
Mercer University. Soon after Tom Holmes arrived there, he found the
most pressing problem to be dealt with was integration.

Under court order and amid student disturbances, the University of
Georgia at Athens opened its doors in January 1961 to two blacks. A few
months later Georgia Tech in Atlanta quietly accepted three black students from Atlanta. All the while southern governors and legislators
shouted, "Never, never!" and threatened to close down public schools
rather than "force our children to go to school with niggers."

Thomas Holmes was called daily to the office of President Harris in
Mercer's century-old Victorian administration building. They continued
reviewing, seeking, planning how best to chart the wisest course for the
university without alienating alumni, trustees, and foundations. The high
point of my day was late afternoon. When Tom came home to Woodlawn,
relaxed in my study—where three windows afforded a pastoral view—he
recounted the Harris-Holmes conferences. Tom's effervescence and
graphic descriptions carried me into the university's inner sanctum, and in
my mind's eye I could see the distinguished educator and holder of several
honorary doctorates pacing the Oriental carpet from massive desk to book-
lined walls and back to swivel chair.

One afternoon in May 1962 Tom said, "A Negro wants to come to
Mercer."

"You don't mean it!"

"Yes, his application was received today. And this is no ordinary
Negro. He's an African, a twenty-year-old student from Ghana. Name's
Sam 'O-Knee.' He's a convert of a Georgia missionary and Mercer graduate, Harris Mobley, who was a member of Tattnall Square while at the
university."

"That's exciting. You will accept him, of course? Will there be any trouble? I mean, how could a Christian university refuse to accept the product of its own teachings? When will he come?"

"I don't know. The trustees will have to vote on whether or not to admit him."

"When will they meet again?"

"In December. He stated in his letter that he wants to come to America and attend the school Mobley attended. He dreams of returning to his homeland to teach and preach and help his people build a better life."

"I was reading the other day that the life expectancy there is thirty-three. Tell me his name again."

"Sam O-Knee."

"Spell it."

"O-n-i. They say he speaks five languages."

Several days later I asked, "What's happened concerning the African?"

"We're still battling it around in committees," Tom said. "But I told Dr. Harris today that Mercer, a Christian university, should do by grace what the University of Georgia was required to do by law."

After careful consideration, Dr. Harris was persuaded that Mercer had no alternative but to open its doors to the African. The next two years, before and after Sam Oni's arrival, were spent dealing with unhappy alumni and trustees. Harris and Holmes coped with nasty anonymous letters and threatening phone calls from preachers, teachers, lawyers, and businessmen, all screaming like George Wallace, "Segregation today, segregation tomorrow, segregation forever." Dr. Harris's life was threatened many times.

But the persuasive team won the battle; in April 1963 the trustees voted to accept the African.

When Oni's plane landed in New York City on August 28, 1963, I was teaching second grade at Whittle School, and 250,000 people, both black and white, covered all the area from the Lincoln Memorial to the Washington Monument. As soon as I arrived home after school, I turned on the TV to hear Martin Luther King Jr. deliver his spellbinding speech:

> I have a dream that one day this nation will rise up and live out the true meaning of its creed: "We hold these truths to be self-evident; that all men are created equal."

I have a dream that one day on the red hills of Georgia the sons of former slaves and the sons of former slave owners will be able to sit down together at the table of brotherhood.

I have a dream . . .

Chill bumps rose on my arms. Not since Winston Churchill had the world heard such a mobilization of the English language. Those words pricked the conscience of the nation and galvanized Congress into passing the Civil Rights Act of 1964 outlawing discrimination in employment, voter registration, and public accommodations.

But federal laws in the making could not change the hearts of the white-supremacy deacons of Tattnall in 1963. They broke the heart of the young stranger from Africa when they sent their pastor to the men's dormitory to inform Oni that he would not be welcome to worship at the church on the campus.

Before leaving Ghana, Sam had been informed of the double standard in this country. So he gathered up his courage and went with the white friend who'd volunteered to be his roommate to Vineville.

When I first saw the pure African that Sunday in September, I was reminded that the miscegenation that racists warned against had been going on in America for centuries. Tall, handsome, Sam Oni was as black as Dole, as black as ebony. And we were appalled to see him embarrassed in the very house of God when, upon the pastor's invitation, Oni and several students walked down to the front of the sanctuary and presented themselves for membership.

The white students were joyfully received, but Oni was singled out. When the pastor came to him, he said, "This is a unique situation. What is your wish?"

Tom Holmes jumped to his feet. "I move he be received," he said, loud and clear.

My heart raced and my mouth went dry as a deacon rose from his back pew, bucketed down to the front, and grew red in the face as he bellowed: "Outsiders are tryin' to integrate 'our' church. Mercer couldn't be satisfied to go out on the streets and get a Macon nigger. They had to go all the way to Africa."

Nevertheless, by a show of hands, Oni was accepted, and many members were friendly. But he later received anonymous letters saying he wasn't wanted except by a few from the university.

In an effort to soften the slings of outrageous prejudice for the young African, we arranged a dinner party in our home for him. Calling it a United Nations Dinner, we invited a student from Japan, one from Denmark, another from Germany, Kathy's friend from Cuba, and Oni. He wore his colorful tribal robes, engaged in brisk conversation, and behaved as a perfect gentleman.

On the day President John Kennedy was killed in Dallas, we buried my aunt and playmate Rachel, dead of breast cancer at forty-four, in the lonely graveyard of Davisboro. My grief was double that November of 1963.

A year later, in December 1964, Tom was called to be pastor of Tattnall Square, "the church-on-the-campus." Before he gave them an answer, Tom met for several talks with two of its leading deacons. They stated that the church had made a mistake to deny Oni entrance, and it had suffered. Students and faculty members had left in droves to attend Vineville, because that church had accepted the African convert. The deacons said they thought the time had come to accept black students, "if they really come to worship, not to create a disturbance—and we certainly need to go after the students again."

So Tom resigned his Mercer position and accepted the call of the Tattnall Church. And we settled into our sixteenth home, the church's spacious bungalow manse, in March 1965. Gladys Johnson came to help me with housework twice a week. And in my study-bedroom stood a huge desk for my writing. From my chair I looked out on a gorgeous green wood and lush grasses.

That same month racial revolution exploded in fury in Selma and Montgomery, Alabama. Aunt Lou's children were repulsed on the outskirts of Selma by state police armed with billy clubs and whips. Yet, like beautiful horses running wild, Negro preachers and young people marched on, joined by white preachers, priests, and nuns from the North. Reverend James Reeb was beaten to death. Viola Liuzzo, a white housewife, was shot.

Each incident brought me more distress. Should I join the struggle in Alabama for human rights? No, it didn't seem right to leave husband and home, go that far away. So I watched and waited for my time to act.

On the first weekend of June 1965, Tommy graduated from Lanier High

School, and Tom and I celebrated our twenty-fifth wedding anniversary. Then Edward Simmons, Kathy's husband of six months, graduated cum laude from Mercer. And Dr. Harris conferred an honorary doctorate upon the pastor of the church-on-the-campus. Now Tom was "Dr." Holmes and stood on the threshold of his finest hour.

In July he appointed a committee to decide what to do about seating African Americans at services. White students were again filling up the pews on Sunday mornings, and eventually some of the several black students now attending Mercer would want to worship at Tattnall Square. The church wouldn't want an "incident."

Tom, in agreement with his associate pastor, Doug, wanted to invite the Negroes. But he must wait for his deacons. In spite of their promises, the deacons' plan was simply that—to wait, say nothing, do nothing, and hope the trouble would go away.

So the tension increased.

33 *A Woman's Liberation*

Nearly a year later, in June 1966, I was teaching remedial reading to forty black fifth-graders on Macon's south side. Under a Negro principal, the school was the city's first integrated public school faculty. Two weeks into the six-week summer session for elementary boys and girls, on a Thursday night, I said to Tom, "I'm going to Atlanta this weekend to see Mother and Pa-Pa."

"I wish you wouldn't go right now!" Tom flopped down on the cool blue sheet of our new king-size bed. Turning his long frame over, he lay on his stomach and propped his chin on the pillow. Fingering the chintz-covered headboard, he said. "We might have *visitors* Sunday. I'll need you."

"We always have visitors," I said, "when the students are on campus."

"These visitors are special. They're *Negroes*. Doug called today and said seven or eight have asked permission to come Sunday morning."

"You don't mean it!" Excited, I pulled myself to a sitting position with both hands on gown-wrapped knees.

"I do mean it."

"Are they students?"

"Summer school students, members of Upward Bound, a government program. Title I, the same thing you're doing. Only these are high school kids."

"What did you tell Doug?"

"I told him to tell 'em to come. Heck, it's not a church unless it's for everybody, is it?"

"Of course not! You know how I feel. And if you didn't let them come, I'd lose respect for you. These preachers who send them word that there's a church for them down the street make me sick. I think we should've invited them."

"We did. We had a sign placed in the student center inviting all students to our services. They're students too, aren't they?"

"Sure. When they read a sign saying, 'Y'all come,' they think it means them too. After all, everything's integrated now except the churches. I'm glad they're coming. Maybe they'll bring new life into this dead old institution."

"Well you'd better get ready to move," he said, half teasing, half serious.

"I don't care. It's time some preacher took a stand, and you have the courage to do it."

"I want you to sit with them. Ask Annette to sit with you."

My heart skipped a beat. "I'll be happy to," I said. Fixing my gaze on the double window opposite the bed, I reveled in the beauty of pale apricot walls and matching drapes. A soft breeze through the open windows billowed the center sheers. *If church members react in anger, we'll lose this house. It belongs to them, and we'll have to resign and move again.*

But haven't I committed my life to this cause?

Saturday night as we were crawling into bed I asked, "Are they really coming?"

"I understand that three are coming."

"Three? What happened to the others?"

"I don't know. I want you to sit with them."

"Yes, it's all arranged just as you asked. Annette will sit with me. Do the ushers know they're coming?"

Tom raised his head and bellowed, "Do you think I'm going to let my church be blasted in headlines all over the world for turning Negroes away? Why, if the deacons knew what we've arranged . . . ! Boy, when they find out, will they be mad!" Then gravely, sadly, lowering his voice, he added, "We might have to move, darling. I might get kicked out."

"But you couldn't tell them not to come!"

"I would've lost all respect for myself if I had."

Too excited to sleep, I saw my students, bright, alert, brown faces clear and glistening, clothes clean and neat, their young minds eager and unprejudiced, loving each new word and rhyme I introduced. *Although sometimes slow to grasp new technical skills, they're dynamic, the most responsive group I've ever taught.*

For centuries their race has made them victims of deprivation, unspeakable poverty, and illiteracy. Just like people everywhere, these children hope for love, happiness, and prosperity; they feel pain, anger, and disappointment; they suffer sorrow and embarrassment; they rejoice in victory.

To me they seemed no different from any other roomful of school children. I sometimes found myself, crayon in hand, standing at the green board in front of them wondering how anyone could hate those most human of all human beings, the nation's children. Especially my own church people, who stood in God's house Sunday after Sunday and sang to the One who died for all mankind. The hypocrisy I saw in the churches filled me with despair. I found more "Christianity" in the public schools!

In spite of my turmoil I slept, waking Sunday at dawn to the chirping of sparrows and mockingbirds, remembering *The Negroes are coming.* Leaving bed and slumbering husband, I walked barefooted down the carpeted hall to the kitchen softly repeating, "The Negroes are coming." Anticipation surrounded me as I reached for the coffeepot, drew water, measured coffee, turned on the electric range.

I hate to give up this kitchen. It's spacious, cool, clean. I've loved working in it. But Tom couldn't tell them not to come, and I love him the more for it. Are not these among Aunt Lou's children, whom I vowed to help?

We've moved sixteen times. I'm forty-seven and Tom's forty-nine. And though he's a man of many talents, he decided when he accepted this pastorate a year and a half ago to concentrate on preaching. If he's discharged, no southern church will want us.

I set the breakfast table for two, then galloped out to the mailbox for the morning paper. *The Negroes are coming and we are going. Where will we go?*

On the screened porch next to the kitchen, I sat in a comfortable long blue chair to sip hot coffee, scan the headlines, and read Ralph McGill's column. I usually managed this pleasant ritual without any mishap. But this was no ordinary morning. My hands trembled. The *Atlanta Constitution* slipped to the concrete floor and hot coffee sloshed from the brown cup and soaked through my thin yellow robe and nightgown.

This is surely the "something big" God has been preparing us for. Not the steepled church on Peachtree, but the cross at Tattnall. Our lives are in His hands, and He will carry us through any storm.

At ten o'clock, my heart hammered while I stepped into a pink linen shift and zipped it up the back. Tom usually did this for me, but my excited husband had already zoomed off in his little brown Rambler. Standing before the mirror, I quickly checked to make certain the lace on my slip didn't show and no run had started in the seamless nylons. *I hope this pair will last until after next Sunday.*

My hammering heart jumped into my throat. *We may not even be here next Sunday!*

Reaching Tattnall, next to the university, I parked the car in front of the men's dormitory where my father, brother, husband, and son had all resided during their student days. I cantered down the tree-lined street toward the church, heart pounding, heels clicking out a rhythm on the pavement: *The Negroes are coming!*

I must calm myself, try not to look excited. People must not suspect anything, think we've plotted or planned. Oh, I hope they'll be nice to those students, because if they're not, if they turn Aunt Lou's children out, I'll have to go too.

I'll take no privilege they can't take.

Annette Highsmith met me before eleven at the designated pew. Sixty-seven and the widow of a Mercer professor, she walked with a crutch. But Annette possessed the enthusiasm and freshness of a child, the sparkle of a May morning. And she got around faster than I, because she lacked my timidity. While the organist played meditation melodies, we quietly saved space between us for the "angels unaware."

Our eyes were riveted to the side door. Dozens of white students entered, but we saw not a single African-American. Unknown to us, two young men came in the front entrance and found seats five rows behind us.

Dead silence hung in the newly decorated temple as Dr. Thomas Joseph Holmes, clad in navy pinstripe, opened the huge pulpit Bible. Tom read from Acts 3:6: "Silver and gold have I none, but such as I have give I thee: In the name of Jesus of Nazareth, rise up and walk." Seeking to lead our church to become more relevant, to help our members overcome racist attitudes inbred since birth, Tom had skillfully, lovingly begun to preach a series of sermons from the exciting book of Acts. By revealing to them the radical Christianity of the Jerusalem church, he hoped our congregation would catch the vision to commit to the mission of the Good Shepherd and of renewal.

As Tom proclaimed the gospel of love, peace, and brotherhood, the black persons I'd known passed before my mind. Lucy, Aunt Lou, Nannie and Dole, Fannie and Jim, Leila, Belle, Flossie, Stephan, Nincompoop, Sarah Simpson and her son.

When the last amen was sung, Annette whispered, "Let me know what happened."

At that moment, I turned and saw the two black youths. The fifteen-year-old high school students from Toomsboro were neatly clad in black trousers and long-sleeved white shirts.

"Look behind you," I whispered.

Annette's face lit up. "Let's go speak to them," she said.

Suddenly I was afraid for those who paid our bread and board to see me shake the hands of black visitors. Anyway, they were being swallowed by the dispersing worshipers making their exit through the front door.

I said, "They're leaving. We can't reach them that way. Let's go out the side door and meet them as they walk toward Mercer."

But Annette wheeled and ran, hobbling, on her metal crutch, the flowers on her beige pillbox hat bobbing. And I, making my reckless choice, raced behind her, heels clicking upon pavement. Gray-haired parishioners stared, bewildered, at their undignified preacher's wife calling "Hello!" to this man, that woman, but not stopping for handshakes lest the young men get away.

Finally we sighted them in front of the building as they stepped off the sidewalk and onto the street, where people were crawling into their parked cars.

"Wait, boys!" shouted Annette as she lifted her free arm.

Dozens of white faces glared, and I was caught. It was too late now. The youths turned, looking a little scared. Annette stretched out her white palm and clasped the young black hands.

Reaching over the fender of a blue car, its occupants aghast, I shook our visitors' hands and said, "I'm Mrs. Holmes, the preacher's wife. We're glad you came today. We hope you'll come again." And I meant it. But I hadn't meant to make a spectacle of myself on the sidewalk before the entire congregation.

Steely eyes glowered at me from cold, white faces, freezing me out of the denomination my husband and forebears had belonged to down through generations. But at last I'd done what I'd always wanted to do. I'd shown my friends how I believed a Christian American should treat members of another race. I was clean inside, but so nervous my stomach hurt.

Back home, the telephone maintained an eerie silence all afternoon. Thinking we had gone to Atlanta, church members kept phone wires buzzing to one another, unaware that a car problem had halted our trip. At dusk, after Tom returned to Tattnall for Training Union and I was alone, the phone finally rang throughout the rooms.

"Is this Mrs. Holmes?"

"Yes."

"I'm a newspaper reporter. I hear nigras came to your church this morning."

My heart hammered and my knees ached. The anger in her voice and the way she mispronounced the word gave her away. She was no newspaper reporter. She was a deacon's wife, and she was threatening me. I'd have to choose my words carefully. Was I ready for Tom to lose his job? Ready for us to lose our home?

"I don't think that's anything to get excited about," I said, hoping she wouldn't notice how my voice shook, hoping I'd say the right thing, trying not to discriminate against the nice young men. "I teach blacks every day at summer school, eat lunch with them every noon. And the sky has not fallen in."

"I hear you shook their hands. How did you feel?"

Trembling overtook me. *We have no home except the one they, the congregation, provide. When we redecorated this neat beige brick bungalow and settled in a year ago, we thought we were fixed until retirement.*

My mind shot back forty years to Riddleville, to Aunt Lou singing about Jesus bearing her burden, and hopscotched to the day she died, when the blacks' burden had become mine. *I've borne that burden forty years, and I'm not going to carry it another day.*

"Liberated!" I shouted. "I felt liberated!"

34   *A Badge of Honor*

As I hung up the phone on the taunting woman, realization hit me like a thunderclap—*this is Someday!* All the pieces of my life zoomed together in one magnificent whole. Wandering from room to room, goose flesh on arms and knees, hands clamped to head, mouth in a broad smile, I wanted to cry and clap my hands and shout and sing. *So this is what it was all for! By segregating me in childhood, Mother inadvertently prepared me to help free blacks from the injustices heaped on them, free whites from our burden of guilt. In spite of my timidity and fear, this is the work God created me to do!*

And I've thought my life insignificant!

After evening worship one of the deacons attacked my husband angrily: "You'll be voted out for lettin' them niggers in here this mornin'."

I shuddered to see the man so enraged, and in a house of worship. He had been our friend. Chairman of the building and grounds committee, the five-foot-five, slim deacon cooperated with me last year in redecorating the parsonage, landscaping the lawns. Now gray eyes bulged from his red face, and gold-framed glasses slid downward on his nose. "You're lower down than any dog," he declared to my astonished husband. "You knew last night them niggers was comin'. Why didn't you call one of us and we would've had 'em thrown out?"

Thomas Holmes towered over the little deacon like a Great Dane over a bantam. "That's exactly why I didn't call you," he said, without anger. "I didn't want pictures of the church I pastor spread over the front pages of the world tomorrow morning showing grim deacons turning away God's children from God's house. Nor did I want those nice young men so embarrassed."

"Well, you're through here. I'm goin' to have you voted out."

"You may vote me out," Dr. Holmes said, raising his Bible high in his right hand, "but you called me here to preach this gospel, and as long as I'm here I will preach it. This book says, 'My house shall be called a house of prayer for all nations.' And while I'm your pastor, we'll not turn away any person who seeks to worship."

"I intend to get up here next Sunday morning," said the bantam, "and make the biggest fuss ever made in this church. I intend to have you fired, you and your associate pastor, and that music director too."

"You've got one vote," said the tower.

"I've just got one vote, and I'm just a little man, but . . ."

"You certainly are a little man, just about as little as any man I ever saw," Tom said, still without rancor in his voice.

Until midnight, back home in *their* house, hostility dogged us through the telephone.

"You have betrayed your people."

"We'd hate to lose you, Brother Holmes. But you're destroying the temple."

"We're mad with Grace. She shook the niggers' hands, but didn't shake ours."

From the moment of that declaration, I became afraid. Not of losing our job and home and salary, as fearsome as that might be, but of the Ku Klux Klan, of losing our lives. Or that we might still, in some way, *misuse* them.

Before the sun was up on Monday I was sipping coffee on the porch and praying in the cool morning air. Catapulted into unfamiliar, awesome territory, we were like horses loosed from bridles plunging into the unknown, where every action might be misunderstood, every word could be misquoted. I prayed that we would behave as true Christians and feasted on words of the Sermon on the Mount while cardinals and robins pecked flower seed at the bird feeder.

> Blessed are ye, when men shall revile you, and persecute you, and shall say all manner of evil against you falsely, for my sake.
> Rejoice, and be exceeding glad.

At eight o'clock I drove across town and over the Ocmulgee River to the school where my principal, half the teachers, and all the children were black. There had been no trouble since school opened a week before. But I feared there might be. Nervously I cruised along in cool comfort while scores of neatly dressed black children trudged through the dust on both sides of the highway. I wanted to give some a ride, but we had been warned to be careful because of threats from the Klan.

Inside the new, air-conditioned schoolhouse, I told my Negro principal of yesterday's happenings and the possibility of calls from the press.

She assured me I wouldn't be disturbed in my work. By the firm set of her cinnamon-colored face I knew I was safe. Her protective warmth melted the reserve between us. I heard myself saying, "I've always wanted to say openly that I deplore the evils of segregation. My husband and I have been embarrassed because white churches have dragged their feet in the Freedom Movement. We think it is God's movement, and the church should have led the people."

She smiled. "Yes, but it isn't integration you're fighting for. It's human rights."

"I know, and I've waited many years to join the fight. Now suddenly, this summer of '66, my government and my church have given me opportunities. But it does make me nervous. My husband will probably lose his job, and we'll lose our home. We're both past forty and have no savings. And no church in the South will call him once his name is associated with this issue."

"The Lord will give your husband another job, and you another home."

"Yes, oh yes!" I recalled how, in our venture in faith when we resigned Lakewood to return to seminary, all our needs were supplied. "I know what it is to live 'on faith.'"

"Now we're sisters," she said.

At one-thirty I returned, unharmed, to our home. Locking the doors behind me, I wondered if there would be a cross burned in the yard and bricks thrown through windows that night. I rubbed my right hand over the Williamsburg wall covering. How I wished the house were ours! It was spacious, comfortable, lovely. From each window we could see a picturesque view. Behind the dwelling were a wood, a creek, and a quaint bridge crossing the stream. When it rained water rushing over those rocks sounded like an infant Niagara.

Pouring tea over ice cubes, I heard their crackle. *I'll not pack a stem of Fostoria or a Havilland coffee cup in old newspapers until I see the yellow of the moving van out front. Everything in house and garden will stay in place until the very last minute. Until then, this home will be our haven.*

At 2:30 I lay upon the bed to rest. Tom stretched out on the other side, his legs propped up on a stack of pillows. Grieved and shocked by the sorry state of affairs, he had developed a backache so severe he could hardly walk.

But we couldn't relax. Christians called to say, "Preacher, you're right, and we're with you all the way. The church should be open to everybody." Deacons and deacons' wives rang up to harass. "You didn't handle it right; you should have consulted us first. You're splitting our church."

"It's not *your* church," the preacher replied kindly. "It's *God's* church."

Unable to nap, I located a skein of white wool and a needle. I had to stay busy. Propping against two blue pillows, I began to crochet an afghan for our first grandbaby, expected in November. Tommy had gone to work at C&S Bank and married a Macon girl, and now they awaited the birth of their first baby.

The movers and shakers of Tattnall Square were busy too. Telephone wires all over the city were overburdened. By seven o'clock Monday night the church was cracking like San Francisco in the great earthquake. Little crevices cut through families and crumbled thirty-year-old cliques. Watching it was both exciting and agonizing. *But it isn't my husband who is splitting the church. It is Truth separating the Christians from the Club.*

At a special meeting of the deacons on Tuesday night, the men gave vent to their feelings. But the trouble continued. As summer simmered along, emotions rose to fever pitch.

Nevertheless, the prophet continued his announced series from the book of Acts while at deacons' meetings my husband and his associate pastors continued to be maligned. To Tom some cried, "If you would just quit preaching from Acts, our church would be saved, and you could remain in our pulpit." Still Tom continued to proclaim the gospel of love, freedom, justice.

Finally, lines were drawn taut.

Amid the tension summer school ended, the baby's afghan was finished, and I started teaching at the integrated Clisby School. The deacons met in confrontation and voted to recommend discharge of all three pastors. The date of crucifixion was set for Sunday morning, September twenty-fifth.

On Friday, September 2, our church's agony hit the front page of the *Atlanta Constitution.* Through his syndicated column, Pulitzer prize–

winning publisher Ralph McGill broadcast the dispute in our Macon church to the world. His masterpiece ended with a quote from John Hurt, editor of the *Christian Index*: "Holmes' reputation through the years is too well established for the stain [of a firing]; if imposed, it could not be other than a badge of honor."

Three thousand miles away, in Berkeley, where he'd gone for summer school, Sam Oni read Ralph McGill's column. "I needed," he told us later, "to escape the Macon heat and harassment. I was embarrassed and hurt; both my parents had died in Ghana; and I'd been hospitalized with nervous exhaustion in Macon. In California I enjoyed not only respite but also some freedom.

"But when I read in Ralph McGill's column that Tattnall was crucifying my friend for letting black persons come to church, I said, 'Dr. Holmes was the first man in America to invite me to his home for dinner. They must not do this to him and to my people. I've got to return to Macon and tell them that such an action will torpedo their mission efforts in my country.'"

And so the African arrived at Tattnall on the Sunday morning of the vote. But when he tried to enter, he was stopped by two big, burly deacons on the church steps. One seized him in a headlock, the other helped drag him down the steps. A third deacon summoned police, parked conveniently nearby.

From the sidewalk the African gentleman said what he'd come to say: "You send missionaries to my land to teach the word of God. But when I come to your land, I do not find God's love in your hearts. Do you not care if my people perish?"

Oni was held in a police car outside the church until he agreed to go back home, while inside the church Thomas Holmes and his two associates were fired. The vote was 259–189.

One hundred members left with us, giving us courage and comfort. But when some said they wanted Tom to start a new church, he encouraged them to join other Macon congregations.

Before eight o'clock the next morning the phone rang. "I want to speak to Dr. Holmes," said a brittle male voice from far away.

"Who's calling?" I asked.

"NBC News, New York. We want a statement from Dr. Holmes."

The fired pastor took the phone in the bedroom. "I feel no malice, only sorrow that a Christian church would allow itself to be shattered over the seating of all people who desire to worship."

He hung up and began to unbutton his pajamas. In the kitchen I opened the refrigerator to get out the bacon.

The phone rang again. "This is CBS News, New York," said another clipped voice a thousand miles north. "I want to speak to Dr. Holmes."

Tom read his statement, and as soon as he replaced the phone, it rang a third time. "This is ABC News, Chicago." Then UPI news services called from New York. WSB-TV Atlanta rang up and arranged to fly two men down for an interview to be aired on that evening's newscast.

By 10:00 A.M. all the major networks had called for statements and the news was on television and radio every hour on the hour across the nation. It made headlines in Ghana and Argentina. Sadly, Sam Oni was quoted as saying, "My faith is almost shattered." Editorials were written that appeared in newspapers and magazines all over the world.

At 12:30 that day a slim, clove-colored man knocked at my front door. White-headed, he held his black chauffeur's cap in his hand. His wife, Gladys, smiled beside him, her dark eyes dancing, her black hair sleek and glistening.

"Mrs. Holmes," said Henry Johnson, in a voice thick with feeling, "I've heard what they've done to you and Dr. Holmes. I saw them hold the African in that police car. And I've come to tell you that if there's anything Gladys and I can do to help you move, we'll be glad to do it."

"Thank you, Mr. Johnson! But you've got your work to do."

"That's all right. I got permission to come, and I've got the whole morning off. We want to help you."

Then I saw that the black house man who had many times let me into the Harris home and served me food from the president's table had not come to my front door this day as a servant. He had come as an equal. I hadn't cried during the entire crisis. But now a loosening inside somewhere allowed tears to spill. "Mr. Johnson," my voice wobbled, "I've always wanted you and your people to know that I think segregation is evil. It has worried me for forty years. Now you know."

"Now I know," he said softly and smiled. "Don't mess up your face. You've got company coming."

I wondered if they'd heard down at Manchester, over at College Park, back in Riddleville. A car door slammed in the drive and two young men with television cameras sprinted toward the house. The telephone rang.

"Mrs. Johnson, you can answer the telephone and pack my china," I said. "They said we could wait a month to move. But we're moving tomorrow. Mr. Johnson, I hate to leave my rosebushes. If you would please dig them up for me, I would be very grateful."

And as I watched cameramen transform the book-lined study with hot, bright lights and yards of electric cords, I was more emancipated than I'd ever been since first I heard Aunt Lou singing about her burdens.

BOOK FOUR *Reconciliation*

35 *Providential Pulpits*

Leaving the fine manse to go into a four-room apartment on Vineville Avenue was the easiest move we ever made. Besides Henry and Gladys Johnson's, other grateful hands helped. Dr. Harold McManus brought a carload of students to transfer furniture on and off the U-Haul truck. Head of Mercer's Christianity department and a Ph.D. from Yale, McManus stood in our kitchen for five hours helping Gladys pack china, cooking pots, and assorted paraphernalia.

Since the agony of Tattnall began in June, letters from friends had trickled in. But on the heels of Tom's firing, communications from people we'd never heard of flooded our mailbox. From New York to San Francisco, Denver to Palm Beach, they expressed astonishment, outrage, sorrow. They surged with hope and congratulations that not one but three white ministers in the South loved their black brothers enough to suffer persecution for them. Phone calls came from California and Dallas, Atlanta and Baltimore, Little Rock and Memphis. Cablegrams arrived from Africa and Asia and the West Indies.

While I continued to teach remedial reading at Clisby School, Tom received several job offers—none from southern pulpits. The name of the man who had sat on dozens of boards and committees and spoken to the Southern Baptist Convention in Houston and in Chicago now bore the stain of "nigger lover." No pastor of a lily-white congregation wanted that stain to rub off on him.

Therefore the first sermon Tom preached after his ouster was at the synagogue in Macon, on Brotherhood Night. Rabbi Annes introduced him as "a man who understands what brotherhood means."

A church in Boise, Idaho, telephoned three times with a job offer. Other bids came from Georgia College in Milledgeville and from an insurance company. Sargent Shriver, director of the Office of Economic Opportunity, wrote to thank Tom for his work with underprivileged Negroes at

Mercer. Then Shriver's office called him five times to set up a Washington date to talk with Tom about going into government service.

Instead, Tom followed the request of Dr. Harris, who asked him not to commit himself until the Mercer trustees met in October. When they convened, they named Tom assistant to Dr. Harris, to take on special assignments and sit in as president while Harris vacationed in Scotland.

But Tom learned, when he went out one day to play golf with a preacher friend who had remained loyal, that his name had been rubbed off the roster of the Idle Hour Country Club.

Meanwhile, he got more requests to preach. There was a sermon in Athens, another in Milledgeville, one at Clairmont Hills in Atlanta, a weekend revival at integrated Mount Zion in Macon. Following these, he preached several Sundays at Woodland Christian Church in Macon. And Dr. J. T. Ford invited Tom to speak from his pulpit in Alexandria, Virginia.

Even at these pulpits, they downplayed controversy by introducing him as "former pastor of Manchester, College Park, and Northside Drive." Each time they omitted Tattnall as though it were a thing of shame. What in my eyes was Tom's finest hour appeared to be a disgrace in the eyes of many others.

Saturday became the saddest day of the week. For thirty years Tom had used Saturdays to visit members and put finishing touches on his sermons. Now he had no members to visit, no sermon to prepare, nowhere to preach.

On one such afternoon in April, he mourned on the sofa while staring at a ball game on television. His long legs stretched before him, feet propped on the blue ottoman. Though there was much merriment on the tube, Tom's face was glum.

Throughout the years I had seen him cry only three times. The first time was at Manchester, when one of his members, a railroad engineer, was killed in a collision of two locomotives. At the scene of the wreck, we saw the body, burned beyond recognition. The forty-year-old engineer left a wife and three young children. Tom possessed a soft heart for his people, and as he reported the horrible scene to his congregation later that morning, he collapsed in tears, his voice breaking, and he had to leave the room. Following, I saw him cry uncontrollably. He cried when his mother died, and the day John Kennedy was killed. Now I wondered how long it had been since his face split into a smile, his eyes crinkling at the corners in the dear old way.

"Tom," I said, "you're depressed because you have nowhere to preach."

"Nobody wants me." His voice carried bitterness. "I'm a has-been at forty-nine."

"I like having you at home with me on Saturday afternoons, and sitting with me at church on Sunday mornings. But I understand how you feel. You've preached every Sunday since you were nineteen. I know you miss it." Then a light snapped on in my brain. "If you can't preach, you can write! Write a book about Tattnall; tell what really happened."

"No, they would say I'm doing it for publicity, agitating the issue, exploiting Tattnall Square."

"Who would say?"

"Other preachers."

"You're thinking about whites. Think about blacks, how much it would mean to them to know that a white man cares for them. Remember Henry Johnson? When he moved my rosebushes from the Tattnall parsonage, he brought an azalea also. 'That wasn't my azalea,' I said. 'It's yours now,' he said."

The face of the rejected preacher relaxed into a smile, and I laughed out loud. "Let's move back to Atlanta, Tom, move away from all this hatred and bitterness and rejection in Macon. Let's go to Atlanta, and we'll both write."

"They want me to come to the School of Pharmacy. They need nearly three million dollars raised for a new building, another million for endowment."

"Ask Dr. Harris to appoint you. Please, I'd love to go back. I believe we'd be happier there."

And so we did. In the summer of 1967, seven years to the day after we left the capital for Macon, we returned to the schizophrenic city on the Chattahoochee River. In May 1968 the *Atlanta Journal* staff wrote:

> There are two Atlantas.
>
> . . . There is an Atlanta where a sapphire-colored cocktail lounge swirls slowly as part of the city's burgeoning skyline . . .
>
> The people in the other Atlanta, mostly Negroes, can stand on broken-

down stoops and cracked sidewalks and see the bar in the sky. To them, it might as well be a spaceship.

They cannot see the faces of the people inside. The distance between them is too great.

On the last Monday in November, carrying a sackful of groceries for the Thanksgiving feast we would share with Mother and Pa-Pa, Kathy and Edward, I climbed the green-carpeted staircase. Tom met me at the door of our Roswell Road flat. He was smiling, his eyes wrinkling at the corners in the old lighthearted way. His voice contained the effervescence I loved.

He took the burden from my arms, saying, "A newspaper reporter is on the way here to get a story on me for the Thanksgiving issue of the *Journal-Constitution,* what I'm doing, how I feel one year later. Get out the scrapbooks and letters."

Excited too, I scurried around the four rooms putting away turkey, cranberries, and celery, pulling down scrapbooks from closet shelves, and recalling the wonder and anguish of those early days after the firing and how I'd clipped and pasted hundreds of letters and newspaper stories.

Outside the high-rise, treetops towered and pine branches glistened in warm sunshine. An autumn breeze played through the Chinese chimes hanging from the roof of the porch. Leaves floated to the floor of the tiny forest, spreading a scarlet, plum, and amber carpet. Gone was the grief of rejection and ostracism.

Dick Hebert arrived at two o'clock. He pored over our memorabilia and interviewed Tom until 5:30. Then on Thanksgiving morning the newspaper carried Tom's picture and a lengthy story: "Dr. Thomas Holmes is a preacher without a pulpit, a teacher without a classroom, a man wrenched out of the life he had loved."

On the other side of the city, in black Atlanta, another preacher read the same story over a plateful of sausage and grits. A former classmate of Martin Luther King Jr., the Reverend Walter McCall gulped the moving account of Tattnall Square along with his coffee.

Our Sandy Springs telephone rang just as Kathy and Edward joined us in the great room for a late breakfast in the sun-splashed nook. Answering, I heard the crisp diction of an unfamiliar voice asking for Tom and handed the phone to him.

"Dr. Holmes, you don't know me. My name's McCall. I'm a preacher, pastor of Providence Baptist Church and head of the Christianity department at Morehouse College. I've just read your story in the paper, and I got so full I couldn't finish my breakfast until I'd called you."

"Thank you, Mr. McCall. You're very kind to call me, and I appreciate it."

"Just call me Walter."

"Okay, Walter, and you call me Tom."

"Tom, you can preach in my pulpit. Our people would be so happy to have a man like you, a man who has given up so much for us."

"You're very kind. And I'd like to come some time."

"I'm inviting you to come Sunday morning."

"This Sunday?"

"This Sunday."

"I'll be happy to come!"

"And my wife and I want you to come to our house today, eat Thanksgiving dinner with us. We've got a turkey in the oven right now. We'd be honored to have you come and bring your wife."

"That's mighty kind of you, Walter. But we've got guests. Our daughter and her husband are here."

"Bring them too."

Tom laughed. "We expect my wife's parents as well. But we'll be glad to come later. Give us a rain check."

"How about tomorrow morning for breakfast at ten o'clock?"

"Tomorrow? Wait a minute. Let me ask my wife."

The next morning we set out at nine-fifteen, driving south through a gray fog, then west towards Adamsville and Baker's Ferry Road. Hearts pounded with exhilaration and wonder, for none of us had ever eaten in a black home before. With startling logic Kathy summed it up: "But we've eaten their cooking all our lives in our homes, churches, and restaurants," she said.

Finally we came to number 4196, a white brick house. Janet, the McCalls' attractive seventeen-year-old daughter, opened their front door. "Come in," she said, and led us through the hallway and dining room and down a step into the well-appointed living room. Taking our coats, she disappeared, and Walter and Anna Mary McCall entered, followed by three black men clad in business suits.

Walter gripped our hands and made introductions all around. C. B.

Feagin, a six-foot-four public school teacher of English, and John Tyler, a slender assistant principal of a high school, were deacons in Walter's church. Dr. Sam Williams was professor of philosophy at Morehouse College, pastor of Friendship Baptist Church, and a member of the Atlanta school board. All of them had been involved in the Movement.

From the moment I saw the pretty face of Anna Mary McCall, I knew we'd be good friends. A woman of about forty, she sat at the head of the table beside her husband. I sat between two black men and across the table from two more. Turning to chat first with Feagin and then with Tyler, I heard Mother's voice in my head: "Never look a colored man in the eye; he might rape you. If you meet one on the street, look the other way, or run."

No, I wouldn't dream of embarrassing these gentlemen! The shreds of my white-supremacy schooling evaporated like mist dispersed by the rising sun. Since my youth I had felt like a hypocrite for ignoring black men, for humiliating other human beings when I wanted to be kind, natural. *Mother should see her child running free!*

On the other hand, thank God she can't!

Our black-and-white company talked and laughed and helped ourselves to steaming dishes of delicious sausage, bacon, eggs, cheese grits, butter, toast, preserves, and coffee.

Then Mr. McCall laid down his fork and addressed Tom at the other end of the table: "You know, Dr. Holmes, whenever one of you white preachers is discharged from his church for trying to help us Negroes, we Negroes should show our gratitude. That's why we invited you here today. When I read your story Thanksgiving morning, I wept and said, 'Here is a man who cares for us.'"

He said "Knee-grows" with pride. I heard the crash of a hundreds-of-years-old barrier collapsing. In its place a bridge of understanding raised graceful arches, stronger than steel. Here at last someone understood; they were not embarrassed by our firing but proud of it, acknowledging that Tom had been persecuted for their sakes.

Everyone talked at once, restraints gone. Our inhibitions vanished, color disappeared. We were just a group of human beings rejoicing together, recounting sufferings and triumphs.

On Sunday our children and I rode with Tom to Providence Church on

Larkin Street at the edge of the Atlanta University Center, which was composed of Morehouse, Spelman, and Morris Brown Colleges, the Interdenominational Theological Center, and Clark Atlanta University. The schools had been started by the Rockefellers soon after the Civil War. Providence was housed in a red brick building with stained-glass windows in pink and lime green. Pale green paint colored the interior walls, and apple-red wool carpeted the aisles.

African Americans of various hues—men, women, children—packed the pews. Walter McCall, black as a pure African, stood behind his oak pulpit. A cross, lit from inside, was suspended above his head. He presented the white preacher to his fashionably dressed flock as "a man who cares about us, the man who was fired from Tattnall Square for preaching the Gospel."

"Brothers and sisters," he said, "when I read in the paper Thanksgiving morning about this man and his act of love, I was eating my breakfast. But I got so full, I couldn't eat any more food. The story I was reading was food enough. And I went to the telephone and called this modern-day Paul and invited him and his family to our home to eat and to our church to preach."

I could feel their rapture ripple through the room, sense their love. From the throats of hundreds of Aunt Lou's children, amens and soft murmurs of thanksgiving rose, instantaneous and volcanic, tingling my limbs and moistening my eyes.

Then Tom towered above their pulpit, his head almost touching the lighted cross. "Brothers and sisters," he said, "I know what it means to be rejected, for I have been rejected. But God restores my soul. Today my cup runs over."

White and black connected like a handshake. Warm tears slid down my cheeks. I sensed the Spirit of the Almighty, Dove in flight, sweeping over the congregation. I breathed a prayer of thanks.

My hero continued his sermon, "The Kingdom of God," by proclaiming, "God became more real to me at Tattnall. Instead of losing faith, as one newspaperman suggested, my faith was strengthened."

African American worshipers have a way of conversing with the preacher. It was like sitting in the middle of a theater-in-the-round. Amens, at first barely audible from the deacons' pews on the left of the podium, now rose louder from front, rear, right, left. "Amen! Amen!"

"Yes." "Amen!" "Well?" "Amen!" "Preach, Brother!" "Thank the Lord!" "Oh, Jesus!" "Well?"

Gradually I became conscious of a chant emanating from the women's corner on the other side of the rostrum. A little ninety-year-old woman with wispy white hair and skin the color of cloves rocked in her pew, chanting like Sidney Poitier in *Lilies of the Field:* "Amen, amen, amen, amen, amen." She looked like Aunt Nannie come back from the grave. Clad in a black-and-white-checked dress, black coat, and black felt hat, the former slave's anthem rose from pianissimo to fortissimo.

But instead of being drowned out, the voice in the pulpit grew more rhythmic and eloquent. "The Spirit of God came down at Tattnall Square, lifted the roof with dazzling light, drew a plumb line right down the middle of that congregation. One hundred eighty-nine people saw that light, and 100 of them left with us. But 250 continued to dwell in darkness."

"Oh, Jesus!" "Preach!" "Yes, Lord!" "Preach, Brother! Preach!" "Amen!" "Amen!"

"No matter what happens, keep on having faith in God."

"Amen, amen, amen!" Joy soared heavenward as black and white worshipped together.

After Tom finished, Walter stood before his flock and started an old spiritual. His people rose to their feet and sang with him, a capella, repeating and repeating:

All night, all day,
Angels watching over me, my Lord . . .

Listening to the deep-throated vocalizing, the rhythmic repetitions, I felt we were surrounded by a hedge of angels, past, present, future.

When we returned to our home at Old Salem, Kathy rushed to her father, threw her arms around his neck, and spoke for all of us, "Daddy, now I know what the Kingdom of God means. That's the best sermon you've ever preached."

Hugging his daughter, Tom said, "It was the most responsive audience I've ever had!"

Other black pastors invited Tom to preach in their pulpits. And everywhere he went, Holmes was introduced as "a man who cares for us, a man who gave up his job for us." He was greeted with shouting and singing from a people who for centuries had suffered rejection, hatred, and murder. I marveled that people of color could still look at a white face and smile.

But these people possessed a depth of spirit, a breadth of soul I'd never witnessed before. We concluded that whites who pushed blacks out of their assemblies were the losers. It was like eating strawberry shortcake without the strawberries.

At Paradise Church on Bankhead Avenue one Sunday morning in January of that momentous year, 1968, a seventy-year-old man lifted up his voice and wept while Thomas Holmes proclaimed the glad tidings. Wiry, gray-haired, he sat on the end of my pew. His cry rang through the sanctuary, shook me like the sound of sirens announcing the end of World War II. He seemed to be saying, "At last you come saying you love us, that now we can be friends, the walls between us broken down. We're not just 'niggers' any more. We're as good as anybody. Waited all our lives, as did our grandparents and great-grandparents. For three hundred years we waited for you to accept us as equals. And now that you've come, others will follow."

Why, oh why, did I wait so long? I asked myself.

At Mount Zion Second Baptist on Boulevard one February Sunday, I found a pew near the back, picked up a hymnal, and sang with the congregation my favorite hymn of freedom—and theirs—"The Battle Hymn of the Republic." Then the choir and congregation sang the hymn I'd not heard for thirty years:

> I must tell Jesus, I must tell Jesus,
> I cannot bear these burdens alone;
> I must tell Jesus, I must tell Jesus,
> Jesus can help me, Jesus alone.

As I listened to 199 Lous sing the washerwoman's mournful song that started me on my awesome pilgrimage, I came to a moment of truth. *I'm not free yet. I have to come full circle, all the way back to the village. I must return to the columned cottage, now more than a hundred years old, where Mother watched over her child, taught her what the soul is and how to read and write, pray and sing, love my neighbor as myself.*

I have to stand again beneath the spreading pecan trees where Aunt Lou labored and lamented her burdens, where I first heard the African's cry for justice in America. I have to see again the slave cabin where I saw the washer-woman die. I must find Nannie Lee and her children, tell them I care. I need to know how they are getting on.

Because I will never be free until they are free!

36 To Make Amends

On a bleak Sunday afternoon of February 1968, Tom had been summoned to conduct the funeral of one of his former members in Manchester. In dear, familiar Meriwether County, we drove past peach orchards, their rows upon rows of short gray trees spreading spindly branches like hundreds of bare hands, palms turning upward, fingers reaching for the sun.

But there was not a glimmer of sunshine. Snow was predicted by nightfall. Like our hearts, the sky was leaden. At the edges of fields, patches of yellow daffodils swayed in winter wind. Last summer's cornstalks were ragged ballerinas bent to the ground. Shreds of dirty cotton in the deserted patches clung to brittle brown bolls like grimy-faced white children to their dark mammies.

Unpainted Negro shacks sat empty now, their porches and steps sagging, windows and doors stripped away by wind and left to rot in sun and rain. Their former occupants had fled to Atlanta, Detroit, New York, Los Angeles to seek a better life—higher wages, freedom, justice. Instead they found cities overcrowded by disappointed, frustrated masses. Here in the South, rotting privies and old wooden wells scrunched under rusty tin roofs, their chains and buckets idle, spoke of an era long since gone.

In late afternoon, when black snow clouds hovered in the northeast and snowflakes fluttered in the air, Tom parked our Rambler in front of the Marshalls' neat white cottage on unpaved Dunn Row. My heart raced as I contemplated the tidings I'd come to share with my former maid-of-all-work.

Fannie opened the door. Her head was wrapped in a printed kerchief that framed her strong black face, now wreathed in a smile. Jim's white-fringed head appeared behind her as I went into Fannie's outstretched arms.

In their small living room, two faded couches adjoined at right angles, lining the outside walls. I sat on one and Fannie sat opposite her former employer in a comfortable armchair. Jim and Tom sat side by side on the other sofa. On a coffee table in front of our knees rested a huge family Bible atop a starched white crocheted doily that curled up around the Book. Beyond the table, a red-flamed gas heater hissed in a small fireplace.

Eager to tell them why we had come, I waited only for greetings all around. "Did you hear what happened at Tattnall Square down in Macon?"

Years of mistrusting hypocritical whites had taught people of color caution and concealment. "No," said Fannie.

"I heard a little some'pin' about it," said Jim, scratching his curly head.

"Well, I'll tell you. Tom was fired because he wanted the church open to black students from Mercer University. One of the students was Sam Oni from Africa, convert of missionaries from Georgia. And when Tom lost his pulpit, we lost our home also, the very same day.

"But we don't feel bad about it. We were glad at last to say to the world that we care for your people, and we're tired, really tired, of seeing you discriminated against. We waited years for the opportunity to help demolish Jim Crow laws.

"And it was partly because of you, Fannie, and you, Mr. Marshall. Do you remember that day you came to me crying because you couldn't vote?"

"We remember," Fannie whispered.

"Well, I never forgot it. It has worried me all through the years, haunted and driven me to do something about injustice.

"I should have gone with you that day to the polling place. I should have escorted you there and seen to it that you got inside the booths."

"You were pregnant with Tommy," said Fannie softly.

"I was out of town," Tom said. "I guess it's a good thing I was. I might have knocked somebody down had I been there. I remember how mad I was when I got back and Grace told me."

"I remember what you said." Fannie's voice was husky. Her head tilted to the right, and she twisted a wrinkled white handkerchief in her creased black hands. "Mister Tom, you said, 'Just keep on workin' and prayin' and singin' the song the Lawd gives you to sing, and some day things will be different for you and your peoples. A just God always hears the cries of his children. Just keep on singin' the song the Lawd gives you to sing.' That's what you say. And that's what I done."

"And He has heard," said Tom. "Things are getting better now. Martin Luther King and his brave followers have made marvelous strides."

"Let me tell you how that story end," said Jim Marshall. "You know I served suppers for the Kiwanis Club in Manchester. The next Monday night after that election, I decided I had to say somethin' to those mens, but I had to find a way to say it. You know a nigger man can't come right out and say what he think to a white man. He have to resort and pretend. So that night I pretend to be sick, all bent over like I was sick whilst I serve the plates and the coffee; and I moan and I groan.

"And directly, Mr. Peters, he say, 'What's the matter with you, Jim? You sick or some'pin'?'

"And I say, 'Yessuh, I's sick. I gotta move, I gotta move to Talbotton, can't serve your suppers no more.'

"'Why, Jim?' they all say. 'How come you gotta move to Talbotton?'

"''Cause they let niggers vote in Talbotton, and they don't here.'

"'Ah, Jim,' they all say. 'We's goin' t' fix that. You just wait. You gonna vote here.'

"Well, it weren't long 'fore Mr. Peters's nephew, Mr. Hoke, run for the legislature. And Mr. Peters, he come to me and he say, 'Jim, round up all your folks, get 'em to the polls to vote for Hoke. He's runnin' for the legislature, and he a good man.'

"And I did, and we all went and voted, and we sent Mr. Hoke to the legislature."

Tom slapped his knee, threw his head back and laughed. "You put one over on them, Mr. Marshall. Good for you."

"Yessuh!" Jim nodded, rocking forward from the waist and smiling broadly. Fannie rocked and smiled, too, while I clapped my hands and laughed with them.

Then Tom arose and plucked the Bible from its curly white nest. "We've got to go," he said. "But before we do, I'd like to read a chapter from this Book." Tom read the first Psalm: "Blessed is the man that walketh not in the counsel of the ungodly, nor standeth in the way of sinners . . ." He finished the Psalm, closed the Bible, and sat down again. No one spoke. I could hear the hissing of red gas flames inside, the wind rising outside, the knapping of plastic on the windows of a back room. Tom bent his long frame forward and said, "Let us have a prayer." Black and white together bowed heads while the preacher prayed. "Lord, thank you for our friends and their faithfulness through the years, their lifetime of hard work and patient waiting for Your hand to move, through them and us."

Suddenly a pent-up praise burst forth from Fannie's heart and fluttered, a barely audible song, upon her lips as she repeated over and over:

Thank you, Lord,
Thank you, Jesus!
Thank you for sending Mr. Holmes,
Thank you, Lord,
Thank you, Jesus!
Thank you for sending Mrs. Holmes!

As we left Manchester, I told Tom, "Now I know God guided Mother, Aunt Lou, and me, preparing us for our mission. I wish I could buy back the old homeplace, rebuild and restore it, give it a new name—Bethel—house of God and gate of heaven."

I rode back to Atlanta awestruck. *God, You chose me, the insignificant, tongue-tied girl from the most obscure village in this country. You chose my five loaves and two fishes to multiply in the most magnificent task!*

I want to go home, where it all started, and put together the puzzle pieces of my life.

Tom could not go with me that spring, but Mother did.

On the first day of April Tom took a jet to New York for four days to call upon pharmaceutical companies on behalf of Mercer's new building on Boulevard for the School of Pharmacy. Pa-Pa, now seventy-four, his hand trembling in the early stage of Parkinson's disease, had gone to Albany to show a film and speak about Baptist Village. He had a driver now and enjoyed these monthly journeys on behalf of the retirement home at Waycross. In fact, he wanted to sell the Decatur house and move into one of the Village's apartments. Keeping up the house and mowing the lawn became heavier each year. But Mother was loath to leave the rooms she'd decorated, roses she'd cultivated.

On that balmy morning, after Tom had left for his flight, Mother and I set out in the blue '59 Oldsmobile for Washington County. I drove along the same route Sherman's army rampaged in the fall of 1864, when he and sixty thousand soldiers tore through the Georgia countryside, leaving in their wake terror, defeat, and destruction. Only a historical marker raised here and there reminded us of the ravages to green meadows and rolling hills little more than a century before. Now redbud and white dogwood blossoms laced through green pine and oak branches everywhere to right and left. In yards and gardens of the sleepy little towns, lavender wisteria, purple thrift, and pink and red azalea bloomed.

"Where does Lucy live?" I asked Mother as we crossed into Hancock County over the bridge that spans the Oconee River. "I want to see her. It's been years since I've seen Lucy." Just how much I'd yearned of late to see my old nurse, I didn't reveal.

"She lives in that little house on the edge of town that belonged to Uncle Tom and Aunt Emma."

"The one Aunt Lou died in?"

"The same one. Uncle Tom told Lucy she could live in it until she died if she'd wash for Aunt Emma."

"That was kind of him."

"Aunt Emma's sister, Mrs. Price, owns the property now. I want to stop at Lucy's for a minute or two. I brought some clothes for her, a red dress, some shoes. You remember how much Lucy liked red dresses?"

Happy to take advantage of Mother's foresight, I parked in front of the ancient cabin of my slave-holding ancestors, my mind and heart in tumult as I beheld again my "burning bush." The crude two-room cabin nestled against piney woods. Three crooked chairs crouched on the rotting porch. The two unpainted front doors were bolted, the wood shutters closed. My old nurse was nowhere to be seen. Clouds of daffodils bloomed in the yard where thirty-seven years before I'd been horrified at Aunt Lou's impoverishment. And where God had commissioned me.

"Lucy!" called Mother.

This is the first time I've set foot on this piece of land since the day Aunt Lou died. It was here that it all began, my pilgrimage to overcome racism. What a strange coincidence that now Lucy lives in this very place! But has Lucy heard about Tattnall? She can't even read and write. Does she know that I love her and her people, that my heart breaks for them? That I always wanted to do something to change the sorry system of segregation, and now I've done a little something?

No, I'm sure Lucy can't comprehend.

"We won't stay but a few minutes," murmured Mother, her white face creased with anxiety. She hurried across the yard to where the kitchen stood a few steps behind the cottage.

"Lucy!" she called.

37 To Go Home Again

As if for the first time I saw the wretched condition of the shanties. Nothing had been done to improve them in the three decades I'd been away. And Uncle Tom had owned this property! He who taught and sang about love of God and brotherhood of man!

Oh, Lord, how our prejudices blind the "best" of us!

If I had some money and land, I'd give Lucy a nice little home. But I don't even own my own.

Then I saw my old nurse. She trudged up from the woods carrying a bunch of golden broom sedge in her sweatered arms. We met her in the open space between kitchen and cabin. Although thirty-three years had passed, she stood smiling before us, as familiar as the morning sun.

The decades fell away. We were nurse and child again.

Mother said, "Whatchu doin', Lucy?"

"Hey, Miz Lila," said the thin brown woman, a smile bursting upon her face, her cheeks dancing up and down in the dear old way. Then, "Hey, Grace," her voice suddenly gruff.

I wanted to touch Lucy, go into her arms, but it was unthinkable with Mother there. *I'll come alone next time.* "You know me!" I said, pleased and surprised, glad she had not called me "Miss Grace."

"Course I know you," said Lucy. "You my baby! I raised you from a baby." Her voice shrill and husky at the same time, she was a thin slip of a woman, now old and bundled in colorless rags, just as she'd always been. Layers of gray sweaters covered a faded cotton dress over a dingy under-shirt visible at the throat; a nondescript, wrinkled scarf wrapped her head. On her feet she wore ragged shoes. The pitiful product of "our southern way of life," after eighty years of groveling in the white world this woman owned nothing but cast-off clothes and a bundle of dried brown grass.

"What are you doing with that?" asked Mother, pointing to the broom sedge.

"I got to build a fire," said Lucy as she walked over to the primitive wash pot and spread the wispy stuff around it. "Got to wash tomorrow."

While I save my back with an electric washing machine, my aged nurse breaks hers using a centuries-old laundry method.

"You better be careful with fire," said Mother. "You could burn up something."

"I ain't gonna burn up nothin'. Hit's ca'm. Wind ain't blowin'."

Mother laughed. "Ca'm! You mean calm."

Lord have mercy, I said to myself. *Nothing has changed here in a hundred years!*

"Wind ain't blowin'," repeated Lucy, pleats between her strange dark eyes. A look of inferiority settled over the ancient face, but only for a moment. Looking at me, Lucy the indomitable bounced back. Her old eyes sparkled, brown cheeks danced. "You come to see me, honey. I nussed you when you was a baby. You didn't know nothin' when I started nussin' you."

A warm glow crept through my heart and spread into a smile on my face. "Here, Lucy, I brought you a dress and some shoes," said Mother, thrusting a Rich's bag out to the mulatto.

"Thank you, Miz Lila."

"Well," I said. "Let's go inside and sit down."

"Ah, we haven't got time."

I spoke up. "Yes, we have. I want to go inside Lucy's house and sit down for a while." *I want to build an altar there.*

"Sure you do, honey," my nurse agreed. "Come on in Lucy's house." She was already up the rickety steps, straightening the crude chairs, opening the front door, and creating a refreshing breezeway through the ancient slave cabin.

Mother looked at the steps and hesitated. She whispered, "I can't go up them steps. I might fall and break a hip or a shoulder."

"No, you won't. I'll help you." Grabbing my mother's arm, I guided her up the ramshackle incline.

Warm spring wind swept through the old slave hut, caressed black and white alike, caring nothing for color of skin but arousing old memories, making new ones. I sat down in a cushionless, almost bottomless straight chair and looked around the room. Lucy sat also. Mother stood.

"This is where Aunt Lou died," I whispered, remembering my shame as I, a child of privilege, dressed in ruffles and lace, beheld the poverty and plight of an entire civilization.

"Yes, this were Aunt Lou's house. Mr. Tom give it to me as long as I live." Satisfaction crept over the thin and withered brown face.

"Well, I'm glad he did. He should have fixed it up, though, before he died."

"Shoot, Mr. Tom didn' fix up nothin'."

"Willie and Cleophas could fix up this place. They sure ought to fix them steps. It's a wonder you don't fall and break your hip." Then turning to me, Mother whispered, "They're sorry. They don't do nothin'."

I was embarrassed. Lucy couldn't help hearing this condemnation of her sons. Although it might be true, I cringed, ashamed that my mother would say so right in front of the other mother.

Lucy pretended she didn't hear, having long ago accustomed herself to white folks' contempt and her sons' indolence. She was too elated today to concern herself, and anyway she'd learned long ago that there's no use fretting over things you can't change. Instead here was something to be happy about: Miz Lila and Grace had come to see her.

She directed her delight toward me. "You come to see me, honey! You didn't know nothing when I started nussin' you." And the brown old wrinkled face smiled again, the wizened head proudly tilted sideways. Her arms folded across her chest; she held her back straight; her legs crossed at the knee.

"Thank God I came. It's so good to be here."

"Ah, you didn't nurse her much. It was Brother you nursed," said Mother, frowning.

"How's Li'l Brother? I wish I could see him."

"Ah, he's got four little children to work for. He's worked to death."

"Lucy," I said. "What is your address? I want to send you an Easter card."

"I don't know," Lucy said. She got up and ambled over to an ancient wardrobe, unlocked it, and took out a long white envelope. "Here 'tis. Here my address. This here a letta' from Evalena."

"Where does Evalena live?"

"She live in At-lana," Lucy said with pride in the granddaughter she'd raised. "She work there. They sure do like her work. They like my baby in At-lana."

"That's where I live. What's her address?"

"I don' know," said Lucy shaking her tied-up head.

"What's her name? Her married name?"

"Miz Gilbert. Miz Jim Gilbert. Ain't her address on that there enverope?" she said, pointing, her voice rising, the pleats deepening between the eyes.

Mother laughed and dropped into a straight-backed chair. "Envelope, Lucy."

Lucy laughed too. "I cain't say hit. I called up Evalena last night, up Miz Price's, called 'lect, or whatsomever you call it."

"Collect," said Mother.

"L-lect, anyhow Evalena s'pose to pay for hit. And Miz Price, she make me pay her a dollar."

"She did?" I said with outrage.

"Yeah, sure did. She say I owe her a dollar; 'clare fo' God, she did."

"She ought to be ashamed of herself," I said.

"Sure had," said Mother.

Opening my purse, I wrote down Evalena's address and telephone number. I found a dollar and gave it to Lucy. I'd given her some oranges, fresh from Florida, and I wished I'd brought something more to give her. But I knew our visit was gift aplenty for the ancient one that day. I decided I would come back again and again with arms loaded to see my dear old friend and learn from her.

"How old are you, Lucy?" I asked, suddenly wanting to know everything about her.

"I don't know," she said, tilting her head as though to say, "You know very well I've never known my age."

"She don't know how old she is," said Mother disdainfully.

"How much schooling did you get?"

"Pa didn't send me to school much. Us had to work when us was li'l, work in the fiel's." Her face relaxed, her brows fell into place.

I was thinking perhaps her father had been born in slavery days, and hoping to pinpoint him in history, asked, "Was your father a slave?" And I saw immediately I had offended my little nurse.

"Naw, 'course Pa won't no slave! Pa was *free.*" She emphasized the word and knit her brows.

"We better go," said my mother.

This time I heeded her admonition, for we had other people to see before sundown. We walked down the rickety steps, I holding Mother's arm, Lucy following, the oldest but most spry. It was then I saw that a piece of wood had fallen from the door of the little black stove in the ancient kitchen house, where Lucy had been cooking a pot of brown beans. A ball of flame upon the worn linoleum had already burned a black patch about the size of a man's hand among the holes and debris.

"Lucy!" I cried. "Your kitchen's on fire!"

She scurried up the stone step and into her cooking room, picked up a dingy rag, and as deftly as a magician, lifted the torch and threw it, flaming, into her stove.

"Lord-a-mercy. You gonna burn up something!" said Mother.

Lucy seized a pitcher of water and poured it over the scorched place on the floor, leaving an acrid odor in our nostrils.

Lucy followed us to the car begging, "Y'all come back to see Lucy, and bring me somethin'."

Mother climbed into the Oldsmobile, and I buckled her seat belt. "I don't know when I'll be back," she replied, her voice filled with woe. "Gainer's in bad shape. He's getting old and feeble. Has to depend on somebody to drive him around."

"I'm coming back in May," I said. "Tom is planning to come to Sandersville to play in a golf tournament. Do you know where Nannie Lee lives? I want to see her."

"Sure," said Lucy.

So we drove away toward the Greek Revival cottage, while the dear old soul stood and watched until our powder blue car was out of sight.

"You didn't have to give her that dollar," said Mother, irritably. "Lucy's got money. Amos says she's got plenty saved up in the bank. He's a cashier there, and he knows. Says she's got a thousand dollars."

"Well, good. They'll need that to bury her."

We reached my childhood home. The stained-glass-highlighted front door still opened into a wide hall. In our old classroom Uncle Herbert languished alone in his rocking chair in the corner, as he had since suffering a stroke five years before. The bachelor was smoking a cigarette and listening to a baseball game on radio.

Smiling weakly, he said, "Hello," as though he saw us every day. But I'd not seen him since Grandma's funeral two years before. His apathy and unshaven face filled the house with gloom. When Herbert's father died, leaving his mother with six young children, the twenty-two-year-old vowed he'd never marry. He'd stay home to take care of his mother. Possibly because of that decision, at thirty-four he had a nervous breakdown, from which he never fully recovered.

The two colonial windows were so soiled you could hardly see through them. While Mother dropped into a chair to chat, I looked around the house. Grandma Mary's clothes still hung in the closet nearby, and old letters, papers, and pictures moldered in Grandma's ancient trunk.

"When have you heard from Lena? George? Cecil?" Mother said.

"We've brought you some oranges, a cake, and some of my homemade vegetable soup," I interjected.

"Put them in the kitchen," he said softly.

I hastened down the wide hall, peeping into each room. Everything was different and yet somehow the same. The wood-paneled walls and tall ceilings were the same. But the furniture was Grandma's and Uncle Herbert's, antique and reminiscent of Rachel.

Letting the screen door slam, I stepped into the backyard and stopped to stare.

Everything was gone!

As though Sherman's army had swooped down and ravaged the area again, only a stump emerged where the pecan tree had once towered, spreading its branches to shade Aunt Lou's washtubs. The tubs were nowhere in sight. Neither was the stand. The walls of the well had been torn down, the wellhead boarded over. All the fences had disappeared. The weather-beaten barn, Abe's cabin, The Closet, our vegetable garden, the hens' nests, chicken houses, smokehouse, pomegranate bush, walnut trees, cornfield—all had vanished. Not even a trace of the silver-sided buildings remained, except in my memory.

Jimsonweed, briar bushes, and crabgrass crept close to the rotting doorsteps. But behind the ruins of the backyard rose tall green pine forests, and now, for the first time in my life, I saw a beauty in my homeland

I'd never seen before. And I thought again of trying to reclaim this old homeplace.

Showers fell as Mother and I cruised through Covington on our way back to Atlanta on April 3. In Memphis, Tennessee, garbage workers were out on strike. I turned on the car radio and heard a man in New York say, "Martin Luther King Jr. will go to Memphis tomorrow to lead a march."

"He's gonna get killed if he doesn't watch out." Mother said.

"I hope not! Mother, there's something I want to tell you," I said as we drove through the rain-splashed streets of Conyers. My heart began to thump. "I'm glad you taught me at home when I was little. If I'd gone to school with other children, I never would have seen the plight of people like Lucy and Aunt Lou. I'd never have understood their heartbreak—the injustices heaped upon black people. That is why we let our church members crucify us at Tattnall. We thought it was time white Christians took a stand for human rights."

For a moment I thought Mother was going to mouth one of her warnings. But instead her face relaxed.

"Mother, you always taught me to be like Christ. And I just couldn't wait any longer to do the thing you taught me to do."

Her face became radiant as she listened.

"You know our witness at Tattnall made news around the world. We've had letters and newspaper clippings from every major city in this country. I'm writing a book about it. Tom's writing a book."

There was a moment of silence while I negotiated through gathering traffic. When she finally spoke, Mother's voice was wistful. "Oh, I always wanted to write a book. But I didn't have enough education."

"I will write it for you, Mother. And I want to thank you, too, for teaching me about Abou ben Adhem. Abou and his 'book of gold' have inspired me all my life to try to love others."

"Spend the night with us," she said as we came closer to Decatur. "Tom won't come home until tomorrow, will he?"

"No."

"Please spend the night with us," she pleaded. She was still smiling, her voice filled with love and tenderness.

I longed to sleep in my own bed, but I could not refuse Mother's child-like plea. I took both our suitcases into my parents' little home.

But it was not to be the end of my struggle to be free.

38 We Shall Overcome

Azaleas—snow white, blood red, and baby-skin pink—draped around a thousand emerald green lawns as I drove northwest from Decatur to Sandy Springs the next day. White dogwood blossoms laced the delicate new green of wooded yards of rich and poor alike. Orange, red, and yellow tulips stood in yards and gardens like little girls arrayed in new dresses and hats on Easter Sunday morning.

But in the midst of the splendor of April in Atlanta in 1968 came news of savagery in Memphis. The eyes of the world focused on us as white racism and black sacrifice met. While the nation hung its head in sorrow and shame, the American dream of liberty and justice for all hung on a hair-thin thread.

On this cloudy Thursday afternoon, thundershowers were forecast. Arriving home, I carried my suitcase inside, opened the sliding glass door and stepped onto warm tiles on our apartment's screened porch to sniff the scents of spring. Geraniums, crimson and profuse, hung in baskets. My "Grace's roses," they were my cheerful substitute for the ones I'd planted and watered and walked away from at Manchester, Macon, and Moore's Mill Road.

I dialed Evalena's number, which I had copied in Lucy's hut.

"Hello," a voice answered from the Grant Park area.

"Is this Evalena from Riddleville?"

"Yes." She hesitated. "Who's this?"

"This is Grace Bryan."

"Why, Miss Grace," said the husky voice. "I don' know when I ever seen you."

"It's been a long time."

"It's been a *long* time."

"Evalena, just call me Grace. You don't have to say Miss Grace. I went to see your grandmother yesterday."

"You did?"

"Yes, I did, and I took Mother. We had a nice visit with Lucy. I was so happy to see her again."

"I know she was glad to see you."

"Yes. But Evalena, I'm worried about Lucy living in that little hut alone. Did you know there are holes in her kitchen floor? And not a single chair has a cushion?"

"Yeah, I know," she said sadly. "I'm going to get her in September, bring her to see me. I'll call you when she comes."

After the call, I closed my eyes for a moment. Headachy and weary from the journey, I rested and read, losing track of time.

Suddenly thunder cracked. My tiny gold wristwatch showed five-thirty. I'd planned to work the chrysanthemums along the garden wall and clean the rooms. But the day was nearly gone, a storm brewing. I jumped up, stuck my feet in brown sandals, grabbed the garbage pail, hurried down the back steps.

Ominous sky draped above, purple and heavy. Again thunder split the silence and rumbled. A west wind rose, tossing green oak branches about. Chinese wind chimes danced, and a big drop of rain wet my graying head.

Back in the living room, I turned on our white portable television to hear the six o'clock news. Tornado warnings were issued for the whole Southeast; I feared for Tom, who this moment was jetting from New York. I brought my bowl of oyster stew to the coffee table and sat down for the Huntley-Brinkley newscast. They repeated that Dr. Martin Luther King Jr. had announced he would defy a court order and lead another mass march in Memphis on Monday in support of striking garbage workers; I recollected Mother's fears voiced yesterday.

Near the end of the newscast, another picture of the civil rights leader flashed on the screen and Chet Huntley spoke: "Martin Luther King has been shot in Memphis as he stood on a motel balcony. He's been rushed to a hospital. A white man was seen dropping a gun and fleeing."

"Oh, no!" I said aloud to Huntley's picture, both hands clasping my head. "Oh no!" Falling face down onto the sofa, I prayed that Dr. King would survive for the sake of his wife and children, and for his people and my people. If he died, the blacks' rebellion and revenge would become open and violent. Rain galloped on the roof. Thunder rolled and lightning flashed outside my sheer-curtained windows. I prayed that Tom's plane would get down safely.

Then I thought of Coretta King, whose home I knew was in that other Atlanta, on Sunset Avenue, in the central city that almost encircled the business district. Has she heard the horrendous news the same way I had—by way of television? Had she been eating dinner when she heard? And her children, what will she say to them? I wished that I might get in the car, drive to her home, put my arm around her shoulders, attempt to comfort her.

But she lives so many miles away. The night is dark, the storm is raging, and the streets are turning to rivers. The city is dangerous for a woman alone at night. Tom is expected home within an hour. And anyway, she doesn't know me. I suspect that a white face she doesn't recognize is the last thing she wants to see at this moment. Could I blame her?

Can I blame black people if they hate all whites?

I had to talk to someone. Walter and Anna Mary! Leaping over to the TV, turning the sound down but leaving the picture on, I dialed the McCalls'.

"Walter, this is Grace Holmes."

"Yes, Grace, how are you?" His Boston-trained voice was crisp and crackling.

"I'm upset!"

"Upset?"

He doesn't know! "Have you heard the news?"

"What news?"

"Dr. King's been shot in Memphis."

"Oh, my God!"

"I heard it on television."

"I'll go turn mine on," he said as though he couldn't go fast enough.

"He's been taken to a hospital," I said quickly. "I don't know what his condition is. And Walter," I said, trying to speak for millions of members of my race, aching to do the impossible—to right the wrongs of three hundred years—and trying not to detain him too long, "Walter, I'm so sorry! Let us pray that his wound is not mortal."

But even as I hung up the phone, I remembered the murder of John

Kennedy and the days of our mourning for him. Turning up the sound, I heard a newsman repeating, "Dr. Martin Luther King has been shot while standing on a balcony. He was preparing to leave his motel room for a meeting. He had just spotted his song leader below, leaned over the railing, and asked him to sing 'Precious Lord, Take My Hand.'"

My heart was stabbed afresh.

Hurrying to get the kitchen cleaned up before Tom got home. I cantered back and forth from living room to sink, eager not to miss further developments, turning the sound up, turning it down, always leaving the picture on, always praying. The dishes finished, I lay upon the sofa again, eyes on the black-and-white screen. Thunder boomed, lightning streaked, and rain splashed onto paved driveways, flowed in rivulets toward the drains.

Atlanta Mayor Ivan Allen heard the news at his home not far from us on Northside Drive and sped with a police escort to the home of Mrs. King. He and his wife accompanied her to Hartsfield Airport to catch a plane to Memphis, to the side of her stricken husband. But at the moment of departure the mayor learned that Dr. King had died. Ivan Allen broke the news to Coretta King in the ladies' lounge.

Meanwhile, Tom's plane landed. He strode through the crowded terminal, unaware of the drama unfolding nearby, and reached home at 8:30. I hurried out to his car in the downpour carrying his big black umbrella.

"Have you heard the news?"

"Yes," he said heavily. "I heard it on the radio after I drove away from the airport."

"Isn't it terrible? I'm afraid for the country."

The next morning I awoke at first light, the memory of the murder piercing me. I put on coffee and opened curtains to a gray dawn. The valley below was clothed with sharp and delicate new greens, while on the hill, azaleas bloomed blood red beneath tall pines. I remembered that today was Friday, one week before our remembrance of the day Christ died. Abraham Lincoln, I recalled, was also killed in April, on Good Friday.

While the coffee perked I went to the front door and picked up the *Atlanta Constitution*, straining to swallow all the big, black headlines in one giant gulp: *Dr. King Shot, Dies in Memphis. Curfew On, 4,000 Guards Called.* And smaller headlines: *Rifle Found, Hunt for Killer Pressed. Presi-*

dent Expresses U. S. Shock: Johnson Tells Sorrow in Call to Mrs. King. Johnson Delays His Trip to Honolulu Until Today.

When Tom awoke he read the headlines, too, and said, "I'm going to see Dr. King's mother and father."

He had met the senior King at a gathering of black and white ministers, where the respected preacher put a fatherly arm around my husband, saying, "I've been praying for you lately."

"I'm going with you," I said, turning on the television.

We stood and listened to summaries of King's life and to the magnificent oratory of this twentieth-century Moses as his speeches were played and replayed. His eloquent voice and soul-stirring words, the prayers, marches, and jail sentences that characterized the life of the hero were intermingled with pictures taken the night of his assassination. Angry blacks dashed through dark streets, their faces illuminated by flaring fires, underscored by siren wailing; police shooting; bricks, rocks, and bottles crashing through glass store fronts in Washington, Chicago, Tallahassee, Detroit, Memphis, and Itta Bena, Mississippi. Tapes of the riots were run and rerun.

By turn, we were thrilled, grieved, horrified; at once transfixed and galvanized to action. We tried to dress and eat All-Bran and bananas without missing a single word, sound, or sight. Then they showed a scene from Atlanta, and I was proud of my adopted city and our mayor. White-haired and handsome, Ivan Allen walked with sorrowing Coretta King from the Atlanta airport after the death message had been delivered. A drizzle of rain fell, and the somber-faced mayor held an umbrella over her hatted head.

"Hurry, hurry!" said Tom. "Get dressed if you're going with me."

I dressed in black. I wanted to show Aunt Lou's children that we cared, that we mourned with those who mourned. My mind vaulted to Riddleville, to Lucy in her shack. It leapfrogged across the state to Manchester, Fannie and Jim on Dunn Row; to College Park and Leila in her dim basement rooms underneath a florist shop; to Baker's Ferry Road in that other Atlanta, where the McCalls grieved; to Grant Park and Evalena. And to the thousands across the land who'd lost their leader. *There must be white faces mourning among the black. One of them will be mine.*

We drove south on rain-soaked Blackland Road between green manicured lawns edged by lilacs, tulips, daffodils, and shaded by giant oaks, pines, magnolias. Like lavender tears cascading down faces of dark-skinned women, wisteria trailed the trunks of tall trees among splashes of pink and white dogwood, reminding me why the month of my birth— and my father's—was my favorite. T. S. Eliot wrote, "April is the cruellest month." *But now we must do what we can to turn King's sacrifice into a symphony.*

Meanwhile, the widow of the martyred King flew north through rain-drops and sun-splashed clouds toward Tennessee. Granddaughter of slaves, Mrs. King rode in the private plane of Senator Robert F. Kennedy of Massachusetts.

Dogwoods flowered in the yards of Daddy King's spacious home. Park-ing the car as quietly as we could, we got out and closed the doors gently, tiptoed up the paved walk, and rang the doorbell reverently. A solemn, brown-faced woman let the three white preachers and me into a large living room. Did she think we strangers had come out of curiosity and superiority? I hoped she would understand that we came purely out of love and shame and mutual sorrow, yet I feared they mistrusted our mo-tives, because our skin was not the color of theirs.

I was introduced to the calm, dry-eyed mother of the martyred civil rights leader. She had no words for me as I gripped her hand and said, "I'm so sorry."

The more emotional father was not as calm. Tom reached his upstairs room before the rest of us did. The heavy-set Daddy King lay on his bed, wearing a dark red robe and covered with a red bedspread. On the floor was a crimson rug. Ringed around his double bed stood four African American preachers, silent and funereal in somber black suits and pol-ished black shoes.

When Dr. King saw Tom, he stretched both beefy arms wide and cried, "Tom, they've killed my boy!" Tears gushed down his round bronze face.

Tom knelt beside his bed. Their arms went around each other's shoul-ders. Their tears mingled.

A warm sun rose over gray-and-green woods outside our apartment on Sunday, April 7. When I went out to the terrace after setting coffee to perk, a sliver of pale pink cloud floated in the eastern sky. Today we would worship and mourn with our friends at Providence.

As we left the apartment, I paused at the door. My mind raced ahead to Larkin Street, pictured our two white faces in a sanctuary of grieving blacks and browns. Would they be angry at the sight of whites, any whites? Would there be some there who wouldn't remember us? Some who didn't know we are their friends? The hysteria that held the country plucked at me as well. No one knew what would happen next, when a bomb might explode, a church blow up, a white shoot a black, a black a white.

But as soon as we reached the red-brick church, I knew my fears were groundless. We were greeted by friendly smiles and warm handshakes and green palm branches. I'd forgotten this was Palm Sunday.

Tears pricked my eyelids. *They remember us. They love; they forgive.* I was further encouraged when I saw Bob Herndon, retired army chaplain, and Dr. Harmon Moore, president of the Atlanta Christian Council. Walter McCall invited the three white preachers to sit on the platform with him.

I sensed in the congregation a sorrow that ran as deep as a mountain gorge, a mourning that would have to wait. Martin Luther King's people had already recovered from the initial shock and outrage of having another one of their sons killed, this time their most illustrious. Their mood had shifted from sorrow to pride and preparation. Thousands would converge upon the city on Tuesday, April 9, for burial of the fallen hero.

Walter referred to him often in the opening remarks of his sermon as "my King." In a voice thick with emotion he rebuked the nameless black youths who hurled bricks through windows of white-owned stores along Hunter Street on Friday night. "My King preached nonviolence. He would have been disheartened to have his followers resort to violence. Please, please, channel your emotions into efforts to help feed the hungry and house the stranger who will be in our midst for the funeral."

The service tranquilized my fears. Since we'd come thus far without violent eruptions in Atlanta, I became more confident that the Dogwood City would come through this crisis well. I caught the spirit of the congregation, which had changed to one of quiet celebration. They seemed determined to spare no effort as the city prepared itself for the funeral.

That day, April 9, would be my forty-ninth birthday. Late the night before, Kathy and Edward drove down from Nashville. A 1964 graduate of

Mercer, Kathy taught at Stratford High School in Nashville while Edward was working on his master's at Vanderbilt. Weary, they merely nodded when I told them, "Tom and I have debated whether we should add our car to the overburdened roads tomorrow. Two hundred thousand are expected to converge upon Atlanta. There will be such a throng, we can get a better view if we watch it on television. And of course, with all the senators and singers, presidential candidates and Jacqueline Kennedy, and other mourners by the tens of thousands, we wouldn't even get near Ebenezer."

But at six the next morning, my heart raced as I read the *Atlanta Constitution.* Not since Sherman's army sacked our city had Atlanta witnessed such a thunderclap of history. I studied the horizon from our damp, warm terrace. The sun rose pale but hopeful behind bars of pink clouds. My black handbag was already packed with extra walking shoes, ready for the funeral march.

By eight o'clock bright sun was soaking up moisture from the grass. Rain clouds disappeared; the mercury climbed. I finished reading the paper. My mind was made up. "I'm going," I said to Tom. "I am going to the funeral. This is my birthday, and this is the way I choose to spend it."

"Okay," he said. "I'll go too."

"That's what we came for," said Kathy. "That's why they gave me the days off from teaching."

"We'll leave at ten o'clock," said Tom. "Let's ask Walter and Anna Mary to go with us." He delayed eating, only drinking his Sanka while he made calls. When plans were formulated he said, "We're going by Dorothy Davis's to pick up a box of sandwiches to deliver to Providence. Then we'll drive to Morehouse. Anna Mary wants to ride with us. Walter has already gone. He'll meet us at Morehouse."

"To Morehouse? But I want to go to Ebenezer and march with the crowd."

The phone rang in the kitchen. It was Brother. "Mother and Daddy are coming here to keep our children. We're going to the funeral."

"Bless their hearts," I said, thankful that even Mother and Pa-Pa supported our going. "Come by our apartment, park your car, and ride with us."

Tom and I, with Brother and his wife, Mary Anna, left our home carrying a box of ham sandwiches. At Walter's house, Anna Mary McCall crawled into our car, and we crawled through Northside Drive traffic while the temperature soared. Tom was right in his decision to go to Morehouse. It was impossible to join the march, to get through the congestion to the faded farm wagon on which King's body lay.

Finally, at one o'clock we found a place to park near the campus. From there our party joined the throngs climbing the hill in broiling sunshine. Mary Anna and Anna Mary, Kathy and I, Tom and Brother and Edward pushed through the multitude of mourners searching for seats.

Television newsmen and cameramen from all the networks sat on high wooden platforms. Young boys perched in tall green trees. History was being made, and here we were in the middle of it, surrounded by sweating, grieving African Americans. In wonder I noticed the great variety of hues. All of us, from ebony black to bone white, silent and somber, waited in smothering heat.

Suddenly I was seized by a moment of panic. Caught in the crush of surging, sweating, grieving humanity, one hundred thousand strong, I feared suffocation and black vengeance, feared that beneath those smooth countenances terrible anger and resentment lurked against any and every white face.

Yet there was no whisper of hostility.

Finally, the family with Dr. King's body and another hundred thousand mourners arrived on foot to jam the green quadrangle of Morehouse College.

"Do not crowd the family," the Reverend Ralph David Abernathy repeated and repeated over the microphone on the rostrum. "Is there a doctor here?" Scores of people were felled by the stifling heat and emotion-charged event.

After Mahalia Jackson sang the soulful "Precious Lord, Take My Hand," Dr. Benjamin Mays, president emeritus of Morehouse College, a sharecropper's son who held forty honorary degrees, a man who had taught and guided M. L. King Jr., rose to read the eulogy.

Then 250,000 people swayed, arms crossed, hands clasped, and sang. Standing between Mary Anna, my sister-in-law, and Anna Mary, my sister in Christ, I held one black and one white hand and added my voice to those of half a million mourners:

> We shall overcome, we shall overcome,
> We shall overcome some day . . .
> O, deep in my heart, I do believe:
> We shall overcome some day.

39 *My Heart Can't Express*

A month and a day after King's funeral, I drove Mother and Pa-Pa to Aunt Mattie's house in Sandersville. After supper, Pa-Pa went to speak at a nearby church about Baptist Village. While Mother and her sister were doing dishes, I slipped out of the white frame Victorian and drove the ten miles to Lucy's. This was one trip I was determined to make alone to speak freely with my old nurse. And to find Nannie Lee, tell her a thing I couldn't in Mother's presence.

Rosy afterglow of sunset descended over verdant countryside when I parked in front of the weather-beaten hut. Lucy Riddle perched alone on her front porch in a hand-hewn chair with a crooked back. Though the air was warm and soft, she was wrapped as usual in old sweaters, and on her head was a black-and-white-striped, red-billed baseball cap. I embraced her slim shoulders, asking, "What are you doing here all alone?"

Wrinkling her mulatto face, she drew her mobile brows into a point above her patrician nose as though to say she was disappointed that I should have to ask. "I's waitin' for you," she said. Then her brows slipped back into place, leaving her face at rest. She stared off into the furry pines across the road.

I sat in the broken chair beside her. "How did you know I was coming?"

The brows quickly formed a "V" again, her voice rose in irritation. "You said you was comin' back in May."

I hugged my old nurse a second time. I had forgotten. "So I did," I said, laughing. "So I did. Lucy, have you sat here every day in May looking for me?"

Lucy's laughter was low and loving. "Sure I has; ever' day in May, I sit here and look for your car to come down the road. I raised you from a baby. You didn' know nothin' when I start' nussin' you. Miz Lila loved for me to nuss you." She raised her eyebrows high above the strange, dark eyes.

I agreed with her, letting her have the solace she deserved. But I yearned to see her neatly, tastefully dressed. The baseball cap looked ridiculous. Suddenly I realized I'd never seen her hair. "May I?" I said as I removed the cap gently. "Lucy, why do you always keep your head covered?"

Quick as a breeze blowing, she grabbed the beanie with both hands and mashed it back upon her fuzzy head. The poor old woman was nearly bald. "Ah, I ain't got no hair. I let that Dickson girl work with my hair when she were pregnant. Now I ain't got none."

I knew it would do no good to try to explain away this superstition, so I said, "Lucy, I've talked with Evalena. She told me where she lives in Atlanta, and I'm going to see you when you come up there to visit her."

"Sure 'nough?" said my little old brown nurse, smiling. "They sure do like my baby in At-lana! She work at the bak'ry. They like Evalena." Her brows knit again under the black-and-red baseball cap. Her eyes fixed on the country field lying quiet and untended across the paved road before her cabin. "I'm going to At-lana to see my baby. They'll come afta' me when I git ready."

It was getting late, and I still had to find Aunt Lou's daughter. "Lucy, do you know where Nannie Lee lives?"

"Sure, she live on Mr. Pate place. She work for Mr. Pate, keep his boy. He sickly, his wife work."

"Where is Mr. Pate's place?"

"Hit on the Bartow Road."

"I want to see her. Will you go with me, show me the way?"

"Yes, I'll go! Lemme lock the house." She jumped out of the chair, locked and bolted the doors, dropped the key into her apron pocket.

I glanced at her chair. She who was eighty-six and deserved a few comforts in her old age had been sitting on a mere broken slat with a hard, straight back. *These last ten days she has waited here and watched for me. I will bring her some cushions next time.*

How sweet she is! How I love her! I helped her into the front seat and fastened the belt around her as though she were my aged mother. Together we drove through the main street of our hometown. I wondered why on earth I had stayed away so long. I kept glancing at her happy face, her nubby brown hands resting in her lap.

As the little gray cabin of Nannie Lee Daniel came into view, my pulse raced. It looked exactly as scores of others had always looked. Perched beside dusty red roads, just across open ditches, they dotted the Georgia countryside. The only visible sign of change in Nannie Lee's house in this fast-changing, affluent society was a television antenna rising above the shingled roof.

In contrast to Lucy's and scores of others, Nannie Lee's dwelling was in good repair. The hard-packed dirt was swept clean. Purple phlox and red verbena bloomed in tubs near the tidy doorstep.

A ferocious German police dog greeted us. Afraid to open the car door, I tapped the horn. The tall, strong figure of our former servant appeared in the open doorway, her dark eyes squinting curiously. Then she recognized Lucy and walked down the wood steps to Lucy's side of the car, bent her angular body to peer inside.

"You don't know who this is," I said. "Do you?"

"I know this Miz Lucy," she said, her voice raspy and reminiscent of her late mother's.

"And this is Grace, Grace Bryan. I've come to see you. And if you'll calm your dog, we'll come in and visit."

Her black face broke into a wide smile, showing white teeth. "Lawd, Grace, I didn't know you. It been so long."

"Yes," I said, getting out of the car and going around to her. We embraced. "It's been too long, thirty years at least. But I've been thinking about you a lot lately and wanting to look you up. I'm so glad to see you! I didn't know where you lived, or even if you still lived. But Lucy was good enough to help me."

"I'm glad to see you. How's Miz Lila and Mr. Gainer and Li'l Brother?"

"Oh, they're fine," I said, opening Lucy's door and unfastening her seat belt. "But I didn't come here to talk about them. I came to tell you something." Then I fell to wondering how to communicate to this woman whom I'd once known as a servant but had never known as a person. This daughter of Africa, of Aunt Lou, whose wails I'd heard thirty-seven years ago and remembered ever since, how best to tell her that it was she, her mother, and her children on that long-ago August afternoon who had shaped the course of my life? Can she comprehend the reasons and the consequences? And have I actually helped to change the climate for her people?

I faced her and blurted, "Nannie Lee, I came to tell you that I love you. Even when I was a little girl, and you and Aunt Lou worked for us, I loved you and your mother. I was there at your house the day she died, and I saw things. . . ." Here I faltered, for I didn't want to embarrass her by revealing just how stricken I'd been at the sight of their poverty and humiliation. "I saw things that saddened me, and I determined that when I grew up I was going to do something to make the world a better place for you and your children."

She tilted her head sideways and wrinkled her dark face with emotion deeper than she could find words for. "Grace," she said, "you're sweet, and I love you too. But why didn't you bring me something?" Then she laughed and, bending over, she slapped her hands on her knees.

"Next time, I will. But let's go into the house and sit for a while."

Most Negro country cabins had been built as cheap and plain as henhouses. Nannie Lee's, owned by the white man for whom she worked, was no exception. Of unpainted wood, it had three rooms. An open brick fireplace joined the two bedrooms and was the only means of heat. Across the back was a kitchen. Walls were finished in natural, narrow wood paneling. There were two small windows in each room covered by skimpy curtains. Water had to be drawn from the well behind the structure near the back door, and a little way behind the well was a privy. However, thanks to Franklin Delano Roosevelt, Aunt Lou's daughter had electric lights.

Nannie Lee led us into a bedroom that also served as a sitting room. There were two double iron beds against the wall, three chairs grouped around the fireplace, and a green linoleum rug on the floor. All was clean and neat, and the three of us huddled close together in the plain, uncushioned chairs. Black, brown and white, we were like the feathers of a towhee. But in the reunion of mind and spirit, color was forgotten. We were merely three women glad to be together.

"Nannie Lee, we've so much to talk about. It's been so long. I'm forty-nine now. How old are you?"

"I'm sixty-two."

"It's been thirty-three years."

"It been a lo-ong time."

"Tell me about your children. Did they grow up all right? How are they getting on?"

Nannie Lee's wide mouth broke into a broad smile, showing her pearly teeth. She laughed aloud and reached for a large frame of pictures hung high above her mantelpiece. Pointing with her dark finger to the images, she said, "This here Tommy, this Ev'lyn, this my baby, Lewis." Somebody had helped them, or they'd helped themselves, got up out of the dusty ditches and cotton fields, left the littered yards. Most wore the academic caps and gowns of graduation from high school and college instead of the rags I'd carried around in my memory.

I squirmed with guilt that I'd done so little to keep my vow; I wished I had somehow helped Nannie Lee's children get through school. Waiting until she hung her treasure back on the wall, I whispered, "I went to Martin Luther King's funeral."

"You did?" chorused Lou's daughter and Lucy.

"Yes. There were 250,000 people there. Half a million came to Atlanta from all over the country, ministers and movie stars, Jacqueline Kennedy and Bobby and Ethel, and the vice president of the United States."

"Dr. King were a fine man," said Nannie Lee.

"It was terrible that they killed him," I said.

"Sure were," said Lucy.

"We all held hands and sang together 'We Shall Overcome.' And we had his father as a guest in our home for dinner."

"Sure 'nough?" said Nannie Lee.

"Yes, we certainly did. Dr. Martin Luther King Sr. ate dinner at our house. Tom grilled steak for him and I served him strawberry shortcake. We invited his wife, but she did not come. Walter and Anna Mary McCall brought Daddy King to our home."

"That were nice!" said Lucy.

"They kilt Martin Luther King just like they kilt Li'l Cha'ly," said Nannie Lee without rancor.

Then I shared with them about Tattnall, finishing, "Tom and I told that crowd, if blacks couldn't go to their church, we wouldn't go there either. For we believe that God's house should be a place of prayer for all people."

"Sure is," agreed Nannie Lee and Lucy. "Sure is." Brown face and black face nodded in assent. A spirit of comradeship prevailed among my mother's old servants and me.

"Once Miss Lila was very sick," said Nannie Lee. "She laid on her bed with pneumonia and high fever. Me and Miss Lucy was in the kitchen. An' I said to Miss Lucy: 'White peoples don't love color peoples.' And

Grace, she were a li'l girl then, and she went an' tol' Miss Lila I say white peoples don't love color peoples. And Miss Lila went to cryin'. And she say, 'Nannie Lee, I love you. I do love you.'"

"Sure did," chorused the women. It was a priceless moment, one I'd waited nearly half a century for.

Then I told them how Tom had been preaching in African American churches in Atlanta, how they loved him.

"Lawd, Grace, de Lawd's got His hand on you!" said Nannie Lee.

I hadn't noticed the daylight fading. But my old nurse, hunched over in her straight chair, sweater-clad elbows on bony knees, began to nudge me into heading back toward Sandersville. "I don't want you out afta dark, baby," she said, her voice gentle, loving. "We better leave."

She was right. But I suspected her solicitations were motivated a bit by envy. The suspicions were confirmed when we parted a few minutes later in front of her hut. The pines were furry black against a dusky sky. "Just remember," she said, "I belonged to you before Nannie Lee."

Yes, I had hurt my old nurse's feelings. I'd told Nannie Lee I loved her, but had not told Lucy. "Oh yes," I said, embracing her slim shoulders, "Of course you did, my dear. I love you, and I always have."

"I raised you from a baby. You didn' know nothin' when I started nussin' you."

"That's right, darling," I said, taking pleasure in her warmth toward me. "You raised me from a baby. You belonged to me first. I love you, and I'm coming back to see you again and again."

The next morning I told Mother about the visit. Her response surprised me. "Why didn't you take me? I want to see Nannie Lee."

"I'll take you now," I said as we packed our face powders and creams, gowns and robes. We kissed Mother's sister goodbye while sparrows chirped and the rising sun turned the old water oaks to shimmering mounds of green.

Fifteen minutes later, wearing a cotton dress, an apron, and sensible black shoes, Nannie Lee stood beside our parked car in Mr. Pate's driveway. Her white teeth gleamed as her bronze face broke into a smile. "Why, Miss Lila, I so glad to see you. How Mistah Gainuh, Li'l Brother?"

"Gainer ain't no count, cain't hardly walk, cain't drive. He's got Parkinson's, has to use a walker. But he just will keep going, speaking to the churches about Baptist Village. He shows the film, raises money for the retirement home. Guess that's where we'll end up."

I would get to see Lucy only three more times. In September 1968, while she was visiting Evalena, I brought her home one day, served her lunch at my table, then drove her to Decatur to visit Mother and Pa-Pa.

Tom and I went back to the village at Thanksgiving, carried baskets of fruit and nuts to Lucy and Nannie Lee. Tom prayed with each of them. As soon as he saw Lucy's hut had no heat, Thomas Holmes first gathered sticks and logs from her yard and, kneeling on the sunken brick hearth, built a warm fire for Lucy.

In December Lucy suffered a stroke. Tom and I went to visit her in the Sandersville Hospital. Tubes snaked from a hissing machine into her nose and twisted, paralyzed mouth. Yet my heart warmed when I saw her dark skin scrubbed clean and her shriveled body wrapped in a white hospital gown and bedspread. She reminded me of a crippled sparrow in the snow.

Eyes closed, Lucy frowned and pulled at her fuzzy hair.

Finding a linen towel, I wrapped it loosely, like a white halo, about her head. Her hand in mine, I said, "Lucy, do you know who this is?"

She opened her eyes. For the first time in half a century, I really looked into those eyes. They were neither black nor brown, but navy! Then I recalled what was often said in the village: her grandfather was white.

I could barely hear the reply that came with great effort. "Sho I know. Hit Grace. You ma baby. I nussed you. . . ."

Smiling, I turned to Tom. "She knows me!"

"An' dat Mr. Ho'mes behin' you."

"Lucy, we've driven all the way from Atlanta to see you because we love you."

A January ice storm prevented me from going to Lucy's funeral, so in March Nannie Lee went with me to put flowers on Aunt Lou's and Lucy's graves, each marked by a bit of colored glass. In the hush of the "colored" cemetery I heard again Aunt Lou singing about Jesus as she scrubbed, heard once more her cry for justice and mercy.

Between fund-raising trips to New York and Los Angeles, Clearwater and Cape Cod, Tom worked on his book, *Ashes for Breakfast*. The title came from Psalm 103:9, "For I have eaten ashes like bread, and mingled my drink with weeping." Coauthored by my brother, Gainer Bryan Jr., *Ashes* was published in May 1969 by Judson Press. Eugene Patterson, editor of the *Atlanta Constitution,* wrote the foreword:

> When Tom Holmes sat down to begin writing this book, he suddenly bent over his desk and wept. . . .
>
> He is not the kind of man who cries easily, nor is he one you would pick out of a Southern crowd as a martyr. To begin with, he is a very tall man, powerfully put together . . . friendly in the outgoing way of the neighborly Southerner—not a purse-lipped reformer, nor a hot-eyed zealot. And in him is the quiet strength and understanding of a faithful pastor who has known a quarter-century of ministry to other people's tears. . . .
>
> If he had been a weak man, these events would not have happened. Had he been faithless, there would be no story. Instead there would have been just another Southern Baptist Church moving along untroubled from Sunday to tranquil Sunday while the conscience of a congregation slept.
>
> But the Reverend Tom Holmes did have faith and strength to match the times.

An autograph party was scheduled at the Baptist Bookstore on the morning of the May 26. Rich's had offered to host it, but Tom thought it more fitting to let the Baptists have the honor. However, when we reached the Peachtree Street shop next to the Hyatt Regency, the manager was shaking like a pine needle in a summer storm. Over the stacks of orange and black books, he told Tom and Brother that the new pastor at Tattnall, a member of the John Birch Society, had telephoned the bookstore manager: "We're closing our account with you and advising other churches to do the same. I'm going to sue Tom Holmes, the Bookstore, the Sunday School Board, and the publisher. And I'm going to get *you* fired."

Undaunted, Tom and Brother sat at the table and picked up pens. Old friends arrived to buy *Ashes for Breakfast.* A hundred people came throughout the morning—former church members, cousins, new friends, old friends—among them Dr. Verdery and Walter McCall.

Threats from Tattnall's new pastor were reported in the *Atlanta Constitution.* UPI called Tom for comment. The day after Tom appeared on a television talk show, the pastor of Tattnall telephoned the station demanding equal time. He sent out letters and phone calls, breathing fire and smoke. After two printings totaling twelve thousand copies, *Ashes for Breakfast* was banned. Frantic friends called to ask where they could find the book.

It was hidden under counters in Baptist bookstores across the South. The New Orleans Store planned to display *Ashes for Breakfast* in their booth during the Southern Baptist Convention in early June. They also planned an autograph party. Both events were canceled without comment.

However, in the spring of 1970 Tom and I excitedly began to assemble our traveling wardrobes and passports for a speaking tour in the British Isles. Marshall, Morgan, and Scott of London brought out a paperback edition titled *Almost All Are Welcome*. Sam Oni's picture, snapped as he was being ushered down Tattnall's steps by a burly police-deacon, adorned the cover. But before we found our birth certificates, our London publisher called to say, "We regret, Mr. Holmes, that British churches are canceling your engagements. Word has come to them from Nashville that you are not a true representative of Southern Baptists."

The book was published in Germany in serial form by the magazine *Die Gemeinde*. And in November 1970, before it went out of print in 1971, *Ashes for Breakfast* won Author of the Year Award for nonfiction by the Dixie Council of Authors and Journalists. As late as the 1980s we still received requests for *Ashes* to be republished. Our efforts came to naught.

Meanwhile, I returned to visit Nannie Lee at least twice a year, taking presents of food and clothing. In Nannie Lee's birthday cards I also sent checks. I mailed boxes of gifts to her and her grandchildren for Christmas. When Nannie Lee's daughter lay dying of cancer, I fetched flowers and a note to her. If this was patronizing, we never noticed. I did the same thing for white friends in the affluent north side of Atlanta to show my concern and sympathy when needs arose.

Nannie Lee and I exchanged letters. Despite errors in grammar, for she had only a fourth-grade education, I treasured her notes, especially the first, written in lead pencil on notebook paper soon after Robert Kennedy was killed:

June 10 = 68
Hello Mrs. Holmes,
. . . My Heart is full of Sanddness Over the tragedy We are had. . . .

Grace I sure have talk about you and your Mother Since you all was here I was so glad to See you My heart cant express all I dident thank you all would every thank enough to come to See me anymore but I See it Was a Mistake and you Cant Imagine how proud I was to See you and Your Mother and I do hope We Will Live to See each other again if it the Lord will and we must pray that the people Will do Better and Stop So much killing Nothing Cause it but Sin Every thing So God Keep your Heart Budden all the time Grace can you remember what I said when your Mother was So Sick I'll take that back now I Said then White people dident Love Color people Yes Some Of them do I Belive you do and they is few more do you Sure have Prove it and I do belive it and I no I Love You I will close You and Your Husband Remember me in your prayer

from Nannie Lee Daniel

40 Discontent at Holmeland

In 1971 Pa-Pa broke his hip and underwent surgery. The hip healed, but his mind never did. He needed nursing care around the clock. So Mother, in a desperate, tearful decision, sold the little house in Decatur and moved Pa-Pa by ambulance to Baptist Village in Waycross.

At the nursing home Mother hovered over Pa-Pa, even though the staff urged her to relax in her apartment nearby. She found it impossible to turn over to strangers the care of her husband of more than fifty years. Although seventy-eight years old, Mother trotted daily back and forth from her bed to his, complaining all the while of high blood pressure, swimming in the head, aching feet and knees, fading eyesight, loneliness.

In 1973 Tom and I bought an acre of land in Coweta County, thirty miles southwest of Atlanta. There, near Gay, the country church Tom had long ago pastored and was called to lead again, we built our dream home. "Holmeland," a beautiful cypress house, rested beneath tall pines where whippoorwills called to one another at twilight. We planted a feast for nose and eyes—magnolia, gardenia, boxwood, dogwood, wisteria, redbud, lilac, forsythia, rose, camellia, azalea, holly, sasanqua. We set out bulbs of daffodil, hyacinth, and lily. Tom also established and tended vegetable gardens and an orchard full of peach, plum, pear, and fig trees, grapevines and blueberries.

During our first August in the country, we invited Mother to recuperate with us after cataract surgery. "Mother's room" was the first one we had finished—a room with a large closet, private bath, her own bed and dresser.

So she left Pa-Pa to have the surgery in Atlanta. The first week in the country she lay, content, upon her old iron bed in "her" room, the pink gingham draperies drawn, a handkerchief over her eyes to keep out the light. Morning and night I gently removed the surgical patch, bathed her precious eye. At first she loved my ministrations, cooing, "You are so sweet." "You're a precious daughter."

But as the hot autumn weeks dragged by, Mother continued to lie on her bed with the curtains drawn, handkerchief over her eye as she'd done in Riddleville every two weeks with her sick headaches. Daily she complained that her eye was getting no better. "It feels like something's in it," she'd say. I drove her thirty miles back to Atlanta to keep the doctor's weekly appointments. We even made appointments between appointments.

Mother grew more melancholy as the September days cooled, the pyracantha berries reddened, turnip greens sprouted in the kitchen garden. By the time October arrived, she had stopped saying her daughter was sweet. Instead she spoke often of other daughters who provided permanent homes for their mothers.

But I was not some other daughter. She was not some other mother. We were Lila and Grace, and we could not live together.

When October came and the little hickory trees turned to scarlet, Mother still moaned and muttered in her darkened room. "My old aching knee just hurts all the time. There's something in my eye. Gainer's never gonna be any better. My sisters were lucky to die young. They were spared this suffering."

"When do you want to go home, Mother?" I asked as gently as I could that October Thursday.

"Home!" she spat out. "I haven't got a home. All I've got left is a sick and helpless husband."

"Why, Mother, you do have a home, a beautiful home at Baptist Village. It's the loveliest, cleanest retirement home I've ever seen."

"Don't call that home! Call it Down Yonder. One room, I've got one room. And I have to get in that crowd of old, sick folks to eat. I never did like going out in a crowd every day, keeping my hair fixed up all the time. Ain't got no hair no way. Think I'll have to buy a wig.

"I don't see why I have to go on living. What have I got to live for? I'm just in the way everywhere. I wish I could go ahead and die and be done with it."

Heaviness in my chest, I tiptoed out of Mother's dark room, padded down the carpeted hallway, around her oak table in the dining room, through the sun-splashed kitchen with its bay windows. The grass was still emerald. Chrysanthemums ringed our small lawn. Last week I had reveled in their jeweled tones. Now they looked much like dead cornstalks brown and bent to the ground.

Joy has fled Holmeland. Depression sits upon our doorposts. I've looked after Mother six weeks, and my mouth is full of ulcers. My tongue is sore from biting it.

But there was something I could do. While at the shopping mall that afternoon, I telephoned Brother. When he called Mother at sunset, she accepted his invitation to visit them in their spacious home in Lawrenceville. "I will come for you Saturday," he said. We all went to bed happy and relieved. Or so I thought.

The next morning after Tom left for his office, Mother put on her faded blue dress and blue slippers with furry trim and wandered about, her cane going thump, thump, thump upon the parquet. "My old knee hurts, there's something in my eye. Don't wanta go Down Yonder. Don't wanta go to Lawrenceville either."

I stood in the kitchen peeling a seedless California orange and browning her whole wheat toast. She tottered from east wing to west, front windows to back, out onto screened porch, back into kitchen. I bit my tongue again. The ulcers burned.

Mother faced me across the breakfast bar, her hair wispy gray, her face a frozen frown. She wore no powder or lipstick, only the patch over her wounded eye. The other, greatly enlarged by the top of her trifocals, terrified me more than ever.

"Why don't you want me to stay here with you?" she demanded. "Why did you call Brother to come and get me?"

Grinding pain invaded my chest. My fingers shook. I laid down the stainless steel knife and answered as gently as I could. "Mother, it's your depressions. They get me down. Tom can't stand for me to get depressed." *Blame it on Tom.*

Her eye widened behind the trifocal at her daughter's forthrightness. "But, Grace, that's the way I am."

Why, she's proud of her melancholia!

I unleashed my tongue. "Yes, I know. You've been that way all my life! You unloaded your lamentations on me year after year since I was little.

I've been crushed for fifty-five years, because you refused to tell your troubles to anybody but me!

"For half a century, I've carried a burden no daughter should ever have to bear. You ran down Pa-Pa, Grandma, all the family. It was all I could do to have a normal relationship with *anybody* in the world. That's why I broke down at College Park."

"Well!" Hurt pride swelled like an arthritic hand. "I've worn my welcome out here! I offered *my* mother a home with me after Mr. Jordan died."

"You had sisters to help you—Aunt Mattie, Aunt Evelyn, Aunt Maude. Anyway, Daddy hasn't died."

She ignored my last remark. "Yes, I had sisters."

"So Grandma had four homes to go to. I have no sister. You often told me you sure didn't want any more children after you had us."

"Well, I had everything to do by myself. No car, no telephone, no money. Had to draw water, build fires, bring in wood, teach school, sew, cook, can, garden."

"Yes, yes, I know. And I appreciate everything you did for me." We sat in the dining room chairs, her old Queen Anne oaks Tom and I had restored. I shuddered with fright; remorse overflowed me. I had made my seventy-eight-year-old mother feel unwelcome.

"If I just hadn't given away all my furniture. Lord-a-mercy, I pray! I wish we hadn't sold our home in Riddleville. I wish we had kept it. I gave up my home for you, so you could get a college education."

"And Brother."

"Yes. I've lived my whole life for my children."

"Mother, you and Daddy made that decision without asking me. I didn't want to go to Bessie Tift. I wanted to go to Mercer, live in a dormitory. But moving to Forsyth is the best thing Daddy ever did for us. I am very grateful to you for my education, for the sacrifices you made."

"We should have gone back to Sandersville after Gainer retired. If we had, I could have put him in the nursing home there and lived among my people."

"It's not too late. We'll help you find a place, Mother. You can have all your furniture back, everything. I will help you. I'll go to Sandersville and find you a little house."

But it was too late for gestures, too late to learn how to make Mother truly happy. She went back to Waycross and Pa-Pa, discontented. My attempts to show repentance and love to my old nurse and to Aunt Lou's children had been gracefully accepted and returned. But could I ever make peace with my own mother?

Pa-Pa died a year later. We took his little body back to Riddleville for burial beside his parents. People came from all over Georgia for the memorial service in the new brick sanctuary of the church his grandfathers had founded. While three preachers spoke and the organist played "Beyond the Sunset" and his gray casket was lowered into the ground, one question went through my mind: "What will we do with Mother?"

Church members served lunch to family and visitors in the dining hall. Then my old home stood open to us once more. Uncle Herbert sat in his usual chair smoking a cigarette, and aunts, uncles, and cousins ate again in the dining room where Mother once served chocolate meringue pie to family, relatives, and visiting preachers. Even Nannie Lee came to share our grief beneath the hand-hewn rafters.

But she segregated herself in the kitchen as always. She neither sat nor ate. One of my aunts noticed her, frowned, and spoke as harshly as mistress to slave, "Nannie Lee, do you live near here?"

"Yes, I live t'other side your mama's old house. Moved there last year."

"Well, why don't you come up here and help us sometime?"

Stunned, Nannie Lee said not a word.

I was embarrassed for my black friend. The enormous humiliation imposed on her pressed me under its ugly weight, took my breath away. I wanted to say, "How dare you treat my friend like a slave to be summoned to your door?"

But another of my aunts entered the kitchen, saving both Nannie Lee and myself from a hurtful scene. Ignoring Nannie Lee, the other aunt asked, "What will you do with Lila? She's not happy at your house; she's not happy at your brother's; she's not happy at the retirement home."

I regained my breath. "She's going home with me for two weeks. After that, I don't know. We looked for a little house over in Sandersville but found nothing suitable."

Before my father died, Tom and I had gone to Pa-Pa's doctor's office to inquire about him. But the doctor wanted to talk about Mother. "Your daddy is going to die. When that happens, Grace, you cannot take your mother to live with you. You owe something to your husband. He comes first with you."

"And something to myself."

"You cannot take your mother," he repeated.

So someone else has witnessed Mother's shenanigans! "I've often wondered what's wrong with my mother—feared she was mentally ill."

"I call it meanness. She's just mean."

My wicked relief at this pronouncement by a professional man lasted but a moment. Suddenly I felt compassion for Mother and jumped to her defense. "She lost her father when she was a baby. Her mother married again, a man who'd been trained in cruelty at the infamous Andersonville prison camp. She was a victim of the Civil War!"

Realizing I'd raised my voice, I quickly lowered it again. "I love my mother very much. But you are right. I cannot live with her. Knowing that one day I will stand where she stands now, old and sick and lonely, and my children will not want me only multiplies my grief and guilt."

But Tom and I did bring Mother, along with pots of yellow mums sent as a memorial by friends, back to Holmeland the day after Pa-Pa's funeral. Early the next morning I was sitting in my rocker in the great room when Mother suddenly stood beside my chair. Her statement settled my dilemma: "I will make my home at Baptist Village. That's the place for me. Everything's arranged for me there. No steps anywhere, doctors and nurses nearby. I'm not going to be happy anywhere, anyway. So I'll just stay there. You and Brother come to see me as often as you can."

Brother and I took turns, one of us visiting Mother each month. Because Baptist Village was a day's journey from our homes, Harvey Mitchell, who had loved my father very much, gave us lodging there. During our stay, we would take Mother out to eat, take her shopping, visit with her in her room.

Every week we wrote letters, and Tom and I telephoned frequently. During each summer she spent two weeks with us at Holmeland and, at Christmas time, another two weeks.

As I readied her room for Yuletide 1977, I reminisced about the woman who'd given me my first Christmases with their sparkling trees, cuddly dolls, and divinity candy. In those long-ago Decembers, pretty, dark-haired Lila cooked the best divinity I'd ever tasted. I could still see her grating mounds of fresh coconut for bowls of ambrosia and three-layer cakes.

Now I tried to relate those memories to the eighty-three-year-old woman whose thin white hair was hidden under a brownish-gray wig. For the past three Noels, Mother and I had worked together making candy, pies, and cakes in Holmeland's sunny kitchen. I bought the juiciest oranges, finest coconut, and plenty of sugar, thinking the traditional preparations for Christmas would make her happy. But she complained all day. "This grater is no good. I can't grate coconut on this thing. Can't crack pecans with these sorry nutcrackers, and you've got no picks to dig out the nuts. I can't measure sugar and butter with your measuring cup. Wish I had mine. Do you know what happened to my cups when we divided my belongings? All of my things are gone with the wind."

It was all I could do to keep from falling into her slough of despond and pulling in husband and children behind us.

But I loved Mother too much to leave her among strangers at Christmas. As I pulled out recipe books to begin baking, I prayed, "Oh God, help me! There must be a better way to celebrate than working myself into a migraine cooking all the dishes that look like the pictures in a book about colonial Williamsburg!"

Put the recipe books away. This year, don't bake sweets. The work will tire you, put frowns on your face and pounds around your waistline. Thirty years you have celebrated the birthday of Christ the King by cooking.

Remember how in recent years you sang carols as you chopped sugared cherries, pineapples, nuts; creamed butter and eggs? But you've never taken time to learn the words of those songs beyond their first stanzas.

This year, learn all the words. They tell of the Christ who turns sorrows into songs, hostilities into hallelujahs. Sing "Silent Night" to your mother, "Away in a Manger" to your grandchildren. Joyfully I put away the recipes and ran to practice all the carols in the hymnbook. But I found I was too unskilled to play piano and sing simultaneously.

At Mercer I knew an English professor who strummed an autoharp while he sang folk songs. It looked so simple. If only I had one! I took my idea to my husband. "Please, Tom, I want an autoharp for Christmas so I can sing carols to Mother."

"You shall have one, my dear. Anything to keep Mother happy and help you through the holidays."

Meanwhile I would learn the lyrics, be ready for Christmas Day. I found poster board, wrote the words large, and stood them up on Mr. Pat's cupboard in the dining room next to the old oak table, now an oval with three leaves added. I memorized all of "Silent Night" while wrapping presents with red ribbons, decorating the fir tree with tiny white lights and angels, decking the mantel with boughs of holly. Every sunset when Tom returned front his office in the city I asked, "Has the harp come yet? I need it to practice on."

I learned all the words of "Joy to the World" while changing Mother's bed, spreading clean sheets, vacuuming her room. My yoke was easy, my burden light. When had I quit dreading her coming?

She arrived December 17, leaning upon her cane, clad in her faded, unfashionable blue dress, bundled in her old black coat with the flat mink collar. As always she wore her wig. Voicing familiar complaints, she went immediately to bed. We didn't know arteriosclerosis was thickening the inner walls of her arteries and cutting off circulation to her head, knees, and feet.

At dusk on Christmas Eve, store-bought cakes and cookies nestled in kitchen boxes. Fragrances of scalloped oysters and roasting turkey permeated the house. Mother napped in her room. Our children would arrive within the hour, bringing suitcases and pajamas. There was space enough at our Holmeland for all.

Sinking into my easy chair in the great room, I surveyed our Christmas scene. Flames danced on the hearth and warmed my knees. Presents were piled beneath the sparkling tree. Only one thing was missing, the gift I still yearned for. *Did Tom not get the harp after all? How can I make Mother merry?*

Then Tom strode in and laid the treasure upon my lap. "It came today from Chicago," he said. "There was not one like this to be found in Atlanta. Read the instructions."

Lovingly, as though unfolding the blankets to adore a newborn baby, I examined my new instrument. Shaped like a grand piano, it was fashioned of shiny wood and strings. My husband, the guitarist, began instructing me.

"Thank you! Oh, thank you so very much, my darling."

41 *Harp and Song*

I had never played an autoharp before, never held one in my hands. But the instrument and I knew instant affinity. I began to stroke and sing. It was easy, as though I'd been strumming all my life. To my amazement, I discovered a richer quality in my voice than I ever dreamed my amateur talent could raise.

The harp was magic!

In her quarters Mother woke. The strains of Joseph Mohr's "Silent Night" flowed in and out the rooms. She rose from her bed, put on her blue bedroom slippers, and crept into the living room, lit by firelight and star-shaped twinkles on the tree. She sat near the fire, her aged face relaxing, becoming serene. Finally she spoke in awe, "I didn't know you could sing like that."

"I didn't know it either, Mother. Tom gave me the harp. And God gave me the voice, I guess." I began singing the second stanza. Mother wept.

When I finished, she said, "You sing as beautifully as Norma Zimmer. I want you to come to Baptist Village and give a concert like Mrs. Boone's daughter. I would be so proud!"

After dinner I continued the strumming and singing until midnight. Before daybreak on Christmas morning I began with Isaac Watts's "Joy to the World." Throughout the season, husband, children, grandchildren, and Mother joined in. She forgot not only her aches and pains but also her hostilities. Parking her cane in a corner, she listened to our music night after night—and even played the piano again! Her face grew merry with laughter, her ancient eyes glistened like angels' wings.

It was the best Christmas we'd ever had, a miracle that lasted far into the new year. When I visited Mother at Easter on my spring break from voice lessons at Mercer in Atlanta, she was still serene and smiling. Everywhere we went at the sprawling complex, Mother was greeted by smiles and cheers. Lady after lady said, "Your mother's a wonderful person."

She had arranged two miniconcerts for her daughter, one in the chapel, one in the dining hall. "Mother, you should have been an artist's agent, a public relations person!" I told her. Among the songs I sang for them were "Danny Boy," "Grace Greater Than Our Sin," and Mother's favorite hymn about heaven, "Beyond the Sunset."

Transformed, her face radiant during my visit, she didn't complain about a single thing. Every time we parted for an hour or two, she said, "Be sure to bring your autoharp when you come back to my room."

She arrived for her summer visit on August 7. When I went to her room to help her unpack, I found her weeping.

"Mother, please don't cry. It's summer, and tomatoes are ripe in the garden. We'll have vegetables on the table and music on the porch."

"I'm in bad shape. And you and Brother live so far apart."

"But we've got cars, and we can get together."

By the end of that week, Mother's suffering was so acute that I called the doctor and took her to the hospital for vascular tests. Before the end of the month Mother underwent surgery to clean out arteries and veins.

She had set me completely free just before she was wheeled out of her room for the operation and Tom prayed as I held her hand. "I know," my mother said, "that I didn't give you enough freedom when you were young. But I wanted you to be pure, to be special."

Her confession startled me, coming as it did after all the decades. Tears burned behind my eyelids. I squeezed her hands saying, "It's all right, Mother. Everything's all right. I love you."

During her surgery I found Mother's last letter, penned on a scrap of paper the night before and left for me in her hospital room.

> I've been made ready for the day tomorrow. . . . The Lord is my shepherd and I'm in His hands.
>
> . . . Sing for me "Grace, Greater Than Our Sin" and "Beyond the Sunset."
>
> I do not fear death, but rather fear the ills of this life. Yours and Tom's love support me. . . . I am ready to depart and be with Christ and my loved ones in heaven, or to struggle on here as may be the Lord's will. Thank you for all your goodness with all my heart.
>
> I'll see you sometime, somewhere.
>
> Tenderly, Mother

On Friday, September 13, 1978, in the very early morning, I held her cold, still hand until it became marble in mine. Brother prayed at the head of her couch, Tom at her right. A hospital chaplain appeared from the shadows and stood at her feet. I watched my dearest friend sink into ever-lasting sleep, and I whispered a prayer.

I closed her eyelids and felt no guilt over her "cold, dead body," only sadness. *Mother, why did you have to go just as we were getting to be good friends?* Sorrow and joy mingled with the shadows. *Now who will I sing to?*

We told Dr. Jacobs to call Mayo's Funeral Home in Sandersville, then drove through the moonlit countryside to Holmeland. I looked at the lovely landscape by the light of a silver, late-summer moon, hearing my mother's voice repeating and repeating, "I didn't give you enough freedom," "Sing for me," and "I'll see you sometime, somewhere."

As I crawled into the bed at 5 A.M. wearing white socks on shock-chilled feet, I still felt no guilt. I knew I had done all one crippled daughter could do for her crippled mother.

When I woke at seven, there was an ache in my head and grief in my heart. *Mother is dead.* I went to the telephone and called my daughter. I could not say I had bad news. Neither could I say I had good news. So I said, "Kathy, I have news."

"What news?"

"Mother is dead. She died at three o'clock this morning. I was holding her hand."

We cried together, relief, sorrow, and joy washing over me. "I'm so glad we had good times together this last year. I'm so glad she was staying here with us when she died."

To the end of that summer and beyond, Mother's spirit lingered like the bittersweet scent of white chrysanthemums sent by Rachel's son and his wife. Every morning I remembered that Mother was dead. She'd never return wearing her rusty old blue-and-white dress and her frozen frown, never send another letter, never sew another dress.

How grateful I was for the autoharp and songs that last Christmas, so that our last days together were joyous! As I thanked God for my freedom from the burden I'd carried so long, I realized that Mother, too, had found release. She who had been a strict keeper of the law had not learned to know Christ—who came to fulfill the law—until she heard her daughter singing the Good News. And Mother had finally, truly found peace through those gospel songs!

There remained only the job of disposing of her things. Brother would fetch them from Waycross tomorrow. Today was Saturday, September 23, cool on the green-carpeted porch at 7:30 in the morning. A chorus of crickets' chirping rose up from the forest. On its tall stem, a late rose bloomed, pink like Mother's last gown.

"Bury me in pink," she'd said. She even wrote it in her funeral plans. "There's a pink lace dress in a box at Baptist Village. Or if you can't get to Waycross, just buy me one at Mayo's Funeral Home, something simple, something pink."

We had decided on a nightgown, for after all she was asleep. In the gray casket her body laid on soft white satin, thin silver hair framing her aged face, peaceful at last. The same face that most of her life wore furrows and frowns was now free of anxiety, relaxed and resting.

The next week in Mother's room at Holmeland boxes were stacked on top of boxes. The suitcases would contain gowns, combs, compacts, safety pins, Kleenex tissues carefully folded. My mother's things. To every item clung her smell, a mixture of mustiness and Coty powder. My nostrils filled as soon as I opened the door.

Those smells brought Mother back to life. Quick as a doe, I closed the door and hurried down the hall before I could be overcome. Her words followed me. *You'll be sorry when you see my cold, dead body.*

No, I will not be sorry. I did the best I could do for you, Mother, all through the years.

But one day soon I will have to stay in that room, open all the cartons, go through all the dresses, coats and suits, piece by piece by piece. I must decide what to do with them—scarves, handkerchiefs, fans, wigs.

It's the wigs that haunt me. They are Mother's taupe-colored hair without Mother's face and eyes.

I shuddered. *I, alone, must dispose of Mother's personal things, and the sooner, the better.*

Then I remembered last night. I wept at church while they sang:

Out of despair into raptures above,
Upward for aye, on wings like a dove, . .
Jesus, I come,
Jesus, I come.

A perfect description of Mother's passage! I picked up the harp, strummed, and sang the words over and over. After lunch I went back into

Mother's room, singing. I threw open the windows to cool autumn air. In the hatboxes I found hats dating back to the thirties: purple, pink, black, green. *Never mind the smells. My mother's in Paradise now. She'll never need these chapeaux to wear on the streets of gold.*

Getting out suitcases, I put gowns in one, slips in another, underwear in a third. *I'll finish the task this week, then call Mother's son and grandchildren to come Sunday and get the items they want. I'll take all the rest back to the land between the rivers, let Nannie Lee distribute them to her family and friends, Aunt Lou's children.*

The unusable I threw away in ragged boxes held for twenty, thirty years. With them I threw away guilt and grief. As I discarded, I sang. All week I worked with windows and doors open to autumn breezes. Drifting in and out and through the rooms, they cleaned the air, scattering Mother's scents away to the treetops, through the green pines and yellowing maples.

I gathered two dozen filmy scarves, wrinkled and scented with Mother's perfume. Tumbled in the dryer with wet towels, the colorful material came out smooth, smelling like new. Then I carefully folded and stacked them, sorting according to size and shape, thinking of the loved ones who would have them: the green for Tommy's wife; the lavender for Kathy; the ballet dancers for our ballerina granddaughter; the yellow for granddaughter Rachel.

Suddenly I was enjoying the ineffably sad task, thinking of Mother in her heaven-home beside the shining river. In the last days of her final year we had become as close as Naomi and Ruth.

I know who I'll sing to! I'll join the choir at Second Ponce de Leon Church and sing to a thousand people every Sunday. By live television, I'll even sing the Good News to fifty thousand.

Yes, Mother, I will sing for you!

EPILOGUE

Thomas Holmes died on January 3, 1985.

A decade later, the Southern Baptist Convention issued a long-overdue public apology for its attitude and treatment of blacks. Today the message "of both judgment and hope" in Thomas Holmes's book, *Ashes for Breakfast,* rings out as clearly to concerned Christians as it did when Tom first wrote it.

Grace Holmes continues to write. She lives in an apartment in Decatur, Georgia, and still sings with the Sanctuary Choir. On special occasions she still sings solos, now with a piano accompanist, and conducts music for vespers at a Decatur retirement home.

INDEX

Mitchell, Harvey, 292
Mobley, Harris, 224–225
Moore, Harmon, 273
Morehouse College, 171, 249–251, 274–275
Morris Brown College, 251
Mount Vernon Academy, 3, 41
Mount Vernon Association, 53
Mount Vernon Institute, 61
Mount Zion Baptist Church, 246
Mount Zion Second Baptist Church, 253

Nannie (servant), 11, 43–45, 62, 232, 252
NBC News, 239
Newnan Central Baptist Church, 116, 165
Nincompoop (child), 209–211, 216, 223, 233
Northside Drive Baptist Church, 191, 195–196, 218, 246

Oconee River, 40
Ogeechee River, 40
Oni, Sam, 224–227, 239–240, 256, 285
Ophelia (cousin), 7, 47

Paradice, Gussie, 205–206
Paradice, Harry, 81–82
Paradise Church, 253
Parks, Rosa, 177
Pete (uncle), 36, 91
Piedmont Hospital, 131
Pirtle, Albert, 191–192, 212
Plymale (dean), 94
Poitier, Sidney, 252
Protests: Selma and Montgomery, Ala., 227
Purnell, Pat, 157–159, 172, 293
Purnell, Tom, 159

R. D. Cole Manufacturing, 165
Raleigh, N.C., 157–159, 162

Raven, George Washington Henry Lincoln Jefferson, 175–177, 180
Raven, Honey, 175–177, 180
Rawlings Sanitarium, 52
Reeb, James, 227
Rehoboth Association, 54
Reidsville State Prison, 222
Rich's Department Store, 106, 115, 149–150, 222, 261, 284
Riddle, Anderson, 41
Riddle, Claudia, 20–21, 33, 65–69, 128
Riddle, Cleophas, 20, 46, 62, 67, 75–76, 262
Riddle, Gozella, 20, 62, 67–68
Riddle, Lucy: attitudes of whites toward, 17–18, 93; daughter's death, 65–66, 67–68, 69, 128; death, 283; Grace visits, 259, 260–264, 277–278; Grace's memories of, 201, 204, 232, 266; Grace's relationship with as child, 16–17, 19, 89; and Lila, 18–21, 33–34, 55–57; living conditions, 68, 260–262, 264, 267–268; as nurse and maid, 6, 22, 47, 56, 64, 73, 75, 76, 92; trip to fair, 55, 59; trip to Nannie Lee's, 278–279, 281–282; mentioned, 26, 49, 194
Riddle, Willie, 46, 62, 65–68, 75, 262
Riddleville, 40–41, 52–53, 60, 69, 75, 85, 91, 112, 212, 223, 234, 241, 271, 288, 290–291
Riddleville School, 94–95
Rivers (reverend), 60, 63, 75, 78, 183
Robertson, Ruth, 111
Roosevelt, Franklin D., 110, 280

Sandersville, 13, 21, 25, 33, 52, 92, 107, 264, 277, 282, 290–291, 297
Sandersville High School, 83–84, 94–95, 100
Sandersville Hospital, 283
Second Ponce de Leon Baptist Church, 299